Rajiv Gandhi

Rajiv Gandhi

Breaking New Grounds

B. K. Ahluwalia
S. Ahluwalia

COSMO PUBLICATIONS

RAJIV GANDHI—Breaking New Grounds

Made in India

First Published 1985

Published by:
COSMO PUBLICATIONS
24-B, Ansari Road,
New Delhi-110 002 (India)

Printed at:
Pearl Offset Press Private Limited
5/33, Kirti Nagar Indl. Area,
New Delhi-110015

PREFACE

There were Cassandras galore in the country who questioned the wisdom of the Congress (I), leaders who turned to Rajiv Gandhi to assume the high office held by his mother till she was cut down by assassins. The sceptic drew attention to the relative youth of Rajiv and his lack of political experience. How could he keep the warring sections within the Congress in line? How could he bring peace to Punjab and Assam which had baffled the sustained efforts of his mother?

It was not the best of times, for one so young and inexperienced in the complex art of politics to take up the challenge. Punjab lay like a millstone on the nation's neck and Assam was smouldering. The Mizos were restless. There were other reports of separatism or parochialism from various corners of the country which did not augur well for the future.

India's neighbours were not friendly. Pakistan assumed bellingeren postures. It was suspected of getting arms far in excess of its defence needs, of backing the extremists in Punjab. The influx of Bangladeshis into neighbouring Indian States and the unresolved question of sharing of the Farakka waters kept India and Bangladesh at loggerheads. Nepal was sizzling with immense fear of its big neighbour. Sri Lanka was unsure of India's intentions on the ethnic disturbances in the Island State.

A lesser man would have cowered under the challenges. Not Rajiv. He was made of sterner stuff. He ordered a national poll to find out whether the people wanted him at the head of the government. He was not willing to rule by proxy. The people backed him fully, absolutely.

That gave him the democratic right to take firm decisions. He bacame his own master. He brought changes in the budget to give an impetus to industry and trade which he felt would give a boost to production and also increase employment opportunities.

He released the Akali leaders, sent a confidant with the necessary skill and competence as Governor of Punjab, held behind-the-scene negotiations with Sant Longowal, Tohra and Badal, and finally worked out a compromise which holds out peace in Punjab. Problems of Gujarat and Mizoram are in the anvil, awaiting a solution. Rajiv Gandhi is determined to sort out the problems, to restore sanity to the political arena, to give a big hand to nationalism. With the great skill he sorted out the Assam problem and the Memorandum of Settlement on the Assam problem was signed between the representatives of the Government and the leaders of the Assam students union and the All Assam Gana Sangram Parishad at the residence of the Prime Minister, Mr. Rajiv Gandhi, in New Delhi, on August 15, 1985.

At the same time, he has been playing a major role on the international arena. He is continuing the tradition of former Prime Minister. He is using his good offices to bring the ethnic conflict in Sri Lanka to an end. He has been a catalyst in the NAM movement. Science and technology sharing between the developed and the developing nations is a topic dear to his heart. His visit to the superpower nations have conclusively proved his competence. 300 days have slipped by. 300 days of creative activity. 300 days of dedicated pursuit of the objective which are dear to us all. 300 days of ceaseless quest for peace and amity and friendship mark Rajiv's captainship.

It is this golden period which comes in for critical assessment by the authors who are well-known for their continued interest in the national movement and the progress of the nation.

The authors are grateful to Prof. K. Swaminathan and Sarva Shri V. Narayanswamy, J.P. Uniyal and R.K. Murthi who were good enough to offer them useful suggestions. We thankfully acknowledge the complete cooperation and help we received from the publisher—Cosmo Publications. They have brought out the book in a record time.

B.K. Ahluwalia
Shashi Ahluwalia

B-13/505, Lodi Colony
New Delhi-110 013.

September 14, 1985.

LIST OF ILLUSTRATIONS

20. Releasing a commemorative stamp on Mrs. Gandhi.
21. Addressing the annual convocation of Vishwabharathi University at Shantiniketan, April 12, 1985.
22. Garlanding the statue of Dr. B.R. Ambedkar on the occasion of his 94th birth anniversary celebrations in New Delhi, April 4, 1985.
23. Inaugurating the Extraordinary Ministerial Meeting of the Coordinating Bureau of the Non-Aligned Countries on Namibia and the Commemoration of 25th anniversary of SWAPO, April 19, 1985.
24. Lighting a lamp to mark the inauguration of Indian Parliamentarians' Conference on Population Development in New Delhi, May 13, 1985.
25. Inaugurating the National Solidarity Day to commemorate the 80th birth anniversary celebrations of the late Fakhruddin Ali Ahmed in New Delhi, May 13, 1985.
26. Being received by the General Secretary of the Soviet Communist Party, Mr. Mikhail Gorbachov, at Kremlin Grand Palace in Moscow, May 21, 1985.
27. Laying a wreath on the tomb of Unknown Soldiers at the Kremlin Wall, May 22, 1985.
28. Exchanging documents with Mr. Mikhail Gorbachov after signing two agreements on behalf of their Governments.
29. Oh his arrival at the end of his 6-day official visit to the Soviet Union, May 26, 1985.
30. Receiving President J.R. Jayewardene of Sri Lanka on his arrival at Delhi airport, June 1, 1985.
31. With the Prime Minister of Egypt, Mr. Kamal Hassan Ali (extreme right), on his arrival at Cairo International Airport, June 5, 1985.
32. With the Egyptian President, Mr. Hosni Mubarak, at the official talks in Cairo, June 6, 1985.
33. Talking with the President of France, Mr. Francois Mitterrand, at Elycee Palace in Paris, June 6, 1985.
34. Hosting a dinner in honour of the French President, Mr. Francois Mitterrand, in Paris, June 9, 1985.
35. Before boarding a superfast train in Paris, June 9, 1985.
36. Watching from the driver's cabin of the superfast train in Paris, June 9, 1985.

37. Addressing a joint Press conference with the Prime Minister of France, Mr. Laurent Fabius, June 9, 1985.
38. Being received by the President of Algeria, Mr. Chadli Benjedid, on his arrival at the airport, June 10, 1985.
39. With Mr. Chadli Benjedid, President of Algeria, June 10, 1985.
40. Acknowledging the greetings on his arrival at Washington Monument grounds, June 11, 1985.
41. With the U.S. Secretary of State, Mr. George Shultz, June 11, 1985.
42. With President Ronald Reagan & Mrs. Nancy Reagan in USA, June 12, 1985.
43. Looking at an exhibit in the Festival of India in USA, June 12, 1985.
44. Addressing the National Press Club in Washington, June 14, 1985.
45. Receiving a plaque by the Chairman of the Indian National Congress of America, Mr. Kamal Dandona, June 14, 1985.
46. Fondling a child at Geneva, June 16, 1985.
47. Accepting Lenin Peace Prize on behalf of late Smt. Indira Gandhi, June 17, 1985.
48. Addressing 71st session of the I.L.O., June 17, 1985.
49. Paying homage to the body of Air Chief Marshal L.M. Katre, Chief of the Air Staff, July 2, 1985.
50. Addressing a Press conference in New Delhi, July 7, 1985.
51. Visiting the historic Roopmati Mahal in Mandu of Dhar district, July 12, 1985.
52. With the new Chief Justice of India, Mr. P.N. Bhagwati, after he was administered the oath of office and secrecy, July 12, 1985.
53. Listening the problems and grievances of tribals of Kathiwada village in Jhabua district of Madhya Pradesh, July 12, 1985.
54. Wading through mud in a tribal village of Madhya Pradesh.
55. Distributing sweets among the children of a primary school of Dugli in Madhya Pradesh, July 14, 1985.
56. Unveiling the statue of Kamaraj in New Delhi, July 18, 1985.
57. With IPS Probationers when they called on him in New Delhi, July 19, 1985.
58. With Mr. Won-Kyung Lee, Foreign Minister of Republic of

Korea, when the latter called on him in New Delhi, July 19, 1985.

59. Exchanging documents with Sant Longowal, President of Akali Dal, after signing a Memorandum of Settlement on Punjab issue, in New Delhi, July 24, 1985.
60. Inaugurating the Ministerial Meeting on Global System of Trade Preferences at Vigyan Bhavan, New Delhi, July 25, 1985.
61. Watching the working of a hand-pump in Themgar Panchayat block, in Orissa, July 26, 1985.
62. With the tribals of Sinapalli village in Orissa, July 26, 1985.
63. Crossing the Sundar river after visiting Borda block in Orissa, July 26, 1985.
64. Acknowledging the greetings of the crowd on his arrival at Bhubaneswar airport, July 26, 1985.
65. A tiny parrot comfortably perched on the hand of the Prime Minister, Mr. Rajiv Gandhi, while Smt. Sonia Gandhi looks at it curiously at Sakhatora village, July 26, 1985.
66. Going round Sakhatora village in Orissa, July 26, 1985.
67. Receiving an idol of Laxmi from the Chief Minister of Andhra Pradesh, Mr. N.T. Rama Rao, after inaugurating the building of Andhra Pradesh Assembly in Hyderabad, August 3, 1985.
68. Looking into a microscope to see how the forensic tests are conducted in the laboratory at National Police Academy, Hyderabad, August 3, 1985.
69. Taking keen interest in the latest methods being adopted by the police in investigating murder cases at the National Police Academy, Hyderabad, August 3, 1985.
70. Looking at the advanced aeronautical facilities in the HAL Complex during his visit to Hyderabad, August 3, 1985.
71. Addressing the employees of Defence research establishments after laying the foundation-stone of the Research Institute, IMARAT, DRDL in Hyderabad, August 3, 1985.
72. Addressing Assembly members after inaugurating the building of Andhra Pradesh Assembly in Hyderabad, August 3, 1985.
73. Laying the foundation-stone of the Research Institute, IMARAT, DRDL in Hyderabad, on August 3, 1985.
74. Receiving the leader of the Chinese delegation, Mr. Li Dongye, Minister of Metallurgy, August 7, 1985.

75. With the leaders of the Opposition at a meeting in New Delhi, August 7, 1985.
76. With the Minister of Foreign Affairs of the Democratic Republic of Afghanistan, Mr. Shah Mohammad Dost (extreme left), when the latter called on him in New Delhi, August 7, 1985.
77. Listening to the grievances and problems of the villagers of Kherwada, August 8, 1985.
78. In a tribal village in Udaipur district to study the progress made in the implementation of various welfare schemes, August 8, 1985.
79. Receiving the Tilak Award-1985 conferred posthumously on Smt. Indira Gandhi from the Governor of Maharashtra, August 8, 1985.
80. Addressing a large gathering of tribals at Kanwai village in Rajasthan, August 8, 1985.
81. Witnessing a desert tribals' cultural show and the sun-set at Sam sand dunes in Jaisalmer district, August 9, 1985.
82. Enquiring from tribals about various welfare schemes and the benefits reaching them at Nichlagarh village in Rajasthan's Sirohi district, August 9, 1985.
83. Listening to the problems of a tribal inside a hut in Deldar village in Rajasthan, August 9, 1985.
84. With the tribals of Bhilon-ki-Dhani village in Rajasthan in Jaisalmer district, August 9, 1985.
85. Addressing BSF Jawans at Tanot in Jaisalmer district, August 10, 1985.
86. Speaking to a weaver at the weavers shed and their Co-operative Society at Kabir Basti in Jaisalmer district, August 10, 1985.
87. Visiting the Victory Pillar at Tanot in Jaisalmer district on August 10, 1985.
88. Along with Sonia Gandhi enjoying a ride on a bedecked camel in Rajasthan, August 10, 1985.
89. Joining steps with the tribals in a colourful folk dance at Nichlagarh village in Sirohi district, August 10, 1985.
90. Looking at the exquisite marvel of art architecture representing the age-old culture of the country in the world famous Dilwara Jain Temples of Mount Abu, August 10, 1985.

91. Looking on as the Memorandum of Settlement of the Assam problem is being signed by the Government representatives and the leaders of the All Assam Students Union and the All Assam Gana Sangram Parishad, in New Delhi, August 15, 1985.
92. Looking on as the Union Home Secretary, Mr. R.D. Pradhan, is exchanging documents with the leaders of the AASU and the AAGSP after signing the Memorandum of Settlement of the Assam problem, August 15, 1985.
93. Offering flowers at the Samadhi of Mahatma Gandhi at Raj Ghat on the occasion of the 38th anniversary of Independence in New Delhi, August 15, 1985.
94. Inspecting the Guard of Honour at the Red Fort on the occasion of the 38th anniversary of Independence in New Delhi, August 15, 1985.
95. Unfurling the National Flag at the ramparts of the Red Fort on the occasion of the 38th anniversary of Independence in New Delhi, August 15, 1985.
96. Addressing the Nation from the ramparts of the Red Fort on the occasion of the 38th anniversary of Independence in New Delhi, August 15, 1985.

CONTENTS

i

LEADER IN THE MAKING

Nations never allow vacuums at the top. And every time vacuum is created, it is filled up quickly. The process of such filling may vary. It could be through democratic process, or through revolution, or through right of inheritance.

It was a vacuum which was created when assassins moved India's Prime Minister, Mrs. Gandhi, down with a spray of bullets on a bright sunny morning in October. For a moment, it looked as if the sun had set on India. At 9.30 on October 31, 1984, the dynamic lady who had weathered many storms lay sprawled on the ground, a dozen or more bullets having criss-crossed through her soft, small figure. The darkness which enveloped men's hearts was frightening. Yet the gloom did not last long. For the 'son' rose to the occasion. Rajiv Gandhi agreed to captain the ship of State.

The folkfore of politics, writes Shri N.C. Menon, makes it clear that great cataclysmic events often produce great men. We can all think of examples when a traumatic national event ennobled an individual who had previously, and accurately, been viewed as undistinguished. Such a person is Prime Minister Rajiv Gandhi. He has grown rapidly in stature. He is quick study. He has the ability to go through twenty-hour days without losing his cool. This in short is our dynamic Prime Minister who is in a hurry to take the nation with all speed into the 21st century.

Soft-spoken, affable and mild-mannered, Rajiv Gandhi became the Prime Minister at the age of forty. He is the youngest Prime Minister of the country and is, perhaps, one of the youngest elected heads of government in the world. His mother, Indira Gandhi, was eight years older when she first became Prime Minister in 1966. His illustrious grandfather, Jawaharlal Nehru, was 58 when he became free India's first Prime Minister. Rajiv Gandhi was born on August 20, 1944, in Bombay. He was only three when India became independent and his grandfather became Prime Minister. His parents moved to New Delhi from Lucknow. His father, Feroze Gandhi, became an M.P. He was known as a fearless and hard-working parliamentarian.

Rajiv Gandhi spent his early childhood with his grandfather in the Teen Murti House, where Indira Gandhi served as the Prime Minister's hostess. He was educated at Welham Prep school in Dehra Dun and then Doon School. After leaving school, Mr. Gandhi went to Trinity College, Cambridge, and then shifted to the Imperial College, London, where he did a course in mechanical engineering.

At Cambridge, he had met Sonia Maino, an Italian who was studying English there. The two were married in New Delhi in 1968. They stayed in Smt. Indira Gandhi's residence in New Delhi with their two children, son Rahul and daughter Priyanka. Theirs was a very private life despite the surrounding din and bustle of political activity.

Rajiv Gandhi's bookshelves were lined with volumes on science and engineering, not works on politics. Music, however, has had a price of place in his interests. He likes Western and Indian classical music as well as modern music. Other interests include photography and amateur radio. His greatest passion, however, has always been flying. On returning home from England, he joined the Delhi Flying Club, went on to obtain a commercial pilot's licence and became a pilot in Indian Airlines, the domestic national carrier, where he was later made an examiner.

Mr. T.N. Ninan, the noted journalist, has given a glimpse of the student life of our new Prime Minister in an article entitled "A Gentleman in Politics" published in India Today.

According to him Rajiv Gandhi was a shy boy who sat 26 years ago at the dinner table in Doon School's Kashmir House, almost hiding from his visiting grandfather, Jawaharlal Nehru, at the senior table in the centre of the room. In class he occupied a back bench. Outside it, he played the regulation games without distinction, occasionally broke bounds and stole forbidden leechis from the school trees, but generally kept out of harm's way. Younger brother Sanjay would break a friend's tennis racket because he undercut a market that Sanjay had set up for lime juice in the school, but Rajiv seemed neither enterprising nor destructive. He was liked, but not "popular", a well-behaved lad but not a sissy. In 1960, he just failed to become a prefect, and passed the senior Cambridge examination in the second division. It didn't seem at that time this boy was meant to shape a country.

Soon he was at the Imperial College in London. After a year, he moved to Trinity College, Cambridge, for a course in mechanical engineering. "Didn't study at all, really," he said once in explanation of the continued lack of educational distinction. And at home in India his mother fretted, writing letters which suggested that she expected Sanjay to take care of his older brother.

Money was tight in England: some £ 620 a year of which £ 460 went in fees, and board and lodging expenses. There was not much left after that, so Rajiv sold ice-cream, worked in a freeze factory, then in a bakery (where he seems to have won a prize for a record quantity of baking), and plucked fruit. But the one who got himself a car was Sanjay, who was doing a stint with Rolls-Royce in Crewe.

Rajiv was good-looking and the girls were interested. But he dated them without conviction, accompanied male friends to pubs where he did not drink (He remains even today a man who is happiest with gallons of Cola), and debated what was wrong with India in the way that political university union, remained unaffected by the Beetles wave, wondered how he would attend a dinner at the High Commissioner's place without a jacket (friends found him one that fitted), and went his mundane way, not flaunting his family connection, making few waves. At a party, he met Sonia Maino, who had come up from Italy, to do a year's course in English. M.O. Mathai wrote tartly some years ago that this was the best thing that Rajiv did at Cambridge. Rajiv has said he thinks so too.

As a child, his ambition was to become a pilot. After receiving training at the Safdarjung Flying Club in New Delhi, he acquired a commercial pilot's licence and became a co-pilot in Indian Airlines.

Mr. Rajiv Gandhi was a man who would have preferred to fly planes. Instead, destiny has decided to seat him in the political cockpit of the world's largest democracy, says Jugu Abraham.

Four years ago, Mr. Rajiv Gandhi had openly expressed dislike for politicians who, he felt, were full of "wheeling and dealing and intrigue." Even his wife seemed to think so. In an interview, he admitted that Mrs. Sonia Gandhi "was dead against the idea of my getting into politics." Unlike his brother Sanjay, he was fighting shy of the Khadi cap.

The death of Sanjay seemed to twist his destiny. The successful Indian Airlines Avro commander who was trained to fly Boeings hung his pilot's cap when his younger brother died in a plane crash. The man who once admitted, "I don't know enough about politics", reluctantly got out of his jeans and into Khadi pyjamas nine months after he dithered and finally gave in to the "draft Mr. Rajiv Gandhi campaign". The change had come on the heels of a personal tragedy.

The die was cast when his mother approved the move. On the morning of May 11, 1981, Mr. Rajiv Gandhi paid a rupee for the pink coloured receipt that made him a regular member of the Congress (I) party. The events followed. He filed his nomination papers for the Amethi Parliamentary seat.

Rajiv Gandhi became a man of the masses when he started his electioneering for the 1981 by-election to the Lok Sabha. The constituency was Amethi from where Sanjay had contested and won the election earlier. The polling day was June 14. Summer was at its peak. Yet Rajiv travelled the entire constituency of Amethi.

The Amethi Parliamentary constituency consisted of 5 Assembly segments and each such segment had been further divided into 12 to 15 sectors and each sector catered to about 15 to 20 polling booths. One polling booth had 800 to 1,000 votes and comprised a radius of approximately 2.5 km. There were about 770 polling booths and Rajiv Gandhi had visited almost every part of the constituency, even those villages which were never visited by any incumbent before. It is a predominantly rural constituency. There are only about half a dozen small towns with a population of 10,000 or above.

His workers were the local people working and campaigning almost on their own in the innumerable villages.

Rajiv Gandhi has a bewitching smile, a winning smile...or better still, a Nehru smile.

He introduced a new style of electioneering. He used to tell: "I have come to meet you and know your problems and I have come to make friendship with you... .

"The election you are contesting...It is yours...and the victory that will be, will be yours... ."

His addresses were brief. He began all his addresses with "Mothers, sisters and brothers" (*Matao, behno aur bhaiyo*) and ended with *Jai Hind*, which he said, was an old slogan and had perhaps not been spoken of for some time.

In spite of the brevity, his speeches had a fresh aura about them every time he delivered them. He made no wild promises. He talked only of redeeming the promises which were already made and he vowed to fulfil them all.

He believes in getting the work done. But he asked for the participation of the people as well, for "the Government can provide water but cannot plough the fields; government can set up industries but cannot do their labour...work they ahve to...sweat they have to...". He told them if people participate in getting the work done, he won't be lacking.

He worked hard—15 to 18 hours a day—and throughout. The printed schedules listed more than two dozen meetings in a day, apart from the numerous roadside stopovers and unscheduled meetings.

He stuck to his schedule. He kept his time and was never late.

He did not fumble for words. He was firm and precise. Rajiv Gandhi spoke in a clear, precise measured tone. "You should have no vague concerns, anybody can talk,anybody can break, working and making something is very hard...".

Rajiv Gandhi's audience was generally not very large. It ranged from 150 to 1500. There was not a formally decorated stage. Mostly the whole decoration consisted of some leaves and buntings hung here and there. A cloth sheet spread over a wooden plank was placed on an improvised raised platform. And sometimes he had to just stand on the ground itself and deliver his speech without any sound, system. Stage or no stage he was the same calm, quiet and thoughtful Rajiv Gandhi.

A large number of petitioners thronged his stage very often. Their long petitions and their sentimentally illiterate narrations did not irritate him at all. His patience did not wear out. He sometimes had to spend more time with the petitioners than the time he spent in making his address—distributing thus the healing touch of an apothecary.

"Do not say Rajiv Gandhi...say Mahatma Rajiv Gandhi is contesting the election," said a villager and the campaigner introducing the candidate was baffled and surprised for the people knew more about him and his temperament than the campaigners did.

He seemed to be aware of their ethos, their customs, the temples and the mosques and knew their auspicious days when most of their marriages would take place.

Thanks to his personality, his love for people, in less than a fortnight Rajiv Rattan Gandhi became 'Raju Bhaiya.' The interest he generated was intense, immense and immaculate.

On a number of times after the *Pradhan*, the headman of the village or some other local leader, had said a few words of welcome, Rajiv Gandhi carried the mike of his sound system to an elderly person asking him if he would like to say something.

According to Rajeev Mittal, author of Rajiv Gandhi—The Theme Today:

"This kind of respect and decency mellows all. "Nobody has the feeling of being ignored and this kind of asking by Rajiv Gandhi is a matter of pride for the man, his ordinaryness which may be he has suffered all his life vanishes, he goes home a great man with a bit of history in his pocket."

This is a style, a confidence, gentlemanliness—it is anything but politics tempered with decency and humility, a typical Rajiv Gandhi factor.

After his victory in Amethi, Rajiv Gandhi was breaking new ground in the world of politics. He was the brain behind the mammoth Kisan rally of January 1981 held in New Delhi. In this exercise, the Congress Party got a shot in the arm and the young politician had a taste of the labyrinthine power structure of Indian politics.

In November, 1982, India hosted the Asian Games. The commitment had been made years earlier but by January 1980, when Mrs. Indira Gandhi returned to power, hardly any work had been done to build the stadia and other infrastructure. Mr. Gandhi was entrusted with the task of getting all the work completed in time and ensuring that the Games themselves were conducted without any hitch or flaw. In fulfilling this challenging task he first displayed his flair for quiet efficiency and smooth co-ordination. Thereafter, as General Secretary of the Congress, he started streamlining and energising the party organisation with equal diligence. All these qualities and more came to the fore later in far more testing and trying times.

The next milestone on the road of Mr. Rajiv Gandhi's short journey into the world of politics was the November 1983 AICC(I) meet at Calcutta where it was made amply clear that Mr. Rajiv Gandhi was the force to be reckoned with. Other general secretaries vanished into the background, G.K. Moopanar and Shyam Sunder Mohapatra had to take a side seat. Other leaders like Kamalapati Tripathi were already known figureheads.

Soon after came the phase when Rajiv Gandhi chose party candidates for the Rajya Sabha elections in March, 1984.

But as in the tragic death of his brother Sanjay that resulted in his becoming a politician, another tragedy has propelled him to the honour of being the Prime Minister, clean and controversyless.

ii

MAN OF CRISIS

The real Rajiv was born the day his mother attained martyrdom. He was without a shadow. He was on his own. The millions who saw him on television with his thin, tight lips, moist eyes, his pointed Nehru nose, his determined forehead, were convinced of Indira Gandhi's right choice. At forty he looked exactly forty, and whenever he looked up he seemed to be telling his mother, "I will not let you down, come what may."

This was a new Rajiv Gandhi, the legatee of a glorious heritage, a true son of a rich soil. Seeing him on TV, standing near Indira Gandhi's body, viewers felt secure, assured. The country, they felt, was safe, its destiny in good hands.

The smooth and peaceful succession of Mr. Rajiv Gandhi as the Prime Minister is demonstration of India's quick resilience to brace challenges and of the firmness with which democracy had struck roots in the country. Those who participated in the process brought memorable credit to their deep commitment to supreme national interest.

When Rajiv Gandhi entered public life there was no indication that his apprenticeship would be so short. Mrs. Gandhi was looming on the political scene like a colossus. She was agile, active and brimming with the zest to serve the nation. She provided the nation the grit and the strength to face several problems. Any other person would have gone to pieces under the strain of the high office but Mrs. Gandhi was made of sterner stuff. She fought all divisive forces and did not flinch from decision which led her into the line of the assassins' bullets.

It was in this moment of crisis that the mantle of the office fell on Rajiv.

Rajiv Gandhi was sworn in as Prime Minister shortly before seven on the evening of October 31, 1984, in Ashoka Hall of Rashtrapati Bhawan. The President, Giani Zail Singh, administered the oath of office.

Mr. Rajiv Gandhi's emotion-choked voice could barely be heard as he took the oath of secrecy in English. After being sworn in he went back to his seat in the front row next to Mr. Pranab Mukherjee, while the Cabinet Ministers were being sworn in.

After an exceptionally grim swearing-in ceremony with the Cabinet Ministers and Mrs. Gandhi's top advisers holding back their tears and trying hard to remain expressionless, the President, for once without his red rose in his *achkan*, called Mr. Rajiv Gandhi and hugged him. The new Prime Minister bent his head and closed his eyes gulping while he did so.

Prime Minister Rajiv Gandhi in his first broadcast asked the nation to give him the support and blessings to complete the unfinished work of his mother. A lot was left to be done to fulfil Mrs. Gandhi's dreams, he said.

The new Prime Minister asked the country to remain peaceful. "We should not let our emotions get the better of us" because a step in anger only leads to blunder. He appealed to the people to exercise maximum restraint.

Mr. Gandhi said, "Nothing would hurt the soul of our beloved Indira Gandhi more than the occurrence of violence in any part of the country." It was of prime importance that "at this moment every step we take is in the correct direction. Indira Gandhi is no more, but her soul lives. India lives. India is immortal. The spirit of India is immortal."

The nation, he was sure, would recognise its responsibility and shoulder the burden heroically and with determination.

He said, "Indira Gandhi, India's Prime Minister, has been assassinated. She was mother not only to me but to the whole nation. She served the Indian people to the last drop of her blood.

"The country knows with what tireless dedication she toiled for the development of India. You all know how dear to her heart was the dream of a united, peaceful and prosperous India. An India in which all Indians, irrespective of religion, language or political persuasion, could live together as one big family in an atmosphere free from mutual rivalries and prejudices. By her untimely death, her work remains unfinished. It is for us to complete her task."

At its first meeting under the new Prime Minister, Mr. Rajiv Gandhi, the Union Cabinet on October 31, 1984, offered its respectful tribute to the memory of Mrs. Indira Gandhi and pledged itself to continue the great work of nationbuilding, carried on by her till the last moment. It called upon the people to maintain peace, communal harmony and unity.

The resolution said: "This meeting of the Council of Ministers places on record its profound sense of grief at the tragic death of the nation's great leader and Prime Minister, Mrs. Indira Gandhi.

"The entire nation feels orphaned at the loss of this indefatigable fighter for the country's integrity and unity. The non-aligned movement has lost a great steward and the world, a great statesman. She led the nation through the most difficult years of crisis and external aggression and built a united and economically strong nation which has become a model of self-reliance.

"While offering our respectful tribute to the memory of our great departed leader we pledge ourselves to continue the great work of nation-building which she carried on till her last moment. Mrs. Indira Gandhi lived and died for the integrity and unity of India and we call upon the entire nation to maintain peace and communal harmony and unity."

The Prime Minister, Mr. Rajiv Gandhi, and 15 national opposition party leaders on the night of November 1, 1984, made a joint appeal to people of all persuasions, particularly active political workers and public servants, to exert themselves to the utmost to restore sanity and harmony.

Amid the reports of violence pouring in from different parts of the country, Mr. Rajiv Gandhi warned that as Prime Minister of India he "cannot and will not allow" communal madness to destroy all that the nation stands for.

Mr. Gandhi said this in a two-minute unscheduled broadcast

to the nation on Friday, November 2, 1984, evening reacting sternly to "disgraceful incidence of arson, loot and murder" in different parts of the country, in the last two days.

The following is the text of the Prime Minister, Mr. Rajiv Gandhi's broadcast to the nation:

"It is with heavy heart that I speak to you this evening. While hundreds of millions of Indians are mourning the tragic loss of their beloved leader, some people are casting a slur on her memory by indulging in acts of hatred and violence. Disgraceful incidents of arson, loot and murder have taken place. This must stop forthwith. The Government will ensure the safety of life and property of every citizen irrespective of his caste, creed or religion.

"Indira Gandhi gave her life so that a united India should live and prosper. Anything that creates a division between brother and brother comes in the way of national unity. This violence is only helping the subversive forces to achieve their ends.

"Communal madness will destroy us. It will destroy everything India stands for. As Prime Minister of India I cannot and will not allow this.

"Tomorrow the mortal remains of Indira Gandhi will be consigned to sacred flames. She had said, 'Do not shed blood, shed hatred.' Let this guide us."

Mr. Gandhi appealed to the Congressmen and party workers to go out to the fields and work for the welfare of the poorer sections of society. The Prime Minister advised the Chief Ministers, who were in the capital in connection with Mrs. Gandhi's assassination, to go back immediately to their respective States and keep "a watch on the law and order situation."

The Prime Minister found time to visit the riot-affected areas on November 1, 1984, even when the late Prime Minister, Mrs. Indira Gandhi, was lying in state and the new Prime Minister had to attend to scores of foreign dignitaries.

PM's visit to riot-hit areas was appreciated by many.

The Prime Minister, on November 2, 1984, described the communal frenzy sweeping the country following the assassination of Indira Gandhi as "disgraceful".

He assured the people that the Government would safeguard the life and property of every citizen, irrespective of his caste, creed and religion.

The Prime Minister issued strict instructions to the authorities all over the country to put an immediate end to the spate of violence in different parts of the country in the wake of the assassination of Mrs. Indira Gandhi. He instructed that such incidents should not be allowed to continue at any cost and they should adopt whatever means necessary for it including seeking the help of the army wherever necessary.

The Prime Minister remained constantly in touch with the authorities throughout the day giving instructions above the steps to be taken to tackle the situation. The control room was receiving regular reports from all States about the situation and the same were being passed on to Mr. Gandhi for scrutiny.

The Prime Minister on November 1, 1984, condemnded the violent incidents that had occurred in the capital and other parts of the country following the assassination of Mrs. Gandhi as "an affront to everything that she stood for."

Making a fervent appeal to work for the restoration of harmony and trust, the Prime Minister warned that such violence would weaken the nation.

The appeal addressed to all Congressmen urged each of them, particularly members of the Youth Congress and the students wing, to combat communalism, violence and hooliganism.

"If we shirk this duty, the future will not forgive us," he said.

The following is the text of the Prime Minister's appeal:

"We have lost Indira Gandhi's presence. But her message will always guide us. What is that message? The nation's unity, the country's strength and progress, and harmony among all sections of the people and relentless efforts and courage in the defence of secularism and freedom. It is the lesson she imbibed from Mahatma Gandhi and Jawaharlal Nehru which she passed on to us.

"It is this lesson that has held the Congress together and made it to be the country's main political instrument, but the incidents that have occurred in Delhi and elsewhere since Indira Gandhi's assassination are an affront to everything that she stood for.

"Such violence will weaken us at a moment when we need all our strength. It will only help those who do not wish to see a strong and prosperous India.

"As members of the Congress it is your responsibility to put a stop to violence everywhere and to work for the restoration of harmony and trust.

"I appeal to each of you to take the lead in combating communalism, violence and hooliganism.

"If we shirk this duty, the future will not forgive us."

The Prime Minister made the following broadcast to the nation on October 31, 1984:

"Indira Gandhi, India's Prime Minister, has been assassinated. She was mother not only to me but to the whole nation. She served the Indian people to the last drop of her blood. The country knows with what tireless dedication she toiled for the development of India. You all know how dear to her heart India was in which all Indians, irrespective of their religion, language or political persuasion, live together as one big family in an atmosphere free from actual rivalries and prejudices. By her untimely death her work remains unfinished. It is for us to complete this task.

"This is a moment of profound grief. The foremost need now is to maintain our balance. We can and must face this tragic ordeal with fortitude, courage and wisdom. We should remain calm and exercise the maximum restraint. We should not let our emotions get the better of us, because passion would cloud our judgement. Nothing would hurt the soul of our beloved Indira Gandhi more than the occurrence of violence in any part of the country. It is of prime importance at this moment that every step we take is in the correct direction.

"Indira Gandhi is no more but her soul lives. India lives. India is immortal. The spirit of India is immortal. I know that the nation will recognise its responsibilities, and that we shall shoulder the burden heroically and with determination.

"The nation has placed a great responsibility on me by asking me to head the Government. I shall be able to fulfil it only with your support and co-operation. I shall value your guidance in upholding the unity, integrity and honour of the country."

Even in the midst of the funeral arrangements for Indira Gandhi he did not allow his personal grief to come in the way of his attending to matters of the state, especially those relating to law and order and foreign affairs.

Restoration of normalcy was at that moment Mr. Gandhi's main concern. On Saturday, November 3, 1984, he issued fresh instructions to the defence and police authorities to deploy by the night enough security forces in the Capital to bring under control incidents of violence, arson and looting.

The Prime Minister sacked Delhi's Lt.-Governor P.G. Gavai on Saturday, November 3, 1984, as the Centre took a series of important steps to combat the communal violence that burst into orgies of killings and arson in Bhogal, Mangolpuri and trans-Yamuna areas of the Capital and in some towns of Jammu & Kashmir, Haryana, West Bengal and Madhya Pradesh.

Home Secretary M.M.K. Wali was appointed Lt.-Governor of Delhi and former BSF Director-General Birbal Nath was appointed Home Secretary to take charge of the concerted police and army action that the Government had ordered to ensure the violence, which had claimed about 650 persons, ended forthwith.

In a message to the people, the Prime Minister said on November 7, 1984:

"I thank you all for the sympathy you have shown me in such overflowing measure. You and I have suffered a loss which can never be made good. You and I must work together to continue and complete the tasks which Indira Gandhi left unifinished.

"Indira Gandhi died as she had lived: unafraid, with courage abiding. Her name and her work will remain deathless. Sacred books tell us that death is the gate to immortality. Yet the physical body ceases to be. It must be returned to the elements. There are different ways of doing so, and individuals often indicate what should be done with their body after they are no more. It is a son's duty to carry out the parent's wish.

"Indira Gandhi loved and venerated the Himalayas and drew strength from them. She regarded herself as a child of the mountains. Whenever she was asked where she wished to live, her answer was: high up in the snowy mountains. To others the steep path might be a trial. To her it was exhilarating.

"She said once: 'To us Indians, the Himalayas are not just a great mountain range. They are an inseparable part of the Indian consciousness, standing for eternal values. The magnificence and grandeur of the mountains, the imperturbable lofty peaks, help us to see ourselves and our concerns in perspective. How small, how insignificant we are and, for all our powers of destruction and creation, how helpless we are in the vastness of the universe! And yet we are possessed of something special—an unconquerable soul. This is what enables men and women to bring the impossible into the realm of possibility.'

"Indira Gandhi had desired that on her death her ashes should be scattered in the Himalayas. I shall later this week entrust the mortal remains of my mother to the care of this great Lord of the snows. A portion of these will be strewn at Gangotri, which my mother described as the symbol of the earth's need for water. This sacred spot is the source of the Ganga, the River of India.

"With the scattering of the ashes in the Himalayas will end Indira Gandhi's earthly journey. But the nation's journey continues. Let us walk together, stout of heart and purpose, firm in step."

The Prime Minister on November 4, 1984, completed the process of ministry-making by inducting nine more Cabinet Ministers, 21 Ministers of State and Deputy Ministers. He retained all the Cabinet Ministers who had served with Mrs. Gandhi with the exception of Mr. P.C. Sethi.

Rajiv Gandhi assumed formal charge on November 12, 1984, of the Prime Minister's office at Central Secretariat, which his mother, Mrs. Indira Gandhi, had occupied for 15 years.

It was an emotional moment for by-standers and for him too as he reached South Block at 10.30 a.m. and was ushered into the teak-panelled office by Mr. P.C. Alexander, his Principal Secretary.

Attired simply in his usual white kurta-pyjama, with a shawl thrown around his shoulders to counter the nip of the November morning air, Prime Minister Rajiv Gandhi was escorted by two of his close aides, Mr. Arun Nehru and Mr. Arun Singh.

Since his swearing-in ceremony, Rajiv Gandhi had been attending to the urgent affairs of state from his residence at 1 Safdarjung Road.

After attending to some papers requiring his attention, Mr. Rajiv Gandhi drove to the All India Congress (I) Committee office on Akbar Road for a brief visit. He then went to Rashtrapati Bhavan for consultations with President Zail Singh and be present for the swearing in of four of his Ministers, who had been out of town when designated earlier.

The Prime Minister promised to give the nation a clean and efficient administration which would give no quarter "to the corrupt, lazy and the inefficient" and ensure full protection from outside pressures to those who worked with integrity and dedication.

Spelling out his priorities in his first major policy statement to the nation over All India Radio and Doordarshan after assuming office, the country's youngest Prime Minister said the administrative system needed to be more "goal-oriented." A new work ethic and a new work culture must be evolved in which the "Government is result-bound and not procedure-bound," he declared.

Mr. Gandhi said the broad domestic and foreign policies of his mother's administration would be continued. He called for religious tolerance and harmony since "answering communalism" would only help "subversive and secessionist forces."

The following is the text of the Prime Minister's broadcast to the nation on November 12, 1984:

"Yesterday the mortal remains of Indira Gandhi were consigned, as she had wished, to the mighty Himalayas. Her immortal spirit beckons to build the India of her dreams.

"Mahatma Gandhi breathed new life into our ancient land. He brought us freedom and taught us that the highest virtues are truth, love and non-violence. Jawaharlal Nehru laid the foundations of a politically and technically modern India—democratic, secular, socialist, non-aligned.

"Indira Gandhi built firmly on these foundations. She made the sovereignty of the people a reality and strove to ensure that policies and laws secured their rights. She fought against fanaticism and narrowness in all their forms. She made the nation self-reliant in agriculture, industry and several branches of technology. She battled relentlessly against poverty. Hers was the foremost voice for international peace in our tense and troubled world.

"Most important of all, she infused us with self-confidence and a sense of purpose. She gave us back our pride. This splendid heritage has been left to us by Indiraji. I pledge to preserve this precious legacy and to work for a united, strong and prosperous India, an India devoted to the cause of peace.

"Nothing is more important than the unity and integrity of our nation. India is indivisible.

"Secularism is the bedrock of our nationhood. It implies more than tolerance. It involves an active effort for harmony. No religion preaches hatred and intolerance. Vested interests, both external and internal, are inciting and exploiting communal passions and violence to divide India. Answering communalism with communalism will only help these subversive and secessionist forces. The combined might of the people and the Government will thwart their designs. There is only one India. It belongs to all of us.

"Speedy removal of poverty is our basic objective. The Government is judged by the degree and quality of change it can bring about. Five years ago, when the people recalled Indiraji to office, she promised an effective Government and she kept her promise. Food production and energy output have touched record levels. Science has surged forward. Industry has resumed its dynamic movement. Employment opportunities are expanding. The economy has withstood the most severe natural calamities and international crises. The political and economic standing of India in the world is higher than ever.

"I reaffirm our adherence to socialism and planning. Without planning we could not have reached where we are. Our aim is continuous modernisation, higher productivity and rapid advance of social justice.

"In our plans, rural development will have priority: greater production of cereals, pulses and oilseeds; spread of irrigation; support for small industries and handicrafts and all-round induction of new technology. Large expansion of employment, specially for rural and urban youth, is essential to reduce economic disparities and to ensure social peace. For this, high rates of growth in agriculture and industry will have to be achieved.

"The public sector has played a historic role in laying the foundation of a modern economy. It has to shoulder greater responsibilities, and to become more efficient to generate surplus for investment.

"Within the framework of national policies, the private sector has adequate scope to enhance the productive potential of the economy. But it should acquire the strength that competition provides by reducing costs and absorbing new technology. Both public and private sectors must venture out into new fields, improve quality and develop indigenous technology.

"Kisans and workers are the pillars of our economy. The focus of our policies on their welfare will be sharpened.

"Government will remain unwavering in its resolve to improve the living and working conditions of the scheduled castes, the scheduled tribes, backward classes, artisans, agricultural labour, women and the urban poor. The 20-point programme of Indira Gandhi, which aims to fulfil the immediate needs of the people, will be faithfully and effectively implemented.

"Our greatest wealth is our people. We must enable individuals and families to realise their potential to the full. For this we shall stress programmes of family planning, nutrition, welfare of women and children, control of disease, elementary and adult education, sport and better communication.

"I am committed to improving the quality of service to the people. I want to tell those involved in this task that if they work with integrity and dedication, they will have full protection from outside pressures and interference. But I also want to tell them that no quarter will be given to the corrupt, the lazy, the inefficient.

"Our administrative system must become more goal-oriented. A new work-ethic, a new work-culture must be evolved in which Government is result-bound and not procedure-bound. Reward and punishment must be related to performance. A strong concern for efficiency must permeate all institutions.

"The last few years have witnessed notable advances in science and technology. Indira Gandhi had a fine partnership with scientists, which helped the nation. I shall keep up this interaction.

"The creative arts give to life the vision of inner truth and beauty. We owe much to our craftsmen who have carried on centuries-old aesthetic traditions and to our artists and writers. We have to conserve our priceless heritage and create an environment in which art will flourish.

"Our educational system needs to be reconstructed as a dynamic force for national growth and integration. I intend to initiate a comprehensive review of the system and to build a national consensus for reform.

"For nation-building the first requisite is peace—peace with our neighbours and peace in the world. Our security environment has been vitiated. Sophisticated arms have been inducted on a large scale into our neighbourhood and into the Indian Ocean. We can depend on our armed forces to ensure the country's inviolability. The Government will continue to do all it can for the modernisation of defence and the welfare of our service personnel and their families. I take this occasion to greet our jawans and officers in whose hands the nation's honour and integrity are safe.

"Eminent leaders and representatives of the world's nations came here last week bringing to us their peoples' sympathy. I made it clear to them that India will continue its work for international peace, friendship and co-operation.

"Jawaharlal Nehru bequeathed to us a foreign policy which Indira Gandhi so creatively enriched. I shall carry it forward. I reaffirm our adherence to the United Nations, to the Non-Aligned Movement and to our opposition to colonialism, old or new. We are determined to work for narrowing international economic disparities.

"We want to develop closer relations with each one of our immediate neighbours in a spirit of peace, friendship and co-operation. This is what we have offered to Pakistan. We have always believed that non-interference, peaceful coexistence and non-alignment should be he guiding principles of our relationship. We shall further pursue the concept of common regional development of South Asia. Our relationship with China are improving and we shall continue to seek a satisfactory solution to the difficulties.

"We highly value the wide-ranging and time-tested relationship with the Soviet Union based upon mutual co-operation, friendship and vital support when most needed.

"We have always been friends with both the East and the West, as they are called, and we want better relations between them.

"With the United States of America, we have multifaceted relationship. We attach importance to our economic, technological and cultural co-operation with them.

"I wish also to assure the people of other regions—the Arab World, South-West and South-East Asia, the Far East and the Pacific Africa, Latin America, the Caribbeans, and Western and Eastern Europe—that we are keen on strengthening political and economic relations with them.

"Indira Gandhi reminded us that the most important single challenge before the world today is the threat of nuclear war. We shall continue her relentless crusade against the arms race. She was equally concerned about the global economic crisis. We shall persevere in the efforts to promote a dialogue between the North and the South and to build a just world economic order.

"The assassination of Indira Gandhi is a grave and critical moment. There has been a churning of the subconscious of our people. It is in moments of crisis that India awakens and responds with clarity and new creative endeavour. Out of turmoil must arise an intelligence that builds a vital sense of togetherness, creates order and establishes a deeply human relationship between man and man.

"Our heritage, the most ancient and that left to us by the torch-bearers of freedom, rests on secularism and tolerance. Indira Gandhi gave her life in building an India which was rooted in these basic tenets. We have to fuse the wisdom of our seers with the insights and artifacts of science and technology. We have to conserve and cherish our heritage—political, cultural and philosophic. We have to establish a right relationship with our natural resources, strengthen our newly won self-reliance. With this we must have the courage to boldly innovate, for change is demanded in our methods of work, in the absorption of new knowledge, in the values we generate for ensuring a meaningful and creative life for our people.

"As we build today so will be the tomorrow. Together we will build for an India of the 21st century. Together we will transform what needs transformation. Together we will face challenges and obstacles to progress. Together we will create an India that is strong, wise and great—a flame of peace and tolerance."

Rajiv Gandhi's first major statement, after assuming formal charge of the Prime Minister's office, was very much appreciated and acclaimed both by the Press and the people alike.

On the birth anniversary of Indira Gandhi, Rajiv Gandhi called the nation to fight divisive forces.

He said that people should not respond to Mrs. Indira Gandhi's assassination by showing anger "but by putting all our energies together by sinking our differences and by keeping together."

Addressing a massive public meeting on India Gate lawns he asked the people to remain united and not to forget why the late Prime Minister was killed and which were the forces behind the act. He said by remaining together alone the nation could be kept united.

He said there were some riots in the country soon after Mrs. Gandhi's assassination. People were angry and for a few days the nation was in turmoil. People must remember, he said, that whenever a big tree fell, the earth did shake a bit.

But the promptness with which it was stopped and the way the people united and tried to stand together was noted by the whole world. The world has seen that India has matured into a strong democracy, he said. The Prime Minister said, "We shall take the nation still forward and see that the work started by Jawaharlal Nehru and Indira Gandhi and the work for the benefit of the poor is completed fast."

Mr. Rajiv Gandhi said Mrs. Gandhi's assassination was aimed at not only killing her but at dismembering the whole nation. "But we showed to the world that the foundations laid by Gandhiji and Nehru are not that weak that they can be shaken by a few bullets."

He said people must observe how the forces which were behind the assassination were getting help from abroad. He said, "All our energies are to be used to finish these forces." He asked the people to provide him strength for the job and also keep their calm.

"Sometimes things done in passion or in grief can prove helpful to enemies of the nation," he cautioned the people. "With equanimity the nation is to pursue policies which have benefited her," he added.

The India Gate meeting was organised by the Delhi Administration in memory of the late Prime Minister whose birth anniversary was observed on November 19. Besides the large gathering of people, MPs, Ministers, councillors, diplomats and some prominent citizens were among those present. All through his 16-minute speech Mr. Gandhi was cheered by a responsive audience.

Mr. Gandhi said this was the first birthday of Mrs. Gandhi when she was not amidst the people. Thirty-seven years ago when Gandhiji was shot, he had not really died but kept guiding the nation towards progress. Though Mrs. Gandhi died a few weeks ago, she continued to provide strength and guidance.

He said when a person reached a stature like the one attained by Mrs. Gandhi, her physical body did not remain that significant as her thoughts and what she did and what was her performance as the Prime Minister became more relevant. Her contribution became evident when a comparison was made between India and other countries.

"After 37 years of Independence we can say we are free in all respects," Mr. Gandhi said He said, if a view was taken of India's neighbours or of several Asian and African countries, very few would be found to be democracies and fewer in a position to be able to stand up with as much esteem as India could."

Mr. Rajiv Gandhi told the people that Pandit Nehru and Indira Gandhi had taken the country to a path which made her really strong. And this they were able to achieve only when they were extended whole-hearted support by the people.

Reviewing the security environment around India and the international situation, the Prime Minister said the world climate had shown no signs of improvement.

On the continuing arms build-up by Pakistan, he said the weapons it was acquiring were ostensibly for use in Afghanistan and the mountainous terrain but in reality they were very difficult to be used there. "There is danger of their being redirected against us."

Referring to the country's past experience, the Prime Minister said whenever there was a build-up like this in Pakistan with outside link-up invariably India had suffered.

He said it was essential that the defence forces were ever prepared to defend the unity and integrity of the country. The defence forces had been modernised so that they would always be adequate to their task. The acquisition of new aircraft by the IAF was to ensure that it did not lag behind other air forces of the world.

He stressed the need to pay greater attention to defence research and development. "We must plan further into the future. I get a feeling that when we talk about our own research and development, our perceptions do not go far enough ahead and by the time our research and development had developed something, the world has moved much further ahead. We should try and jump ahead. maybe 10 years or 15 years." he said.

He also stressed the need to bring about greater co-ordination between the three Services at various levels and said that there was greater need for such co-ordination specially among the lower ranks where interaction could make a great difference in the effectiveness of the fighting forces.

iii

THE RAJIV WAVE

When Rajiv Gandhi took over as the Prime Minister, the Opposition began to doubt whether elections to the Lok Sabha shall be held in time. Born and brought up in a family wedded to democratic institutions, Rajiv Gandhi ensured that the general elections to the eighth Lok Sabha were held not only in time but a little ahead of it. The general elections were held on December 24, 27 and 28, 1984.

The Congress (I) gained a hefty three-fourths majority in the Lok Sabha shattering all previous electoral records in the country and virtually obliterating the Opposition in most of the States.

The massive wave in its favour, which was halted only in Andhra Pradesh and Tripura and partially in West Bengal and Jammu & Kashmir, saw the party chalk up a mind-boggling 401 of 495 seats. The party created history by surpassing the record of 371 seats bagged by the undivided Congress under Jawaharlal Nehru's leadership in 1957.

Strangely, the shattering blow dealt to all other national parties by the Congress (I) in this election elevated the regional Telugu Desam of Mr. N.T. Rama Rao to the stature of the single largest opposition party in the Lok Sabha. The Telugu Desam won 28 seats.

The Prime Minister, Mr. Rajiv Gandhi, recorded a glorious victory in Amethi when he won by a staggering margin of 3.14 lakh votes. His sister-in-law, Mrs. Menaka Gandhi, who was his chief opponent, lost her security deposit.

In an open letter to the Prime Minister, N.H. Antia has pointed out that this election has shown that "the common man has lost faith in politics and the politician, and has touchingly placed his implicit faith in you as their last hope. Let those who have been elected on the tickets handed by you not suffer from any delusion that the people have voted for them. The people have only used them as a vehicle to get you, a young non-hardened politician, into a position where they hope you will look after their meagre needs which remain to be met almost four decades after Independence.

"The massive mandate that the people have given you is, I believe, their last trust with democracy. We hope you will justify their trust in you.

"The triumph of the Congress (I) in the electoral battle holds out both a lesson and promise in as much as it is an opportunity as well as a challenge. An overwhelming verdict of this type which is unparalleled in the post-independence democratic annals merits to be analysed in the context of the message conveyed by the electorate to different political parties in the fray.

"The verdict has its clear-cut and implicit aspects. In the former sense the message of the electorate is succinctly and neatly weighted in favour of a strong and stable democratic polity presupposing efficient and well-oiled government and party apparatuses to deliver the goods to the people."

The Prime Minister, Mr. Rajiv Gandhi, has emerged the nation's hero-symbol endowed with freshness of approach and dynamism of youth and infused with an image to enable him to ensure a clean political, administrative and social life-style.

The majority won by Mr. Rajiv Gandhi is unprecedented whose reassurance is accompanied by an equally unprecedented problem posed by the absolute rout of the Opposition for reasons for which it has to blame only itself. This is the lesson of the mandate for those who have been trying to thrive on the deliberately created caste-based and community-based social divides. The poll outcome is a rejoinder to all those who had been basing their calculation on mental "balkanisation" of the country's political entity by fanning divisions of region, caste and creed and the greater rebuff that it conveys to the elements who had gone to the extent of

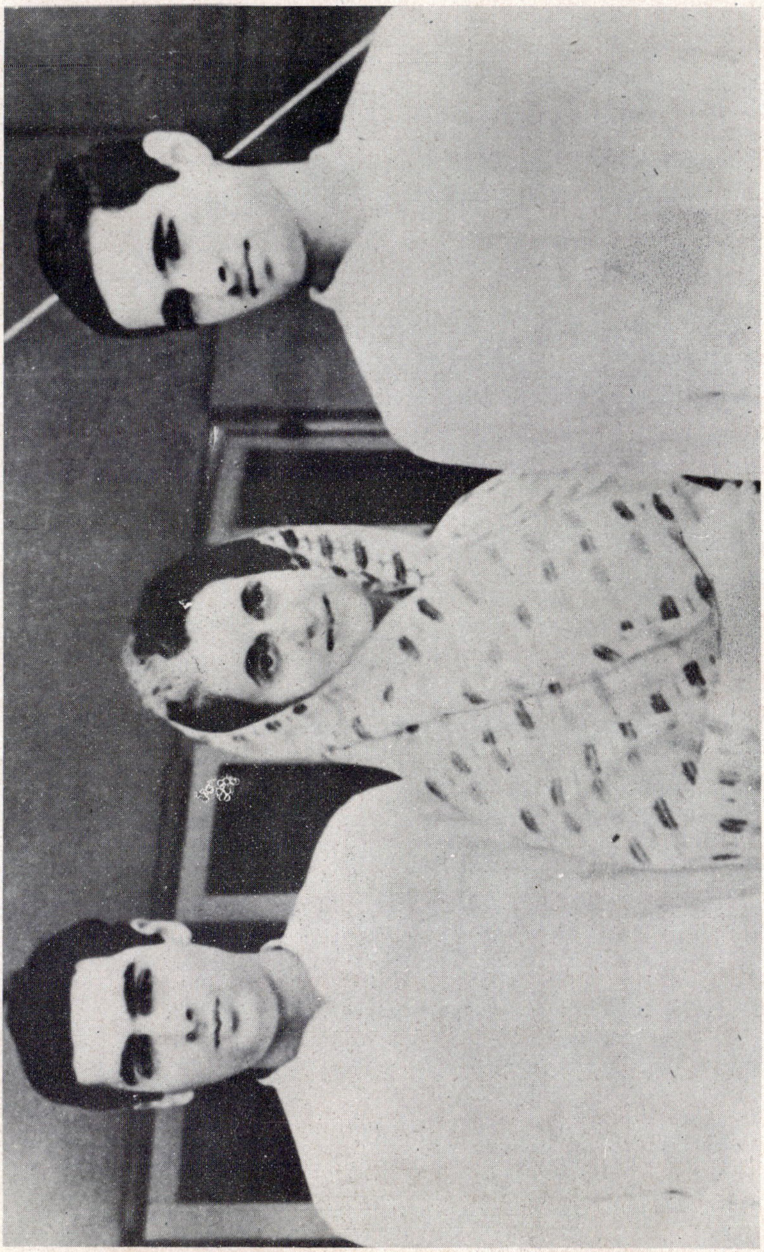

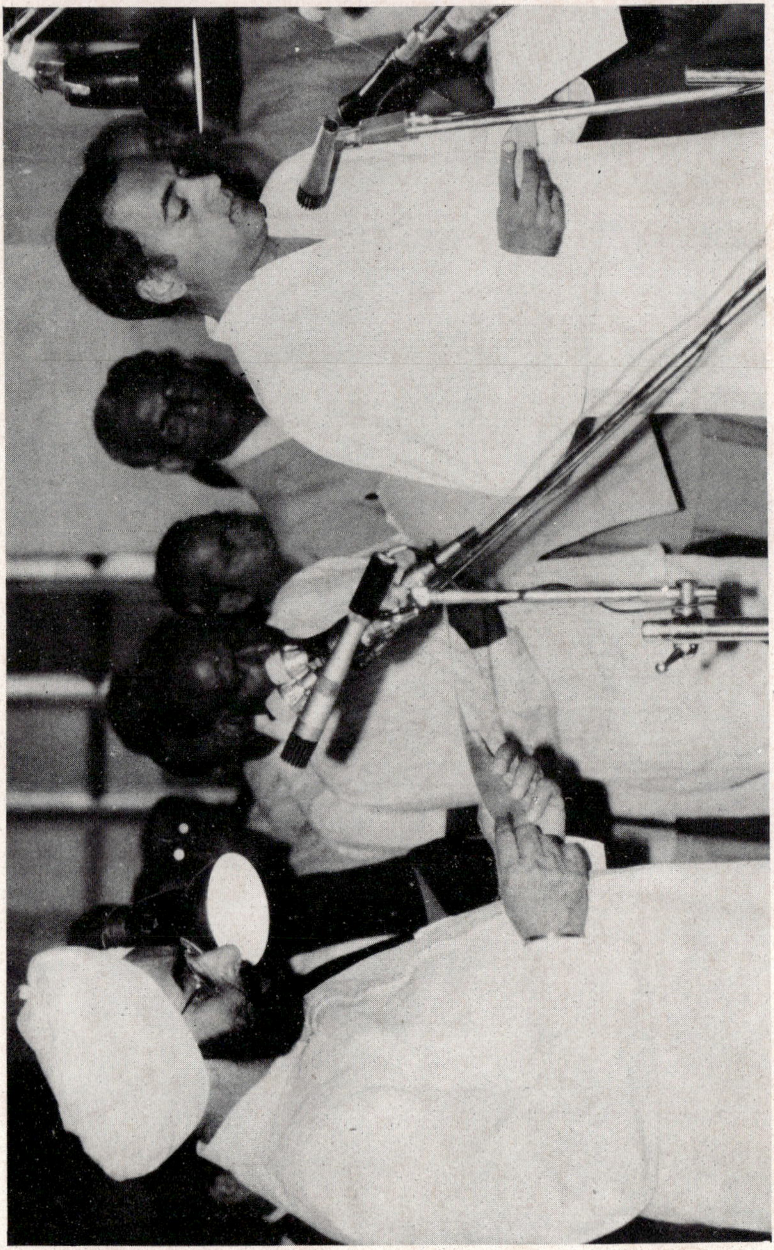

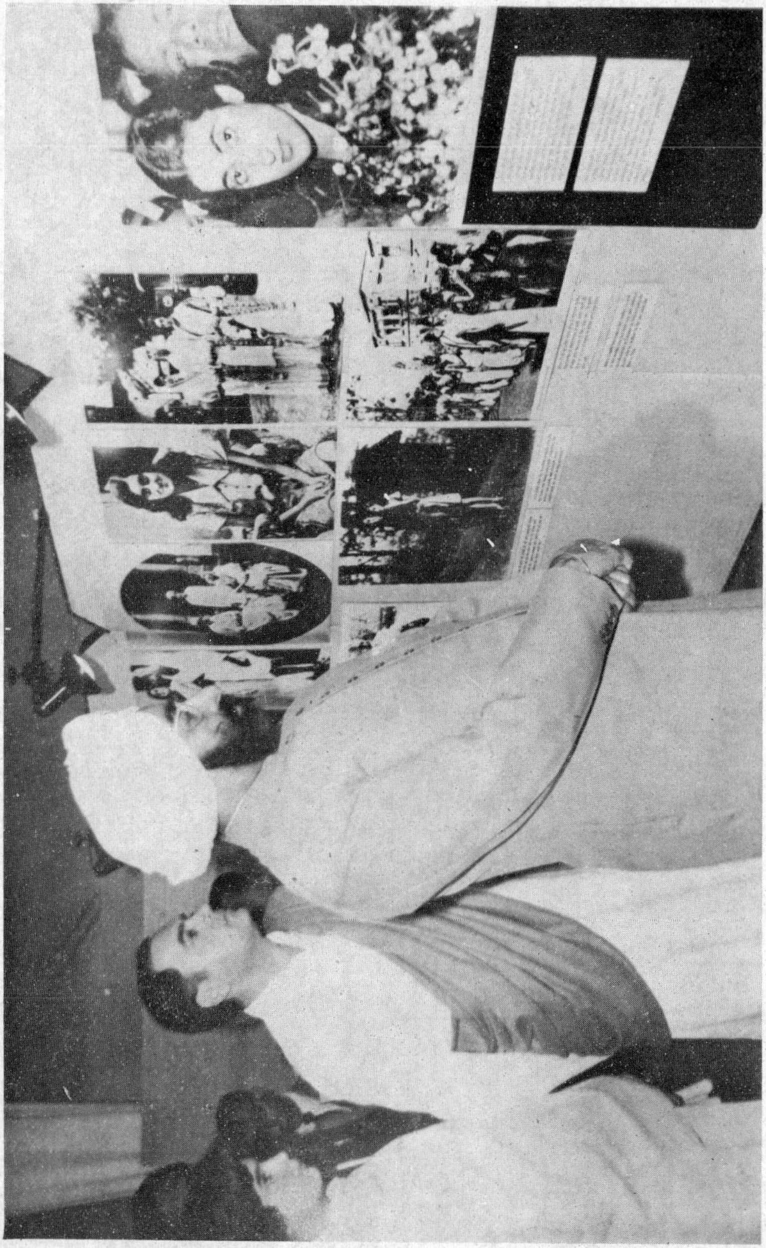

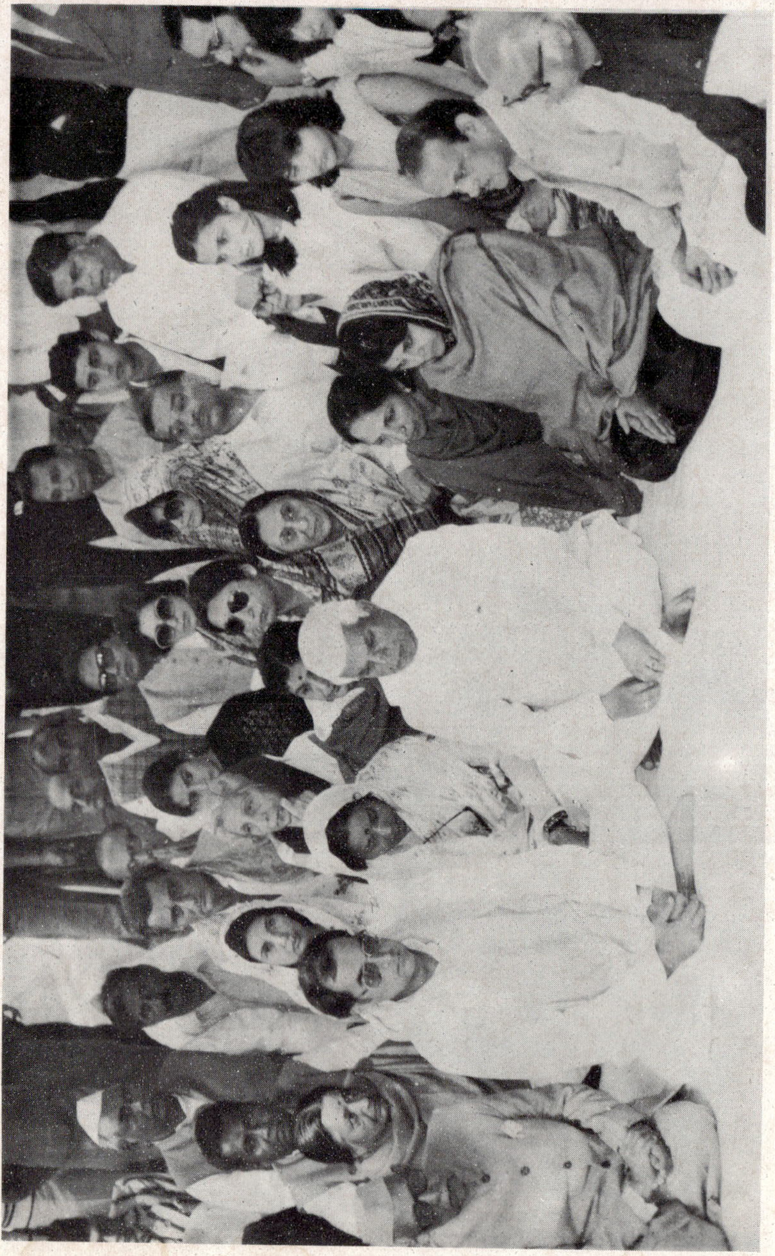

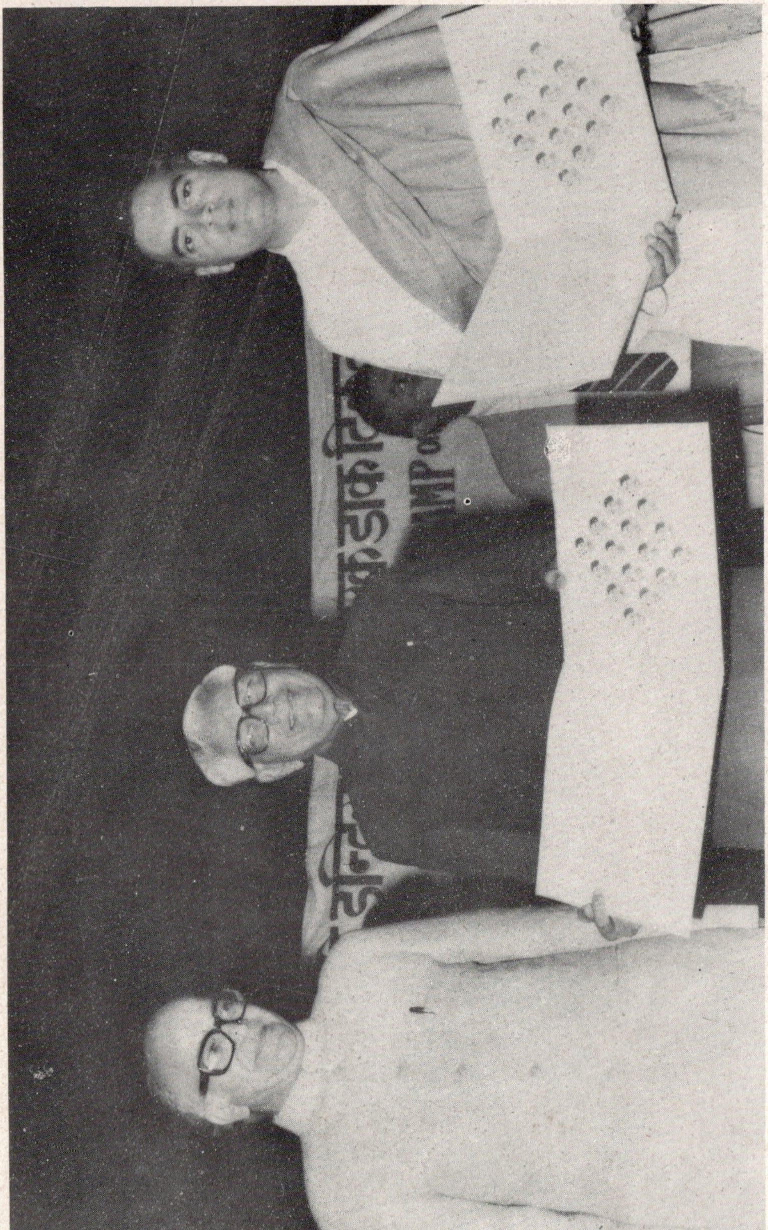

lending themselves as tools in the hands of outside forces of destabilisation aiming to bring about dismemberment of India as a modern nation-state.

Eminent journalists, computer experts and political science pundits have all analysed and explained the unprecedented and overwhelming success of Mr. Rajiv Gandhi and the Congress (I). In fact our youthful Prime Minister has stunned the world by surpassing the election successes of his mother, Indira Gandhi, and grandfather Jawaharlal Nehru. What is the secret of this massive 'swing' and overpowering 'wave'? A combination of the following factors has resulted in this record-breaking poll performance:

The lack of faith among the people in the capability of the fragmented opposition parties to provide a cohesive, stable and dynamic government specially in view of the Janata experiment of 1977;

The inhability of the Opposition to rebut the charge about its ambivalent attitude towards the Anandpur Sahib resolution;

The wave due to the dastardly assassination of Indira Gandhi;

The efficient and mature manner in which Mr. Rajiv Gandhi assumed the mantle of Prime Ministership in the hour of crisis and handled events following his mother's murder;

Mr. Gandhi's assumption of power is seen by many as a much delayed transfer of power to the younger generation as we have been disillusioned by the "old leadership" and its ability to bring about dynamic change in administration needed for the modern technological age. Besides, the new government gives the unique assurance of stability with change;

Mr. Gandhi's personal image also contributed to the victory to a large extent. He exudes an image of a clean, forthright and mature young leader who has become the hope of the nation; and

It is as much a vote for Rajiv Gandhi and the progressive image he has projected as it is for the century-old Congress policies and programmes. It would not be inaccurate to interpret the results as an overwhelming support of the Indian people to Rajiv Gandhi and his 'new' Congress which has promised to carry the country into the 21st century by their progressive policies.

On December 31, 1984, Rajiv Gandhi's new Cabinet was sworn in. It is generally known as the New Look Cabinet. Prime Minister Rajiv Gandhi has been as good as his promise in selecting his Cabinet. He has used his mandate for change with discernment and circumspection. His new look Cabinet is a combination of experience and expertise. While tested war horses like Narasimha Rao, S.B. Chavan and Buta Singh have been retained, Bansi Lal, K.C. Pant, Ashok Sen, Abdul Ghafoor and Vishwanath Pratap Singh are the new Cabinet Ministers.

The Prime Minister has redeemed his pledge on education by appointing a Cabinet Minister in charge of education, perhaps the first time after the death of Abul Kalam Azad. K.C. Pant, the new Minister, has his plate full if he is to wrestle with the problems of reforming the educational system. K.R. Narayanan and Natwar Singh have been brought in as Ministers of State for their expertise. Madhavrao Sindhia is in for his victory over Vajpayee.

The Prime Minister has written letters to several world leaders—including U.S. President Ronald Reagan, Soviet Prime Minister Nikolai Tikhonov, President Zia-ul-Haq and President Jayewardene—expressing his Government's desire to improve relations with their countries.

Mr. Rajiv Gandhi has written these letters in reply to the messages of felicitation he has received on his becoming the Prime Minister of India. He has made use of these messages to briefly express his basic approach in foreign policy.

In his letter to President Reagan, Mr. Rajiv Gandhi has expressed the hope that the potentialities of Indo-U.S. ties would be realised in greater measure in the years ahead. He said it was a matter of satisfaction that recent years had witnessed a marked growth of "our bilateral relations in many fields."

"We also attach the utmost priority to the acceleration of social and economic developments in achieving our objective. I took forward to the further strengthening of co-operation between our two countries."

Mr. Gandhi said his Government had assumed office with an "overwhelming mandate from the people" to safeguard the nation's unity and integrity.

In his communication to the Soviet Prime Minister, Mr. Tikhonov, Mr. Gandhi said he would strive to further strengthen Indo-Soviet friendship and co-operation. Mr. Gandhi said friendship between the two countries had been "mutually beneficial and is in the interest of peace and stability in our region and in the whole world."

He pointed out that the Soviet Union stood by India in times of stress and difficulty.

To President Zia, the Prime Minister wrote about his commitment to the "search for peaceful and co-operative relations" with Pakistan and expressed the hope that the two countries would work together for peace and stability in the region.

Mr. Gandhi said his government wanted to establish relations with Islamabad on the basis of "sovereign equality, non-interference and mutual benefit."

The Prime Minister, Mr. Rajiv Gandhi, reiterated that his Government would give top priority to the problem of Punjab.

In his first address to the nation over Doordarshan and All India Radio after his electoral triumph, Mr. Gandhi pointed out that a Cabinet Committee had been set up to study the problem and to consider alternatives for "a peaceful settlement within a specified time-frame."

The following is the text of the Prime Minister's broadcast to the nation over All India Radio and Doordarshan:

"You have given my party and me your confidence in overflowing measure. Who could ask for more? And how can we prove worthy of it? Only by working for you with unremitting faith and humility, summoning all our reserves of strength and energy, being as unsparing with ourselves as you have been generous with your trust.

"I do not regard it as my victory, or even the victory of my party, which commences its hundredth year of service; it is the victory of the people of India.

"You have spoken clearly and unmistakably. You have given a mandate for unity, for strength, for harmony.

"The whole world sees once again the vitality of India's democratic tradition. The political system built up by our great leaders, Gandhiji, Panditji and Indiraji, has marched to new strength. The election has been a great celebration of democracy. India's ancient heritage going back to the dawn of mankind, stands renewed in freedom.

"The dust and din of the elections are behind us. The passions they generated must now make way for reconciliation. Great tasks wait us and we should approach them in a spirit of togetherness. United, there is no challenge that we cannot meet.

"Secularism is the basis of our unity. Communalism and all other narrow loyalties are incompatible with unity. These elections have shown that our people always rise above these artificial barriers. We have to fight communalism and the suspicion and insecurity it breeds. It is my first duty to safeguard the life, property and legitimate rights of citizens belonging to every faith.

"We must go beyond the prevention and suppression of violence. We must cure the minds where hatred and prejudice arise and grow. We must take the campaign for unity to every village and every street of every town. An ideological battle against communalism, fanaticism must be waged in our schools and universities, in our work places and in our media.

"My Government will give top priority to the problem of Punjab. A Cabinet Committee has been formed to study various aspects of the problem and to look at alternatives for a peaceful settlement within a specified timeframe. In ending the sad chapter of discord, all should co-operate. The Sikhs are as much a part of India as any other community. They have played a heroic role in winning and defending our freedom. I wish to assure them that their life and property will be protected in every part of the country. In Punjab and elsewhere, all patriotic forces must repudiate those who preach separatism and practise violence. There cannot, and will not, be any concession to separatist ideologies and to the cult of violence. India's unity is paramount, everything else comes after that.

"Earnest efforts will be made to settle the foreigners' issue in Assam. The give-and-take of the conference table can yield victories which confrontation cannot.

"In a few months we shall begin the Seventh Plan. The war against our old enemies—poverty, unemployment, disease, ignorance—continues. In the weeks ahead, we shall review our existing policies and programmes to ensure that our basic objectives of growth with justice are realised within the stipulated time-table.

"The public sector will continue to be a major tool of development; deficiencies in performance wherever they exist will be quickly overcome. Far-reaching proposals for change have been formulated and are under consideration.

"Improvement in productivity, absorption of modern technology and fuller utilisation of capacity must acquire the status of a national campaign. I have asked the Ministries of Science and Technology and Industries to prepare specific proposals to achieve these objectives.

"I have reviewed the foreign trade policies and directed that concrete steps should be taken in the next few weeks to give a fresh impetus to our exports.

"The 20-point programme for the weaker sections is being restructured to be more effective.

"Continuing deforestation has brought us face to face with a major ecological and socio-economic crisis. The trend must be halted. I propose immediately to set up a National Wastelands Development Board with the object of bringing 5 million hectares of land every year under fuelwood and fodder plantation. We shall develop a people's movement for afforestation.

"The Ganga is the symbol of India's culture, the source of our legend and poetry, the sustainer of millions. Today it is one of the most polluted rivers. We will restore the pristine purity of the Ganga. A Central Ganga Authority will be set up to implement an action plan to prevent the pollution of the Ganga and its tributaries. Measures will be taken to ensure cleaner air and water in all parts of the country.

"Administrative reform is crucial for social and economic transformation. It is for this reason that I decided to take under my own charge the Department of Personnel and Administrative Reforms. A full-scale review of administrative organisation, policies and procedures is in progress.

"I have asked that the decision-making processes should be decentralised along with enforcement of accountability. Rules and procedures will be drastically simplified to speed up decision-making. Results will take precedence over procedures.

"I have directed all concerned agencies to ensure that citizens get prompt and courteous service from Government departments and agencies. An effective machinery for redressal of public grievances will be set up in offices and departments with large public dealings.

"Action will be taken to rise the morale of public services. We shall prevent extraneous interference in the normal functioning of public services. We must create a new administrative culture for service of the masses. Training of civil servants of all categories will be restructured to develop competence and commitment to the basic values of our society.

"Education must promote national cohesion and the work ethic. The grandeur of our freedom struggle and its significance for national integration have to be brought home to every student. Our schools and colleges should acquaint the younger generations with India's ancient heritage and culture. The curricula and text-books should curb parochial and communal interpretations of our composite culture.

"I have looked at some of the policies and programmes in this field. I have asked that a new national education policy be drafted.

"We are formulating programmes to use on a large scale the new communication technology in our school system. Delinking of degrees from jobs under Government is under active consideration. Steps are being taken to establish an Open University to bring higher education within easy reach of all. The Central Schools Organisation will be expanded. These schools will function as centres of excellence in every district of our country.

"I would strongly emphasise education's organic link with the productive forces of society. We shall reorganise vocational education to align it with industry, agriculture, communications and other productive sectors of our economy.

"We have inherited a well-tested and consistent foreign policy which serves our national interest. We have always believed in working for peace. Our policy is to be friends with all countries on the basis of reciprocity and mutual benefit. Our commitment to non-alignment and a new world economic order based on justice, equality and mutual co-operation is unshakable. This means a total dedication to the twin causes of peace and development. We also believe in safeguarding the independence of States and upholding the principles of non-interference and non-intervention.

"One aspect of our foreign policy needs special attention. We have deep historical and cultural links with our immediate neighbours in South Asia. We share the same memories of foreign rule and look forward to the same prospects of development and a better future for our peoples. I believe firmly that we can work together to realize these common aims. We do have some problems, but we are determined to resolve them on the basis of mutual respect, sovereign equality and friendship.

"In a troubled world, India has a role to play because of its history, its geography and its faith in peaceful coexistence. In trying to live up to our responsibilities, this Government will scrupulously follow the basic approach and principles bequeathed to us by Jawaharlal Nehru and Indira Gandhi. Like them, we shall be dynamic in our responses to the changing context.

"In the last few weeks it was my privilege to have travelled over all parts of our beloved country. I saw millions of fellow Indians face to face. In all the cultural diversity of our people, what stood out was the unity of India. It is a privilege to be born in India, and to be heir to its great civilization. We have so much to secure for our own people and so much to give to the world.

"We are passing through a difficult phase. Our burdens are immense, our road long and arduous. Your co-operation is vital for achieving the national goals.

"I give you my greetings for the New Year. May it bring happiness to everyone.

"From time to time I shall share with you my ideas, my hopes, my struggles. But even more I want to listen to your difficulties, your ideas, your hopes. Together we shall share the burden and the ecstasy of building our India."

Union Law Minister Asoke Sen stated in New Delhi on January 7, 1985, that Prime Minister Rajiv Gandhi had decided to give the "utmost priority" to judicial reforms.

Addressing a meeting of the All India Congress Committee Legal Cell, which invited him and State Minister H.R. Bhardwaj to felicitate them, Mr. Sen said: "We must have a system of justice which would reflect our national aspirations and be dear to the people."

Mr. Sen said, in England, thanks to the legal aid system, every barrister and solicitor is a busy lawyer unlike in the 1930s when only a few barristers could earn a good living from the legal profession. A similar legal aid system had to be introduced in India, he said and hoped to see to it during his term of office that there would be no briefless advocate in this country.

Mr. Sen stated that the Prime Minister had told him to quickly have a judicial reforms plan and push it through.

While introducing far-reaching changes in the administrative set-up, Prime Minister Rajiv Gandhi has created a full-fledged Ministry of Science and Technology and also implemented the Sarin Committee's recommendation about bifurcation of the Department of Posts and Telegraphs.

A new Ministry of Environment and Forests has also been created with two distinct Departments, one of Environment and the other of Forests and Wildlife.

The new Ministry of Science and Technology will have under it the Departments of Science and Technology, of Scientific and Industrial Research and of Non-Conventional Energy Sources.

This will make for greater co-ordination in scientific research and development and also upgradation of technology and development of new energy sources. Matters relating to the National Research Development Corporation, the Central Electronics Limited and the National Information System of Science and Technology will be looked after by the Department of Scientific and Industrial Research. The Commission for Additional Sources of Energy will work under the Development of Non-Conventional Energy Sources.

The creation of a Ministry of Science and Technology is in keeping with the Prime Minister's desire to take the country into the 21st century by building the necessary scientific and technological infrastructure.

The Presidential notification also effects departmental reorganisation in the Defence Ministry, which now has a Department of Defence, a Department of Defence Production and Supplies and a third Department of Defence Research and Development.

The Department of Rehabilitation, which was hitherto a part of the Labour Ministry, has been attached to the Ministry of Home Affairs. The Ministry will now also look after relief and rehabilitation of displaced persons.

Prime Minister Rajiv Gandhi has said that India would like to improve its relations with Pakistan and "finish off this confrontation that has been taking place over the years."

In a 50-minute interview with Times, Mr. Gandhi said India would like a reduction in the level and sophistication of arms which were being supplied to Pakistan.

Blaming the arms race in the subcontinent, he said, "We are in no mood for an arms race. (If) we are forced to, we have to, but we don't want to. We have much better things to concentrate on."

"We would like to reduce the tension between our two countries as quickly as might be possible," the Prime Minister said.

On relations with super powers, Mr. Gandhi said India wanted to improve its ties with the United States in every sphere.

He said: "I see a strong relationship between India and the Soviet Union. We have been friends for a long time. They have been friends when we have needed them. And there are many issues on which we think alike without having to align with the others.

"Of course, this does not mean that we don't want to be friends with the United States. We want to improve our relations in every sphere with the USA but we want to keep our option of individuality open."

Referring to Punjab, Mr. Gandhi said his Government would like to get the Akali Dal's co-operation. Many of the earlier statements and actions of the Akali Dal had given rise to a feeling in the country that the Akalis wanted to "operate outside our Constitution. We would like them to be categorical and say they would operate within our Constitution and find some method of disassociating themselves from the extremists."

He spoke of Sikhs' major contribution to the nation and said "we hope to get an even bigger contribution from them."

Mr. Gandhi said most Sikhs were "very very good citizens. The exceptions are very few and they have been misguided."

On sectarian violence, Mr. Gandhi said: "If you look at the castes, the religious angle, all of our various regional, linguistic groups, each one of them is a prospective danger. But the real danger is economic stagnation. Whenever we have had a problem with the minorities, it has been when there has been an economic problem.

"So in a way there is a problem and in a way there is not a problem."

Noting that the economy was moving well, he said the elections had shown that the country stood united and that "national integrity is a prime factor for everybody."

Mr. Gandhi said his Government would open up more areas

for the private sector to operate in the interest of free growth of the economy.

Prime Minister Rajiv Gandhi has set in motion the process of consultations with the top Opposition leaders to acquaint himself with their views on issues of national importance.

Mr. Gandhi met Bharatiya Janata Party General Secretary L.K. Advani on the night of January 10, 1985. He had already had discussions with Congress (J) Chief Jagjivan Ram and CPI leader Indrajit Gupta.

The problems that figured at these discussions, held at the initiative of Mr. Gandhi, included Assam, Punjab and Sri Lanka.

Mr. Advani is understood to have suggested steps to sort out Centre-State ties and introduction of electoral reforms.

Andhra Pradesh Chief Minister N.T. Rama Rao whose Telugu Desam Party now forms the main Opposition group in the Lok Sabha, specially flew down to New Delhi from Hyderabad to meet Mr. Gandhi.

Prime Minister Rajiv Gandhi on January 12, 1985, urged a departure from traditional ways in the ensuing second phase of the country's developmental effort, putting an end to procedural delays and heavy cost overheads.

Inaugurating the year of the youth, in consonance with the United Nations General Assembly resolution to observe 1985 as the "International Year of the Youth", he enjoined upon the country's young people to rise above regional, parochial and caste differences to help build a strong India.

The Prime Minister, Mr. Rajiv Gandhi, launched the 'Year of the Youth' by inaugurating the National Youth Forum on 'Youth for Unity and National Integration'. Speaking on the occasion the Prime Minister said:

"Today is Vivekanand's 122nd birthday. The message that he gave us is still very valid for today's youth—strength, unity and integration for the country. The responsibilities in front of us today are much more than have been in front of our country for many many years. You are aware of the conditions in the world. You are aware of the tensions within our country. We have to rise above these to unite India. We have to rise above parochial, caste, religious differences, linguistic differences and build a united strong India.

"In recent weeks, we have seen a new upsurge in the youth of India. This must be strengthened and must be carried forward, the youth is always impatient—impatient with procedures, wanting results—and we must work hard towards this. India has gone through its first phase of development.

"Now we start the second phase. We must evaluate what we have achieved. We must consider the progress we have made and we must identify the mistakes we have made, because it is only then that we can correct them and we can move ahead. Today we must look towards the results and the youth must work towards this end—results in every sphere. We have to build the strength of our youth. In India today almost 71 per cent of our population is below 35. India is a young country and India looks ahead to the next century, to a progressive strong country. If we work towards this from today, we will be ready in the next 10 or 15 years. We have to build not just in the traditional ways that we have been building; that has kept us very occupied in procedures, has tied us to very heavy overheads, which we cannot afford to carry any more.

"During the past weeks, I have seen some of the problems that are facing the country and the biggest problem is discipline. Discipline in every sphere—discipline on the street, on the road, discipline in public and at a much higher level, discipline by various Governments—Central Government Departments, State Governments—and this is where we have to tighten up. If we are not able to maintain discipline, we will not be able to progress at all.

"We have to see that the new programmes that are brought in are such that they build the youth, build the character of the youth and in that character they build Indian culture, Indian traditions, Indian values. We have to see that the physical strength, physical condition of our youth is improved. Like Vivekanand said it is not just the mind, but the mind must be supported by a strong body; and that is very essential. We have to concentrate on how we can build our youth physically and make them really winners in whatever field they participate; whether it is sports or anything else, there must be a spirit to win, to give just a little bit more, which is something that is lacking in our youth today. We are very happy to rise to a certain level and then we seem to start relaxing thinking 'I have done my bit.' But it is that final spurt that really makes the difference. This is where we find our youth is lacking. We have to just give that last push to rise above the ordinary, to rise to exceptional level. We have seen whenever there has been a need our youth has stood together and has risen to the occasion; we know that they have it enough to do it. I have seen during the past three or four years that challenges which no country could have accepted, which no country could have accomplished, we not only accepted but we accomplished them and we accomplished them well. This is something that we have to be proud of, but more than that we have to remember that we can do it and we have to keep on doing it and not just give it in a spirit and then relax for five years. We need a continuous push; the country needs a continuous push and India's youth must give it that push today.

"There are tremendous tasks ahead—tasks of uniting the country, of building the country—and this is not the time for us to think of our differences. It is time to get together, it is time to build. The young must look towards the 21st century, build for the 21st century and take India ahead towards the next century.

"I congratulate you for this two-day seminar that you are having. We will be bringing out a lot of programmes for the youth. From your discussions, we will get some more ideas, some new ideas, and we will try to keep this year, the International Youth Year, a very active year for India's youth."

Addressing the general body meeting of the Congress (I) Party in Parliament of January 15, 1985, Mr. Gandhi said his Government had initiated certain steps to resolve Punjab and Assam issues and hoped to achieve success shortly. However, there was a limit to talks and discussions as these could not be carried on at the cost of the nation.

He was of the view that confrontation should be avoided so as to create a congenial atmosphere for finding an amicable solution acceptable to all concerned parties. At the same time, he made it clear that there could be no compromise with extremism and terrorism which must be stamped out firmly.

The Prime Minister's 45-minute, scintillating address in the Central Hall of Parliament was punctuated by applause from the admiring partymen as he touched a wide range of national and international issues. The meeting was attended by over 500 Congress (I) members of the eighth Lok Sabha and the Rajya Sabha.

Maintaining that his Government was taking note of the activities in the neighbouring countries he expressed concern at the influx of 40,000 Tamil refugees into this country in the wake of the ethnic conflict in Sri Lanka.

While reaffirming that it was internal issue of Sri Lanka, Mr. Gandhi hoped the Sri Lankan Government would soon find a political solution to the vexed problem and the Tamil refugees would return home.

Referring to India's on-going dialogue with China to normalise relations, the Prime Minister said the talks were going on well but "we have a long way to go."

Stressing the need for giving a further fillip to the non-aligned movement, Mr. Gandhi maintained that India wanted friendship with each country in the world.

He said this country was not happy at the accumulation of sophisticated weapons in the Indian Ocean, which should be declared as a zone of peace. The naval build-up by foreign powers should be withdrawn from the area.

He described as a 'welcome step' the recent Geneva talks between the two super powers for nuclear disarmament.

Welcoming the newly elected members to the eighth Lok Sabha the Prime Minister exhorted them to take keen interest in the deliberations of Parliament and utilise their tenure as a member of this august forum to serve the people. Having given a massive mandate, "the people are having a lot of expectations from us."

Underlining that the number of Opposition members was small, he stressed that the democratic processes must be maintained. "We shall not suppress anybody by force as we believe in achieving results through hard work," he said.

The Prime Minister, Mr. Rajiv Gandhi, condemned the attempt on the life of Akal Takht head priest Jathedar Kripal Singh near Ludhiana on January 16, 1985.

In a message Mr. Rajiv Gandhi said, "I am distressed at the news of the attack on Jathedar Kripal Singh and two Sewadars near Ludhiana today. The act deserves the strongest condemnation. The use of violence should have no place in a free and democratic society such as ours.

"I wish Jathedar Kripal Singh and the Sewadars speedy recovery."

Nikhil Chakravorty has commented on the performance of

Prime Minister Rajiv Gandhi in the first fortnight after the new Cabinet was sworn in.

"Between the swearing in of Rajiv Gandhi's new Cabinet on the new year eve and its first encounter with Parliament when the Lok Sabha meets on January 15, the fortnight is marked by a series of important announcements of government measures and crowning them all came the Prime Minister's policy statement broadcast to the nation on January 5.

"This policy statement, succinct and clear-cut, reiterated the tested policies that Jawaharlal Nehru first gave shape to and Indira Gandhi pursued and enriched, ranging from foreign affairs to public sector. The common concern for modernising the economy and streamlining the administration could hardly be missed, while the emphasis on reinforcing the unity of the country, looking after its diverse regions, together with specific assurance to the aggrieved Sikh community, could not but evoke nationwide response. Specifically, the decision to take up the Punjab crisis—on an urgent basis, as could be evident from the appointment of the three-member Cabinet team—has received support even from Opposition leaders, engaged now in the frustrating exercise of post-mortem of their poll debacle."

The Prime Minister's prompt measures to tone up the administration has the stamp of youthful exuberence. The reorganisation of Ministries and departments that has been undertaken is a subject on which much may be said on both sides, though the establishment of Ministry of Science and Technology was long overdue. The setting up of advisory panels of experts is a healthy move, the beginnings of which were made under Indira Gandhi.

Rajiv Gandhi's government was responsible for unearthing the biggest espionage of all times in our country.

Taking the House into confidence the Prime Minister, Mr. Rajiv Gandhi, made a statement in the Parliament of January 18, 1985:

"As you know, every Government has to exercise the highest vigilance in regard to the protection of confidential information and intelligence, I reviewed and strengthened security procedures. It came to Government's notice tht certain employees in sensitive positions were suspected to be indulging in activities detrimental to national interests. Some arrests have been made in the course of investigations, which are still proceeding. I am confident that Hon'ble Members would not press me to say anything more at this stage, as it might hamper these investigations."

Prime Minister Rajiv Gandhi on January 22, 1985, asked Chief Executive Councillor Jag Parvesh Chandra to give him "a note on the question of granting an Assembly to Delhi."

The Prime Minister gave the instruction to Mr. Chandra when he led Congress (I) members of the Metropolitan Council to the residence of Mr. Gandhi. The Congress (I) Councillors called on the Prime Minister to assure him that they would implement his policies with dedication.

During the meeting the Councillors suggested to Mr. Gandhi that Delhi should be given an Assembly so that the problems of the people could be solved speedily.

The Prime Minister also asked Executive Councillor (Health) Bansi Lal Chauhan to give him another note on why it was desirable to lift the ban on the recruitment of doctors. Mr. Chauhan wanted the ban to go so that hospitals could start functioning "in full strength."

Prime Minister Rajiv Gandhi accepted on Janaury 28, 1985, the Jawaharlal Nehru Award for International Understanding, conferred posthumously on Indira Gandhi. On that occasion he said:

"It is appropriate that we are gathered here today, six leaders from every Continent appealing for a sensibility, appealing for peace in the world. This was an appeal that Indiraji started in May last year. She had organised this meeting today. Unfortunately, she is not with us to participate in it. But her message of peace, her message going deeper than material values, will be carried throughout the world by others. Her depth in looking at any problem was such that it included a humaneness. She was never satisfied with just the material ends. She wanted to go deeper and to see how humankind could benefit most.

"Peace and disarmament is not new to India. It was propagated by Lord Buddha many centuries ago, followed by Emperor Ashok, and much more recently by Gandhiji and by Panditji. That message of non-violence of disarmament has not changed and I think Gandhiji described it very well; he said that non-violence is not just 'not fighting', it is much deeper than that. It is 'not even thinking of retaliating', it is 'not even thinking of violence,' and only when you achieve this are you really non-violent. It is this towards which the whole world must aim today. Today the world is in a situation where the terrible weapons of destruction that we have built could wipe us off with the malfunction of a small component costing may be a few paise or a few cents.

"She raised her voice against this destruction: she raised her voice not just for India, her voice was for the backward, the deprived, the depressed, all over the world. She fought for the rights of humankind everywhere. She was devoted to two causes throughout her life—India's freedom struggle and India's development, and then the Non-Aligned Movement. They are not really that separate when you look at them.

"The Non-Aligned Movement was a logical development of India's freedom movement. India's freedom movement showed the way to the rest of the colonised world half a century ago. We set a trend and it led to a new freedom for many people in the world. The non-alignment has tried to establish that freedom in the face of neo-colonialism and neo-imperialism and that struggle must still carry on. All her life she fought for what she thought was right. She stood on her principles and on her ideology and no one was able to shift her from that path. She believed that the earth belonged to all of us, not to any great power or any group of powers; and it is our equal right to live on this earth. She fought for a just economic order between the richer countries and the poorer countries. She fought for a harmony between man and nature, knowing that we cannot fight nature, knowing that if we try to fight nature we are the ones who will lose.

"She worked for the best utilisation of our resources. She worked for the protection of our environment. For India she had a very special love; not just for the modern India, for the India she was building but she had a love for Indian traditions, Indian culture, she had love for Indian spirituality. And in modernising India she struggled to preserve these great values of our country. She fought with courage and best example I can give is of her favourite songs by Rabindranath Tagore. Her favourite song was: *Ekla Chalo Re*, which says that no matter what odds are against you, no matter what you have to face; no matter that nobody else is willing to walk with you, if you are right you must walk alone.

"Sir, it is an honour for me to receive this prize on her behalf. The cheque that you have given, I will put into the Indira Gandhi Memorial Trust and we will see that it goes towards propagating her ideals and presenting her view to the world."

Six-Nation Summit on Nuclear Disarmament was held on January 28, 1985. Welcoming the Presidents of Argentina, Mexico and Tanzania and the Prime Ministers of Greece and Sweden to New Delhi Mr. Rajiv Gandhi said: "What brings us together is mankind's highest cause today or ever, namely Peace. We represent not only our own peoples but the constituency of peace which embraces all continents and countries and includes vast millions even within nuclear weapons countries. We reflect humanity's passionate conviction that the earth shall live. That is our mandate. That is the cause for which Indira Gandhi lived and worked.

"In 1944 a great experiment was launched, the United Nations, in the tremulous hope that the thought of war can be abolished from the minds of men. Another experiment was going on at that time—for harnessing the secrets of the atom to military power. The first nuclear bombs were dropped in 1945. The U.N. Charter could not obviously refer to nuclear weapons, but the General Assembly has unequivocally declared that the use of such weapons is a crime against humanity. The five permanent members of the U.N., who have a monopoly of nuclear weapons, claim a kind of legitimacy for possession of such weapons. But to the people of the world, nuclear weapons are in themselves an unmitigated evil and their use or threat of use by anyone is impermissible in any circumstances.

"It is true that no nuclear weapons have been actually used since 1945. The proponents of the theory of balance of terror take credit for this nuclear peace. It is at best a grey peace, precarious and unstable. Production of nuclear weapons is going on. They are becoming increasingly sophisticated. Each improvement in accuracy and mobility makes present agreements so much more fragile.

"Existing compacts deny to non-nuclear weapons States the right to conduct experiments even for peaceful purposes, while placing no restraint on the nuclear-weapons powers in the matter of multiplying their arsenals. This is a discrimination to which we have objected. Much is made of the danger of horizontal proliferation. But the dangers of present stockpiles, their vertical proliferation and the risk of catastrophe by error or design are slurred over. How can one nation be considered more responsible than the rest? Basic problems of sovereignty and human survival are involved.

"The two great powers have recently agreed to resume discussions on nuclear weapons. This is a good development and we welcome it. We want these negotiations not to be confined to ways of dealing with only the consequences of improvements in capacity and delivery systems. They must ultimately address themselves to the basic objective, which is the elimination of all nuclear weapons, as recognised in their statement. Credible and reassuring first steps would be a freeze on further production and deployment of nuclear weapons as well as fissionable material for weapons purposes. This has to be followed by nuclear weapon powers embarking on physical reduction of stockpiles. Furthermore, the discussions and agreements should be more than bilateral; they must apply to all possessors of nuclear weapons. Otherwise the peril remains open.

"The actual prospect of nuclear weapons being used remains where national security is based on the premise of "stability" through extended deterrence or through the building up of defence systems. Every refinement of deterrence, like "flexible response" and "limited" and "winnable" war scenarios, assumes that the use of these weapons can be controlled by increasing their technological sophistication. The qualitative arms race is thus built into the arms control approach. That kind of arms control is in reality no control.

"The dangers have increased of computer errors, systems failures, accidents and misjudgements at lower echelons to whom responsibility is inevitably delegated. There is, besides, the new danger of nuclear terrorism and blackmail.

"Sophisticated weapons are being transferred not merely between members of military alliances but also outside. Global justifications are advanced. This leads to several new local and regional tensions which, sooner or later, are bound to result in physical conflict. This is not mere speculation. It has immediate relevance to the situation in our region.

"Arms race and international tension are inseparable companions. Over the years there has been a heightening of tension all over the world. All multilateral activity is getting increasingly shackled in block rigidities and polemics. There is a spurt in proxy wars and many regions are affected by turmoil directly and indirectly. Therefore, the initiation of a dialogue between the major powers, though welcome, does not by itself free smaller and vulnerable states from the competitive attention of the big powers. Along with dialogue, there must also be a genuine effort not to view all relationships in terms of the global strategic balance and 'spheres of influence'.

"Military spending is rapidly nearing the staggering figure of 1000 billion dollars annually. It continues to rise while the world economy hovers between uncertain recovery and a relapse into deeper recession. This vast military expenditure, apart from causing dissonances in the economies of the leading military powers, has aggravated the problems of global economic recovery and development. Many developing countries face the stark prospect of economic collapse and social upheaval.

"Technological advances are inexorably widening economic disparities among nations. The policies of powerful governments are further accentuating these disparities, building up tensions which bode ill for relations amongst countries. Force cannot find answers to these problems, vision and statesmanship demands a co-operative approach and constructive measures to reduce and remove disparities and ensure a better life for all.

"A new and unfortunate development is the undermining of the various multilateral agencies in the U.N. system. Those agencies have played a notable part in assisting poorer countries in the last four decades. If they are weakened, the ideals of the United Nations, indeed the very basis of international co-operation, would be shaken. A campaign has to be launched in the capitals of the world to reverse this unfortunate trend.

"The threat of first strike is now being used to justify new kinds of arms races. The probability of climatic catastrophe renders the first strike meaningless. The Nuclear Winter hypothesis, which is being increasingly accepted, shows that even a first strike would spell a holocaust as much for the aggressor as for the victims. It underlines the indivisibility of peace and the urgency of disarmament.

"Another matter of concern is the idea of deep strike, according to which conventional weapons could be used for striking at targets at distances up to 300 km. It is claimed that this would lessen the resort to nuclear weapons at an early stage of war in Europe. By blurring the distinction between nuclear and conventional weapons, the possibility of a nuclear war is increased and the control of nuclear arms made more difficult.

"In May last, our six nations called upon nuclear weapon powers to halt the arms race and put into effect a programme for the cessation of the testing, production and deployment of nuclear weapons and their delivery systems. It was endorsed by many parliaments and national groups and evoked positive response from one nuclear weapon power. Today we also ask the powerful to prevent an arms race in Outer Space and to embark on a comprehensive treaty to ban the testing of all nuclear weapons. Prime Minister Palme mentioned that the UN Charter gave the right to every nation to defend itself. We are gathered here today defending ourselves, not with weapons but with words. We will not defend ourselves with war, we will defend ourselves by building a public opinion against war.

"The survival of the human race depends on the demilitarisation of the global surface and on keeping Outer Space free of weapons. We must strengthen the defences of peace in man's inner space as well—his mind, soul and spirit. Mahatma Gandhi, who was alive when Hiroshima took place, declared so preceptively: 'The bomb will not be destroyed by counter-bombs, even as violence cannot be by counter-violence. Let us work to strengthen humanity's faith in itself and its capacity to conquer the peril which has come out of its own technology'."

Mr. Rajiv Gandhi should get full marks for taking a prompt initiative to curb defection malpractices that have reduced Indian politics to a farce—from value-based to money-based. It is no secret that like any other saleable commodity the price tag had got attached to those legislators who were willing to change sides.

The Anti-Defection Bill provided the first major check to the country's political corruption that has been growing systematically ever since Aya Rams and Gaya Rams emerged as new villains of Indian politics.

This new breed of politicians has no scruples about anything. They look for money bags and have successfully turned politics into a lucrative business proposition in collaboration with multi-faceted opportunist leaders.

Intervening in the debate on Anti-Defection Bill, Prime Minister Rajiv Gandhi said in the Lok Sabha on January 30, 1985:

"Mr. Speaker, Sir, this Anti-Defection Bill has been pending for a very long time. I think it was first mentioned almost seven years ago. We have taken it up as one of our first major tasks because we felt that this is an area where public life needs cleaning up. As rightly promised during the debate on the presidential address, our Government has the political will to implement what we promise. We also have promised that we will carry the Opposition with us. And I am happy to say, sir, that we carried almost all of the Opposition with us. There are one or two exceptions.

"We are moving an amendment for removing Clause 2(1)(C). Clause 2(1)(C) allowed a member to lose his membership of the House if he was removed from the party. Logically speaking, this clause should have been there, because like one of our members from the Opposition has just said, if we look at the moral issue and if we decide that the party is the fundamental unit which gets you elected, then you lost the right of that election if you are no longer a member of that party. Like another member has said that 33 per cent for a split is too little and there should be no such thing as a split. There are lots of areas in this Bill which are grey. We are covering new grounds which may not be covered anywhere else in the world. And we have to see how best we can tread along this path. It is better for us to tread cautiously than to make serious errors and repent for them later. So, there will be shortcomings in this Bill. But we see and identify those shortcomings. By removing Clause 2(1)(C) one lacuna comes out and that is that if the House—either this House or State Legislature—is not in session and there is a defection or a split, however it may be defined, but the Government is seen to lose the majority, then there would be a long time before the next session was to be called and this could lead to a lot of horse trading. This was one of the reasons why Clause 2(1)(C) was there. I am sure that this was one of the reasons why one of the opposition parties—more than one—was very keen that this be maintained. We are looking into how to close this lacuna. We have not been able to do it in this Bill itself. But in my discussions with the Opposition we have found a method which we are looking into and hopefully we will be able to put some time-limit, possibly a minimum time-limit, between the suspicion of a Government losing its majority and the test of its strength in the House. We will see whether this can be put in, either in this Bill, may be in the next session, or, if it has to be put in elsewhere, we can do it there as well.

"I do not want to take too much time of the House, because the opinion on this Bill is more or less unanimous and there is not much to debate.

"One point was raised: What is the hurry in having this Bill? We have been waiting 7 years to have this Bill and a lot of damage has been done. This Bill should have come yesterday. Should have come last year. Should have come 7 years ago. We are doing it the fastest that we can do. I feel that anybody who does not want this Bill has to have his own integrity examined.

"Sir, it has been said that this Bill is being brought to keep the Congress Party intact, to strengthen the Congress Party. I would like to point out that the defections are invariably to the Congress Party, and not from the Congress Party. We do not have a problem with people leaving the party; we have a problem with people wanting to join our party. We do not need this to strengthen our party. You can see the strength of our party in front of you.

"This Bill is the first step towards cleaning our public life. We will be taking other steps, electoral reforms, other reforms, and you have my assurance, Sir, that we will carry the whole Opposition with us in these forthcoming decisions that we will have to take.

"Sir, I commend this Bill for adoption. I thank the Opposition for co-operation in formulating the Bill and for supporting this Bill."

Intervening in the debate on Anti-Defection Bill, the Prime Minister, Mr. Rajiv Gandhi, said on January 31, 1985, in the Rajya Sabha:

"Mr. Chairman, Sir, yesterday, the 30th January, we had all gone to Gandhiji's Samadhi to pay our respects and homage. On Gandhiji's Samadhi in very large letters are written what Gandhiji called seven social sins. The first one written there is politics without principle and it was only appropriate that we took up this Bill in the Lok Sabha on the same day. Sir, this Bill covers new ground in our country's history. And whenever we take such a step we cannot even admit that it will be complete and perfect in every way. There may be shortcomings in this. There will be still differences of opinion. But after spending a long time with leaders from all sections of both Houses we have produced a paper which, I think, meets the requirements of every opinion within these two Houses. There were still some parties who wanted a much stronger Bill—not the Congress Party, but definitely three parties from amongst the Opposition groups. But because of rest of the opinion we have produced a Bill slightly softer than they would have liked. The Bill for the first time recognises a political party as an entity. It recognises the factual position on the ground that you win your seat on the ticket of a political party. We try to start with the moral question. The moral question that the voter is voting for a particular ideology is voting that same principles, is voting for a programme and all that is represented in the election symbol of the party on whose symbol he stands and when he comes to the House to be sworn in, he brings a piece of paper, a certificate on which is written the name of the party on whose symbol he won. If we accept this as the starting point, that the voter has voted for a particular ideology, has voted for particular programme, then there are very few questions that can be raised on this Bill.

"Sir, I think the Member has just finished speaking; if he really had something to say, he should have said it while he was speaking earlier.

"Sir, this Bill has provisions for dissent. We have between us decided on one-third as the minimum to show dissent. This has to be arbitrary figure. There were groups, specially one or two groups, which wanted over 50 per cent—again not from our party, but from one of our oppositon parties. There were other groups that wanted it lower, that wanted it at 25 per cent. But unanimously we decided that 33 per cent would be a good starting point. We can watch it from here, see what experience shows us and then, if necessary, take corrective action at a suitable date.

"This Bill also has provisions for a merger. The Hon'ble Member, who was speaking as I came into the House, mentioned aparty joining the Congress Party. We are not opposed to parties getting together. We are not opposed to people dissenting. We are not opposed to a change in view-point. But it should not look as if we are cheating the voter. The voter elects us on a particular platform. If we change our platform then we are cheating the voter and we should go back to the voter and let the voter send us back on our new platform. That is roughly what this Bill does.

"There are a few points which have invariably come up for discussion. One of the points is that this should not have been left to the Speaker or the Chairman. It should have gone to a group or it should have gone to the Supreme Court or it should have gone to the Election Commission. There were all sorts of suggestions. What we have tried to do in this Bill is to make it as black and white as possible so that there are no grey areas where somebody has to take a decision. The decision should be automatic, backed up by a sequence of events which are on records, so that there is no debate about it. We also thought that the operation of the Bill should be quick so that there is no time in which horse-trading can take place and there is no time for a problem to arise. That is why we left this to the Chairman or to the Speaker. If it had gone out, outside the realm of the House, it would have ended up with long debate. We have seen how long it had taken us to get our party recongnised as the true Congress Party. Every case would entail a three or four or five year debate whether it would be in the Supreme Court or in the High Court or in front of the Election Commission. But the fact is that it would have made this Bill totally redundant and this is what has happened to one anti-defection Bill which we have in Kashmir. It has not worked because there was an opening to go to the High Court and to the Supreme Court and it keeps being debated. And any Member who wants such a delay is only showing what his true intentions are and he should spend a little time in introspection and try to think what he is really wanting.

"Some Member, I believe, has said that the Congress wants this Bill because the Congress is scared that the party is going to break up. I have not heard anything so ridiculous.

"If you look at the history of defection, the number of people that have left the Congress are insignificant. I am not talking of splits because splits are different. I am talking of defection. The number of people who have left the Congress are insignificant. The number of people who have joined the Congress are numerous. This applies to the number of people who want to join the Congress specially today, and I am not talking of only workers; I am talking of some of your very senior leaders also.

"So this Bill is not to stop the Congress from breaking up. The Congress has lived, has gained strength for hundred years. We are not going to break up in a few years. If you look at the parties and see which parties are breaking up you will see the shattered remains in your part of the House.

"One member from the DMK Party has just been complaining about some parts of this Bill. But a member from his party was present when everything was discussed and we came to a unanimous conclusion. I wish he will discuss this with that particular gentleman who sat with us in the meeting.

"This Bill is only a first step in cleaning up some of the defects in our political life. It cannot attempt to do everything; it cannot claim to do everything. But it is a starting point.

"We have got other ideas, we will be discussing them with members of the Opposition and I hope we will be able to come to a unanimous Bill on each step. But I would request them, when we have meetings, that they should send the same members to each meeting so that we do not have to start from scratch every time.

"I would like to thank the Opposition for all the co-operation they have given us in this Bill and as I said while answering the debate on the Presidential Address we will be seeking their help in everything that we do. We will be open to suggestions; we will be open to ideas and we will be open to criticisms. We will try to carry the whole House with us on every major step we take".

A commemorative postage stamp on late Mrs. Indira Gandhi was released in New Delhi on January 31, 1985, by the Prime Minister, Mr. Rajiv Gandhi. On that occasion he said:

"Indiraji had many aspects to her personality. With the release of this stamp, the P&T Department has chosen one of those aspects—her crusade for world peace.

"It is appropriate that this stamp has been brought out just after the six-nation summit had successfully concluded and appealed for world peace. This adds one more aspect to that.

"Indiraji fought with courage whatever odds came in front of her. She was not the one to succumb to pressures. She knew what was right, she knew what to be done and she would do it, irrespective of whom she had to face. Today we have to carry on a similar struggle for peace. For the question of nuclear holocaust which is not just isolated to those countries who may be directly involved with the latest thinking the whole globe will be affected by the side-effects of a nuclear war and we must raise our voices to strengthen the movement for peace. We must continue it."

The Prime Minister, Mr. Rajiv Gandhi, inaugurated a two-day Conference of Chief Secretaries of States at Vigyan Bhavan on February 4, 1985, and told them that there was a new mood in the country and it was for the administration and the political system to meet the high expectations that had been aroused. People wanted to see things move faster and more efficiently.

Mr. Rajiv Gandhi said that two of the basic functions of the administration, namely, law and order and development, were interdependent. Without law and order, there could be no development. Many riots had shown that economic disparities had triggered them off.

Faster development was the foremost need. The administration as a whole should be modified to meet the needs and demands of the Eighties, the Nineties and the 21st century. Training had an important role to play in creating a result-oriented outlook and in installing new drive. Many people were stuck in the rut and it looked as though ink flowed in their veins.

The Prime Minister said that if the administrative machinery had to move faster, there was need for a better system of information gathering and information retrieval. Very often, when questions were put to the bureaucracy, the replies dwelt on how much money had been spent rather than what had been achieved on the ground. Mr. Rajiv Gandhi pointed out that for faster development, it was essential to have more autonomy—not only more autonomy for the administration from the political element, but within the various layers of the administration. He reiterated his earlier statement that he would do everything in his power to stop political interference with the administration.

With autonomy went greater accountability. A sense of accountability must filter down to all levels of the hierarchy. What the country needed was a truly professional administration.

India, said Mr. Rajiv Gandhi, had faced a number of challenges and had shown that the system, when clothed with authority and made accountable, could produce as good results as anywhere else in the world.

Administration, the Prime Minister said, was the point where Government met the people. A spirit of friendliness and courtesy must permeate the civil services.

R.K. Karanjia, the noted journalist, met Rajiv Gandhi after he had completed 100 days as Prime Minister and asked him how he felt. "I really feel just the same as I did before," Rajiv Gandhi said.

According to R.K. Karanjia, "the soft, confident voice that spoke with characteristic modesty nevertheless radiated power, and so did the handsome face with the doe eyes, the generous mouth and determined chin—a power that is clean, detached, compassionate, yet decisive and uncompromising. Character is writ over all the planes of his features giving the assurance of a man equal to the job.

"But surely, the hundred days have made some difference to the nation's polity and administration, Mr. Prime Minister? Karanjia asked.

"Not much, I am afraid, in the way of performance," Mr. Gandhi answered. "We have been working on several projects, but they have yet to be implemented. We really had no time. All we have been able to accomplish is to set the bureaucracy moving and working. The Ministries, also, are at their jobs seriously attending to different portfolios and problems.

"So far as Parliament is concerned we have adopted the Anti-Defection Bill quite speedily and smoothly if I may say so considering its chequered course in the past; and we hope it will serve as a deterrent to political corruption.

"In the matter of external affairs, the meeting of the six heads of non-aligned States also went off well, and seems to have created considerable impact. Follow-up action is now being taken with personal calls by us on all the nuclear powers."

All this indicated that a launching pad for performance had been well laid by the Rajiv administration. So Karanjia asked: "When do we take off?" "With the Budget of course," Mr. Gandhi said.

After his clean sweep of the Lok Sabha polls, Mr. Rajiv Gandhi turned his attention to cleansing Indian politics. Whether it is being done on political or moral consideration is debatable. What Rajiv wanted was not merely to clean the party. In fact through a new set of guidelines he aimed to change the very composition of the party. When the State units were asked to submit the list of party candidates for the elections in the first week of March to 11 State Assemblies—Uttar Pradesh, Madhya Pradesh, Himachal Pradesh, Andhra Pradesh, Bihar, Gujarat, Maharashtra, Karnataka, Orissa, Rajasthan and Sikkim—and the Union Territory of Pondicherry, the regional bosses had no idea of the guidelines. When the party bosses submitted their lists, Rajiv sprang a surprise. He asked them to select candidates on the basis of the guidelines and set up panels for selection. The guidelines are generally known as the ten commandments and are given below.

1. It is necessary to ensure that the person nominated by the party has a clean image in the constituency.

2. Loyalists and those enjoying credibility amongst the people should be preferred.

3. No person should be nominated who is a casteist. Every nominee should have a secular image in the constituency and his/her outlook should be pro-poor.

4. A sitting MLA in whose Assembly constituency Congress (I) lost in the last Lok Sabha election should have no claim for the party nomination. Candidates who lost in the recent Lok Sabha election will not be considered for party nomination to the Assembly.

5. The question of nominating a sitting MLA in whose Assembly constituency Congress (I) got substantially reduced margin of votes in the last Lok Sabha election is a case for review.

6. Persons below the age of 45 should be preferred. Approximately 60 per cent of the party nominees should belong to this category.

7. As far as possible, 20 per cent of the party nominees should be women.

8. Adequate representation should be given to Sewa Dal Workers, Youth Congress, NSUI, Mahila Congress and Labour Wing of the party.

9. Due consideration should be given to professionals such as

engineers, doctors, scientists, educationists, management experts and ex-Servicemen.

10. The Congress president may make any exemption in any case.

Yet it is to the credit of Mr. Rajiv Gandhi that more than 800 MLAs and 70 Ministers were denied tickets on the basis of the new guidelines. No Prime Minister in India has ever dared to purge the party on the eve of elections. Leave alone that, no Prime Minister so far has ever taken steps to cleanse the ruling party the way Mr. Rajiv Gandhi has done. What Rajiv did was what both Mahatma Gandhi and Jayaprakash Narayan dreamt of doing. That more needs to be done to purify Indian politics is a fact. But the first step has been taken, says K. Gopalakrishna, a noted journalist.

On February 10, Prime Minister Rajiv Gandhi, launching his election campaign for the Assembly elections in Uttar Pradesh, assured the people that his Government will fulfil all the poll promises made to them.

Mr. Gandhi called upon the people to vote the Congress (I) to power in the States which was necessary for rapid growth of the country. While the Centre only formulated the welfare schemes it was the States that actually implemented them.

He said installation of Congress (I) Governments in the States was imperative for strengthening the Centre.

States like West Bengal, Karnataka and Andhra Pradesh which had non-Congress (I) Governments were economically moving in the reverse gear, he said.

Mr. Gandhi said an opportunity should be given to the Congress (I) for meeting the poll commitments.

The party had promised clean politics and already two steps had been taken in that direction. The first was the introduction of the Anti-Defection Bill and the second the induction of new faces in the list of party candidates.

The Prime Minister said new candidates had been fielded to give a new look to the party as well as to increase the pace of development. However, the denial of ticket did not necessarily mean that it was due to a bad image. The partymen denied a ticket should not get discouraged as their services were required for strengthening the party. Mr. Rajiv Gandhi said the few steps that had been taken so far proved that corruption could be eradicated.

The country could progress only when there was clean politics and the Government was devoid of corruption.

The Prime Minister said his party had promised welfare programmes for the **womenfolk.** The largest ever number of women had been given party tickets and he hoped they would raise their voice for the welfare of women. At the same time the Government had made a provision for free education of girls up to high school.

He said if the Congress (I) was voted to power in the State, special welfare schemes for scheduled castes and tribes and other weaker sections would be implemented.

Mr. Rajiv Gandhi thanked the people for voting the Congress (I) to power in the recent Lok Sabha elections. The elections had shown the world that India was united and looking forward to a prosperous and bright future.

There was a clear indication that the Rajiv Gandhi wave, which played havoc with the national Opposition parties in the Parliamentary elections, still held its sway, by and large, in the Hindi heartland. As witness we have the three-fourths plus majority for the Congress (I) in Madhya Pradesh, the expected 90 per cent tally for it in Gujarat and Himachal Pradesh, the 80 per cent in Uttar Pradesh and 60-odd per cent in Bihar and Rajasthan. With all that, in the Hindi belt as a whole, the Congress (I) has done better than in the 1980 Assembly elections. Beyond the Hindi belt the Congress (I) has emerged with commendable results in the Orissa. The Congress (I) has come through with a sizeable mandate where it counts, but there are enough signals that it cannot afford to rest on its laurels.

Mr. Rajiv Gandhi has emerged as the most popular leader on the Indian political scene according to a recent survery conducted by the G.B. Pant Social Science Institute, Allahabad. In response to the question as to which leader(s) are in a position to solve the current problems of the country, his name has been suggested by over 80 per cent of the respondents. His "background, image and performance" have been the main considerations working in the minds of the respondents, apart from the fact that "he alone can lead a strong government at the Centre."

Prime Minister Rajiv Gandhi is fast becoming a "media star" in the United States judging by the cover stories and commentaries in leading American news magazines and dailies.

Both the Newsweek and the Time vied with each other in projecting a highly complimentary profile of Mr. Gandhi. Time underscored the varied achievements of India since its independence.

The apparent change in the American media perception of India is taken as a good augury for the prestigious "Festival of India" in the United States that Prime Minister Gandhi inaugurated jointly with President Reagan in June.

"For all India's simmering problems", Time said, "Rajiv Gandhi is inheriting a nation that has proved remarkably resilient in times of stress and makes steady progress toward easing its perennial problems of poverty and over-population."

The magazine also noted that after 33 years of planned economic development, "India is emerging as a major industrial and military power and a model for the Third World."

The U.S. media has also commented favourably on the way in which the Indian Prime Minister has constituted his Cabinet ousting some from the previous government, and bringing in a group of well educated technicians, businessmen and diplomats. "Gandhi is off to amazingly fast start," wrote Newsweek. Time has proved this prophecy to be true.

iv

TAKING INDIA INTO 21ST CENTURY

Mr. Gandhi is in a hurry to propel India into 21st century. In the India of his dream justice will be swift and meted out even to the poor.

Prime Minister Rajiv Gandhi said that the government would extend its full co-operation in strengthening the judiciary. He asked the bar to reciprocate the gesture by trying to become a strong, independent and professional body.

Mr. Gandhi was addressing a distinguished gathering after laying the foundation stone of the Rs. 1 crore Bar Council of India Bhavan in New Delhi.

The Prime Minister, Mr. Rajiv Gandhi, laid the foundation stone of Bar Council of India Bhavan on March 19, 1985. Speaking on the occasion he said that the "legal profession in India has developed over a very long period. Today, we stand independent because a large number of lawyers gave up their practice and fought for our independence. It was that foresight that made our Constitution and that laid the foundation of a country which has shown the world that it can not only survive, but can progress while other countries have not been able to do that. When I talk of progress, it is not just economic progress because that in a way can be much easier. In a much broader perspective, like you have just said, Sir, there are very few countries who still have democratic Governments around them. This is one of our major achievements. We are today a democracy because we have established institutions, we have nurtured these institutions, and we have strengthened them. And if our society is to progress, it can only progress on the basis of strong institutions. None of them trying to pull down the other but each of them trying to build up the other institutions. And this is what we must all work for. There have been conflicts between different institutions in our country but we must now try to end these conflicts. We must try to work together to build our country, to take our country ahead. The challenges ahead are tremendous and there is no time to detract from each other. There is barely enough time to help each other to build our country."

Mr. Gandhi added that democracy can only survive if there is social justice to match it. Progress without social justice cannot be counted progress in a country like India. One of the first things that any Government must do, and progress and development is really secondary, is establishment of law and order because without law and order nothing else can work. In establishing law and order, the judiciary, the Bar has to be involved fully. After 37 years of independence, we see certain problems coming up mainly with the speed of justice, and if justice is delayed we cannot really claim that it is being delivered. We have to look ahead and see how we can clear up these roads, how we can expedite justice without diluting the justice, without reducing it in its value. We have to see how our people can get justice not just a question of time, it also is a question of affording it where we have taken some steps and we have shown that it can be done cheaply. It is also a question of physical access. How many people can trek the long distances to High Court? Is it necessary to have a rethink on this, to see how we can make it more accessible to the average person save his time, save his money and expedite the case.

In India justice has been a very integral, independent part of the country, and that is really one of the reasons that we have remained a democracy while other countries have not been able to maintain that. I think one of the main reasons that we are a democracy is there is satisfaction amongst the people that justice is available to them, that development is available to them.

If these two pillars are seen to weaken then the third pillar—democracy—will be very difficult to keep up. And this is what we must all work for, the Prime Minister added.

Mr. Gandhi assured that on the part of the Government there will be full co-operation in strengthening the judicial system, in strengthening it as an institution, and he hoped the Bar to reciprocate and thus raise the professional standard and make it a truly professional profession.

Mr. Rajiv Gandhi stressed the vital importance of electronics. While inaugurating the Seminar on Investment Opportunities in Electronics, organised by the All India Manufacturers Organisation in New Delhi on February 21, 1985, he said: "The field of electronics interests me and is critical for India's growth. Electronics is really like the nervous system of a nation. As a nation evolves that nervous system must evolve with it, just as it evolves with the species. In the earliest species, there were barely 250-odd nerve-junctions. The humans have 15 billion-odd nerve-junctions.

"We need a similar network in our country if India is to progress, if India is to move ahead, if we are to keep up with the world. We missed one bus with the Industrial Revolution. A sudden boost in muscle power, and we were not able to catch up for 300 years. Maybe, we didn't jump on the second bus on time—and that is the electronic revolution or computer revolution—and now we might have to run behind that bus, catch up to it and jump on to it. I think we are capable of doing this.

"Although electronics is an industry on its own, it really must be used to supplement all other industries, updating our older industry, making it more productive, making it more competitive, and really bringing it up to world standards. Today electronics has permeated just about every field—industry, education, defence, information handling. There is no place where you do not have electronics. India is still lagging far behind. I was just told that on an average you have to dial twelve times before you can get through. So, there are these problems and we have to get rid of these problems."

Regarding certain problems with Government policy, especially taxation and duties. Mr. Gandhi said that the Government had been looking at these for the past couple of years. It came out with a completely new package for the electronics industry some months ago, and he hopes that "you will like the package that we shall present you in the next session of Parliament. But I should like to point out that many of the concessions that we gave, many of the reductions in controls, have not been passed on to the consumers in the way they should have been. The Industry has not been as dynamic as it should have been. Well, we shall give you another chance. If it does not work, we shall have to think of prodding a little harder, not by force but by some other means. I feel, for example, that protection should be of only one sort, preferably only fiscal protection and not licence protection, which means that you will have to be more efficient. You will have to compete. You have mentioned import duties, but import duties go together with import protection and there again we have preferably to have only one."

To get electronics really moving in India. Mr. Gandhi added, "We have to go down to the other end of the chain. We are mostly talking about manufacturing and selling. We have to go to other end and produce enough people who will be able to deal with the equipment that you are about to produce, which means a turnaround in our education system. We need many more institutes such as the ITIs, but oriented and run in a much more professional manner, oriented towards more modern fields of technology. We need to really develop a mentality in our people of using modern methods.

"And somewhere along the line in stressing equality and equal right we have gone a little off the track and we have promoted only mediocrity. We have to look at this and once again bring excellence out, lift excellence up and not try to pull excellence down to make everybody equal and mediocre. We shall be looking at this aspect, with regard to the education system, and I hope that this will, over a long term, help industry to develop and expand.

"One of the complaints was the telecommunications system. We have been looking at this sector and I think that in the coming policies which will be put before you, maybe a month from now, you will find that we tried within our resource constraints to do something for telecommunications. We are already looking at the licensing policy; much of what you have said we have already done. It will take some time to get to you. But on most of it, action has been taken pre-empting your thoughts.

"Now to the banking sector, maybe, the less said about it the better. We have not had the time to look at it yet, because the last couple of months have been extremely rushed. I think in the coming months we shall take a deep look at it and it does need a thorough overhaul. Really, what is needed is much more electronics in banking.

"Electronics in India has been developed by the small-scale sector and by the public sector. We have got a very large gap in between. We would like to fill this gap. But while filling this gap we shall try and see that the present industry is protected, not completely but to some extent. We shall in the coming months see that many of the procedural problems that you have raised are cleared. But as we develop new policies, as we move ahead, we shall have to feel our way and get proper feedback from you. Because every step we take will raise new problems, and we would like to get quick feedbacks so that we can take quick action to correct them.

"You will find this Government moving faster than you are moving. The problem will not be with Government constraints or Government restrictions or the time taken by Government but with can you keep up with what we are doing,"

On March 22, 1985, Prime Minister Rajiv Gandhi proposed a new strategy for technology upgradation saying that the Government would concentrate on certain areas leaving others to the private sector so that together key areas in industry came up to the international level in about a decade or 15 years.

He said the Government would come up with a programme for the purpose, hopefully during the current session of Parliament itself and would like the industry to respond to it.

Inaugurating a national conference on exports, organised by the Association of Indian Engineering Industry (AIEI) on the occasion of its 90th anniversary, the Prime Minister said in certain areas the country could afford to be behind one or two generations in technology. But in others, especially the fast growing industry, technology must be up-to-date so that India moved together with the rest of the world.

Mr. Rajiv Gandhi said that India's Engineering industry "is amongst our oldest industries and also the newest, the most modern and between these two extremes we fit in it every type, every technology, every method of working. In a way our Engineering industry is representative of all our industry—small enterprises, large industries, public sector, private sector. It goes right across the spectrum and when we look at it we can see both the problems that India's industry faces and the achievements that India's industry has achieved during these past 35 years. Our growth since independence has been good, but not as good as we would have liked it to be. And if we look ahead to the future, we must grow very much faster to be able to catch up with the world. Our industries have matured tremendously. They have incorporated a very broad spectrum of products but technology in the world is growing very fast and if we are to catch up, we have to move faster than any other country, otherwise there is no question of catching up.

Mr. Gandhi added that "Indian industry has its extremes. It is as good as any industry in the world. It can compete with any industry in the world. The bad, unfortunately, is nowhere near our good, and this is where we must do some work, we must raise the average level of our industry. The fact is that we have certain industries which can achieve this, and for that we have the capability, we have the competence, we have everything going for us, but we must let it seek down to the bottom. The problem is that we don't use the full potential that is available to us. When I said full potential I don't mean just in a percentage of output of a particular factory but in manpower, in human resources, in everything that is available. What we have to see is how we can utilise everything that we have got going for us, and in that I would include many Indians who are not in India today but living abroad who are not finding adequate or employment of a sufficient degree within our country. We must treat them as an available resource, temporarily not in circulation in the country. We must create a climate to bring them back and use them, especially in areas where we feel we need immediate results.

"Quality of our products", the Prime Minister emphasized, "really needs very much to be desired. One of the problems is that we are selling to a captive market, we are selling to a market which is not responsive to quality. We are selling really in an absolutely sellers' market. It will change in our recent policy statement. In our budget, we have tried to change them to some degree. But our market of 700 million is so vast that it is not going to change quickly. The industry will have to change faster and will have to make the market change because ultimately you will be called upon to compete not with each other but with other industries in the world. And we must prepare for that day today.

"Most of our technology", stressed Mr. Gandhi, "is not really up to date. By the time, we buy a technology we start working on it. by the time we start producing, we are already one or two generations behind. Here we should decide what we really want. In certain areas, it is not necessary that we have the most modern technology and it does not matter if we are one or two generations late. But in other areas, even one generation late is too late and we cannot afford to do that, especially in the fast growing industries. We must see that we are moving at least as fast as anybody else and here we must really plan ahead not to look what other people have developed but look ahead to see what they will develop 10 or 15 years from now, and work towards that target so that after a given period, we are together with them, we are not left behind. In this system that we have been following where we see what other countries have got then, we try to make that, we try to either buy the technology, develop the technology, well by definition we are going to be left behind. And we are always going to be behind. We want to change this.

"We will, from the part of the Government, choose a few areas which we feel are important for the Government. Similarly, I would like you also to choose areas which are important for your industries and to concentrate in those areas to make to bring us up on par or ahead of anybody in, let us say, five years or 10 years or 15 years depending on what challenge we put in front of us. We will be bringing out programme on behalf of the Government hopefully during this session of Parliament; and we will put this in front of you. We would like you to respond to it and to help our industry, both public and private sectors, to move ahead.

"One other problem which will come up and which we must address immediately is employment. There are many areas where we just cannot continue with labour-intensive industries. It will just not be feasible after a few years. And we must plan for that day today, which means re-educating our labour, which means re-orientating them to a different type of work. And we must prepare now so that this change-over is smooth, labour is not jobless and in fact, if it is handled well we can have a much larger employment but in different areas and have a much more efficient industry. We must produce a programme which will address this problem.

"For our industry to expand, to grow, we must get many things from abroad, and we must pay for them with our exports. Import substitution has been one of the key factors in our development process and with import substitution, we have been able to develop our own technology in certain fields. But sometimes this has gone astray. It has been brought to my notice that on occasions parts that may cost a few dollars and are not of strategic interest are costing us thousands of dollars because we are substituting them with local manufactures. Now here we must decide what we really want. In certain strategic fields there can be no compromise. We have to develop our technology, our own products but there are other fields where we should take advantage of this, we should not try to develop everything from A to Z in our country all at the same time. We can make a programme over a period of 10 years, 20 years, may be 30 years and say that in these years we can develop so much, next 10 years we can develop so much more and at a reasonable cost we should be able to import these products. But this must be paid for by exports, which means much more competitive market, much higher qualities, delivery schedules and upgrading of technology as soon as possible. You must respond to this. You must be able to increase our export earnings so that we will be able to have this freedom to be able to import a few items which might make our products much cheaper, much more competitive and much more efficient. Our R & D must be developed in such a manner that it really ends up with the finished product. Too much of it is getting left behind in the laboratories today. The technology aspect is not being reflected enough while we are pushing very hard on the science projects. This again is a problem that we are looking at but we would also like you to try and incorporate newer developments into your products and not take advantage of the market that you have sitting in India.

"The Government, as you have seen, has taken very concrete steps to give India's industry a push. The Budget, various industrial policies and we are now going to concentrate on infrastructure to see that you get what you really need. Now, we need a response from you, not just the private sector, may be even more so the public sector. We are not fighting each other—Government and Industry or Government with public sector and private sector—this is a joint venture to take our country forward. And we must look at it as such. And then we will be able to cooperate, get the maximum from what we have, from our resources, from what is available in the country and we will be able to move at a fast pace.

"The last point I would like to raise is sickness which is something which is dragging our industries down. We are not going to put up with sickness. And this will be very clear to you in the coming weeks. We will make it very expensive to go sick and you must also respond by seeing that industry does not go sick or does not go towards sickness. Certain industries must die, we cannot pretend that all industries must carry on into the 22nd century which are going on for the last 300 years but excluding that category we must accept this fact that some industry has to be allowed to die and we must make a panel for somebody who makes an industry which has no reason to go sick. When I said panel I don't mean only the managements, I also mean the financial institutions which are backing them and anybody else who is involved in that.

"Management really is the core of the whole issue. I have seen that even the worst labour relations have changed dramatically when the management has taken a positive step. When the management has been, not necessarily, soft towards labour but when it has been positive in addressing their genuine grievances, when it has been able to think ahead of the unions and see and identify the problems of labour. There are some anomalies in our labour laws, there are some problems, we will be looking at these but the responsibility must lie with management. And it should be a question of pride in one's management that one does not let the industry go sick, that one does not let have strikes and unrest in one's industry.

"The tasks ahead are tremendously challenging. India is ready to go. From the Government we have given it a push, now it is your turn to give it another push."

On March 23, Prime Minister Rajiv Gandhi stressed the need for job-oriented education in the country.

The Prime Minister was addressing the annual convocation of Lucknow University.

In his first convocation address as Prime Minister, Mr. Rajiv Gandhi said: "Your academic education is over. Now you will enter the world. Tomorrow's India will be built by you. It is a very big responsibility. You will have to take it up very seriously. You have to keep in mind that whatever you have been taught is ultimately meant for the progress of all humanity, the whole world and India. You have to channel all your efforts in this direction.

"We are at present engaged in reviewing the educational system of the country. When we think about it we have to see what we want for the future and where we want to take our country. We have to see what we have done in the past 37 years of the post-Independence era, and how far we have been successful in achieving our objectives. How has the situation changed? How has the world changed? How has technology changed and what new shape has science taken? We have to keep all this in mind while thinking about our future. What will be our requirements to take the people of India forward rapidly, to make them strong, to raise their standards of living? We shall have to formulate our system of education after giving deep thought to all this. When we look at our educational institutions today, we find that a large number of people are taught, but education leaves much tobe desired. We do not get what we want. We are not able to help our youth to progress or develop as much as we wish.

"If we have to strengthen our educational system, make it better, then we shall have to start with the teachers, because excellence has to emanate from them. While formulating a new framework for our educational system, we must give thought to them first. As the Vice-Chancellor has remarked, if we want to progress in the present-day world, and if India has to rapidly develop and go ahead, it is essential that we set for ourselves high standards of ideals and objectives. We have to rise and compete with other educational institutions in the world. If our institutions are second class, naturally they will produce mediocrities. I do not want to blame any individual for this. But the weakness is in the system. Today the foremost task is to achieve excellence. How should we improve it further? Only by developing our skills can we achieve rapid progress towards the goal of a strong India.

"What is the position today? In India, nine out of eleven students taking school certificates join universities. This does not happen anywhere else in the world. In other parts, only one out of 10 joins a university. This does not mean that our students are better than theirs; it only means that in other countries 90 per cent people are not required to hold university degrees. Conversely, there is not enough employment here for the university degree holders. There are many people who hold degrees but there are not enough employment opportunities for them. We have to reverse this. We have to see where employment opportunities exist, which type of education will lead to employment and, accordingly, reorient our educational institutions. In factories it is not only the labourers who work. In the present-day world the number of labourers in factories is going down. Wherever people are engaged in large numbers in manual labour, the countries are falling back and are not able to compete with other advanced nations. Employment opportunities are opening out in the field of information handling and service industries. We have to see that our educational institutions turn to this area and prepare the youth for it.

"I find that many women have won medals today. I hope that after winning these medals they will not just go home, get married and confine themselves to home-life. I should like them to take the fullest advantage of their education in such a way that the country is benefited. Many things can be done at home and those activities can strengthen the country's economy. There are many industries in villages also. A new home industry is developing fast and women can employ themselves easily in that area. This industry is known as 'computer programming', which is very easy to handle and brings excellent returns. It can also make the country strong.

"A new generation will arise which will prepare our country for the next century. We have to look to the future and see how we can exploit the new opportunities. You have to remember that in our country you belong to a group who can be counted on the fingers, the chosen class which has received education. Millions and millions of people do not get this opportunity. You should never lose sight of those people. We should always remember that it is they who are the backbone of our country. Therefore when we step into the world and in whatever things we engage ourselves, we should see that we make some contribution to the country so that the poor and backward people are able to raise their standards of living and are able to move above the poverty line. This is a very big responsibility. You have to fulfil this responsibility with great patience and discipline. Always remember that the coming generation of India is the pride of the nation and it has to raise India and take it forward."

Inaugurating the conference of non-aligned and other developing countries on the Role of Women in Development on April 10, 1985, the Prime Minister, Mr. Rajiv Gandhi, said:

"The role of women in developing countries is very crucial to the rate at which a country develops and in many ways is an indicator as to how well the country is developing.

"The non-aligned represents a very large majority of humanity on this earth. We have traditionally fought against imperialism. against colonialism. racism, neo-imperialism, neo-colonialism, against all forms of discrimination and domination. We have fought for an equitable social and economic order. Here, the rights of women and the fight for all these causes, in a way, is similar to the fight for the rights, for the uplift of women in all our countries.

"Women are in a sense a social conscience of a country. They hold our societies together. In developing countries women have been active in all fields and specially they have risen to prominent places in the political field. But, unfortunately, at the lower level we have not been able to give them enough freedom of movement, enough help to rise above the discriminations that they are faced with which have built up over thousands of years of a male-dominated society.

"Subjugation, whether it is of a country, or of an individual, is very similar. And women have been depressed. This fight to bring women out, to bring them up in our society, is no different from the fight of the non-aligned to bring other countries up, to build them, to give them more opportunities.

"Our society's progress can really be judged by how well half our society progress. And if they are to progress fast, half the talent, half the energy cannot be ignored. Women must be allowed full freedom of action and full movement. Women are equal in every way, whether it is their spiritual urge. whether it is political ideals, historically in sacrifices, in heroism, there have been no shortcomings, there have been no differences just because of sex. Women have risen to the highest levels, highest levels of sacrifice, highest levels of heroism. This is evident from all our freedom struggles.

"But now, we have to fight the historical, the social and

cultural backwardness that has been thrust upon women. The male superiority has become, in a way, a vested interest and like all vested interests, it is damaging to humanity. And all of us—men and women—must fight this with all our strength. Women's right for education, for employment, for their growth, for their development must be built and all facilities that we can give must be given to allow this to build up.

"Women's contribution to humanity throughout history today, whether it is in the work place, in society or in the home, has been no less than anybody else's. Still, today, women don't get adequate opportunity in education, in employment. We are trying to change this in India like Smt. Chandrashekherji just said, we have taken many steps for the uplift, for the progress of women. We realise that one of the key factors is education. And as a first step, we have made education free for girls up to the High School stage in India. We will take other such steps to see that women are able to develop in India. In India, women will be equal partners in building our nation.

"The U.N. decade on women has fought for political, administrative, legal, social, economic and cultural equality for women. But really what we have to do is build this into our society. We passed laws, we have conferences, it must permeate down into the hearts of people. And that is when it really will start making a difference.

"As a group women are maybe the largest under-privileged group in the world. And we must fight to remove this disparity. Our last Prime Minister Indira Gandhi had said that 'It is very good to see women in top positions and they get a lot of publicity when they come into top positions.' But it is really at the grass roots, at the daily level that the discrimination must be removed. It is the fight up every rung of the ladder that has to be made easier and we hope that this conference will contribute towards this struggle.

"We are in India for using special programme, having special monitoring to see how women can progress faster. We have had a recent Act in Parliament—Family Courts—to prevent delays. We have had many social groups helping many voluntary agencies. Government action is good, essential but more than that it is the mood in the society which has to be changed. This can be done only with the help of everyone, voluntary agencies, Government agencies, every support that we can gather. These problems are similar all over the world, more so, amongst our developing countries."

The Prime Minister, Mr. Rajiv Gandhi, replying to the debate on the demands for grants of the Ministry of External Affairs, said in the Lok Sabha on April 10, 1985:

"India's foreign policy has been well established for over 37 years now. We are continuing along the same road. Under this foreign policy India has attained a certain position in the world, a certain authority in the world. In a way, our foreign policy was not very different from the course of our independence struggle. It is a development of the same movement on a world-wide basis. We fought against imperialism, against colonialism, against racism, against any form of domination or discrimination. Today we still fight against these wherever they are on earth. Added to these, we have neo-colonialism and neo-imperialism which did not exist at that time. And if you really go down to the basis of our outlook on disarmament, are we not getting back to Gandhiji's *ahimsa* on a wider scale?

"This foreign policy has helped India to gain a certain standing, but more than that it has set certain precedents in the world. It was this foreign policy that started off the Non-Aligned Movement which is today one of the largest movements in the world, and which, I am sure, that history will find, has been responsible for avoiding many tensions and may be even many wars. We shall continue along this road for peace, for disarmament, for a more just, social and economic order.

"Most of the specific points have been covered by the Hon'ble Minister of State, but I should like to go over some of the major areas of concern to the House and to the people of our country.

"We have been taking certain initiatives in our region. We feel that it is important that we develop the best possible relations with all the countries in our region keeping our own basic ideologies, our basic policies intact and not deviating from them. We are following this course. We have taken certain initiatives, with our Foreign Secretary going to these countries. And we hope these visits will help to develop better social and cultural relations between these countries and us. We have to see that the relations in our region grow deeper and that real cordiality is established in

But we must keep one thing firmly in mind. Whatever be the conclusion of this ghastly period in Sri Lanka, it must be such that the Tamils will live in peace and harmony in Sri Lanka for the coming years. We must not look just to one or two years or five years. We must look much further ahead and see that the atmosphere is retrieved to an extent that the Tamils feel safe and confident to live in that country. Nothing that we do must make it such that it will make it difficult for the Tamils to live in Sri Lanka on a future date. Keeping this in mind, we are working towards a solution. We have had contact, on a number of occasions, with the President of Sri Lanka. We have had certain exchanges of communication and we feel that there is light at the end of the tunnel.

"Our relations with the USSR and the USA will be more friendly. The USSR has been an old friend who has stood by us at times when we needed friends. We appreciate this and we shall keep this in mind. With the USA, we are trying to improve our relations. But there are a few points which do seem to stand in the way. One is, as I have already said, the arms supply to Pakistan. The second is that we feel they are not taking enough action on Pakistan's nuclear programme. We feel that equipment is still coming from outside. We feel that technology is leaking and not enough is being done to control that. But we are looking forward to better cultural, better social and better trade relations, and on my visit there, I do hope to bring these points to their notice and we hope we will get a positive response.

"The Non-Aligned Movement has been one of the largest peace movement that the earth has seen and we will be taking more steps to build on this. We are having a Ministerial level meeting on Namibia in Delhi next week which will be followed by a meeting later this year. We have helped the African countries which are suffering from tremendous famine and drought by sending them one lakh tonnes of wheat. This is really an example of where we can help them. We do not have to think back very far to find that India could have been in a very similar position. Merely 20-25 years ago, if we had a drought, we would have suffered in a similar manner. But today, because of our positive policies in developing self-sufficiency and developing ourselves, we are able to send grain to them. This is an area where South-South exchanges are really important because we are the ones who can show them how to rise the region. It is not enough just Governments getting together and signing agreements or pacts. We need something much more long-lasting and deeper in the interests of all of us.

"Our Foreign Secretary has recently returned from Pakistan. There has been some comment about his visit and what was spoken there and what was done. I think, a few things need to be clarified.

"Discussions have been started. But I should like to make it very clear that the talks that we are referring to today are not talks on the 'no war' pact or on a peace agreement or at that level. We are talking of improving relationship, improving exchanges between our two peoples, improving the cordiality between the two countries, because that is what will improve the atmosphere which can lead to a basis for a proper understanding between our two countries.

"I have met President Zia on two occasions—once in Delhi in November and once in Moscow. On both occasions we had very cordial talks. President Zia was very forthright in what he wanted to do to improve relations between our countries. Unfortunately, after the first occasion we had the incident with the jathas visiting Nankana Saheb in Pakistan. After the second talk, we read an interview that he had given to a journal, which again was totally contrary to what he had spoken about. This is just to bring these facts to your notice. We are worried about their feverish purchase of arms and weapons which we feel are well beyond their just requirements. Today we believe that the USA is spending the maximum amount it has ever spent since the Vietnam war drew to an end on armament going to the Mujahideen in Afghanistan. And, as you know, these go through Pakistan. We cannot be fully sure of how much goes where. The sums involved are very very large.

"We do not like what we see about their nuclear programme. We have still no indication that they are not making a bomb. We know that they are getting aircraft, they have got aircraft, which have the capability of carrying nuclear weapons. Just a few days ago, the President of Sri Lanka visited Pakistan. And we were disturbed that he should have brought up the Jammu and Kashmir issue while he was in Pakistan. Simultaneously there is a forum being set up in the United Kingdom which is also opening this issue. I wonder if these are a coincidence.

"With Sri Lanka, many of our Members are very justly agitated.

about that level. And it is an example which is clear and visible to everybody in the world that when it comes to the crux, we have taken the correct path and the others who have got carried away by various theories and various smooth talk, have not been able to rise while India has.

"Through NAM and on other platforms, we shall be taking up, whenever we can, the case for the South African people. It is one of the last vestiges of colonialism left in the world and truly, the whole of humanity should hang their heads in shame till we get rid of this.

"We have taken initiatives to show the world what India really is, not what is perceived in the media, and to this end we held two years ago a festival in England and this year we are going to have a festival in the USA and a festival in France. This will bring home to the people of America and the people of Europe what India really is. We are also projecting our musicians, our dyers, our potters and our village people. We will be taking them to the world and exposing the world to what really is the heart of India.

"The Iraq-Iran war is really one of the most terrible wars after the First World War in the manner in which it is being fought. We have taken various steps, as have many other people in the world, to try and bring this ghastly war to an end. Unfortunately no one is seeing an end to this war today. We shall still be working at this, to try and bring peace in this region.

"The PLO has fought a very brave struggle. We have stood by them in the past because we have felt that it has been their right to have a homeland and we will stand by them in the future also.

"Sir, last but not the least is the question of extremists and secessionists propagating the division of India from their bases in various countries. We have taken up this matter in earnest with those governments. We have applied pressure in whatever ways have been available to us. And we have got some responses. We are looking at this very seriously and we shall continue to do so. India's foreign policy over the years has proved that it was correct not only for India, but for the world, and we shall carry on building along the same lines. Thank you very much."

"On April 15, 1985, Prime Minister Rajiv Gandhi asked top entrepreneurs from abroad to play a supportive role to help the Indian economy grow to a position of self-reliance, ensuring simultaneously equity and social justice.

The Prime Minister said that healthy conditions had been created for foreign investors in India, and indicated that rules would be further liberalised for infusion of foreign investments.

The Prime Minister was addressing 123 executives who had gathered here to attend a two-day "Round Table on India" which the European Management Foundation (EMF) had organised in collaboration with the Association of Indian Engineering Industry. Mr. Gandhi had addressed the executives of Davos, Switzerland, in September last year when he was General Secretary of the AICC(I).

The principal point the Prime Minister made in his address was that the satisfactory performance during the Sixth Plan had brought the country to a position where it could think of moving faster. The round table, he hoped, would enable both sides to understand each other better and see the direction in which the economy was moving.

Inaugurating the Round Table on India, organised by the European Management Foundation, the Prime Minister, Mr. Rajiv Gandhi, said:

"We, in India, are today in a position from which we can move ahead fairly rapidly. From this Round Table, we would like not only you to understand India better, to understand our systems, our policies, our people, but we would also like to learn from you and understand how we could do better, how we could move faster. You will be mainly looking at our economy, the direction it is taking. I would like to just say a few words about it.

"Our economy is based on Five Year Plans. We have just concluded the Sixth Plan from 1980 to 1985. The performance during this Plan was highly satisfactory. Our average growth rate was little over 5 per cent in GNP. The agricultural output in 1979-80 was 109 million tonnes and this year we are likely to go over 150 million tonnes—almost a 40 per cent increase in five years and unlike some other countries, there are many products which we don't count in this agricultural output.

"Our investment rate is high—25 per cent and we have invested heavily in critical areas: agriculture, irrigation, energy, transport, communications. We expect returns in these areas. In spite of this high growth rate, we have managed to keep our inflation rate fairly low. Our balance of payments have been kept well under control. And we have not had some of the problems other developing countries have had. This would be commendable performance under any circumstances. But during this period, the world economy has been going through tremendous pressures and many developing countries, for that matter even some developed countries, have been going through severe difficulties. We, with our economic management, have managed to avoid these difficulties and maintained a good rate of growth.

"During the past Five Year Plans we had established a strong foundation for growth. And it is this that we can take advantage of and build on today. The Seventh Plan, which will be ready in about six months time, will project the policies and strategies for the next five years. The broad-thrust areas are already clear and the details we will have very soon.

"Our basic thrust is for growth with equity and social justice. The guiding principles of our development have not changed since our independence. We have adapted them to the technologies, to the development status of our country as we have moved along. We are planning for 5 per cent growth during this Plan. Our population growth needs decelerating and we are looking at this very very seriously.

"During the past plans we have achieved a fair amount in equalising the various sections of our society. For example, the consumption rate of the poorest has increased while the consumption rate of the very richest has remained the same or declined very slightly. This shows that our policies for upliftment of the poor are working. Our policies for involving the maximum number in the development of India are, in fact, having effect.

"Agriculture is the bed-rock of our economy. Almost 70 per cent of our people live on agriculture. And this necessarily means that our industries must relate to the agricultural sector and be fully involved in our development process. We have progressed very rapidly in agriculture, like I have just said, but there is still very much to be done in terms of the crops, in regions there is still a lot of disparity. Industrial growth must be parallel with agricultural growth, for us to get maximum benefit from both sectors. Our basic policy for agricultural growth has been irrigation and fertilizer to put it very crudely into two boxes, and remunerative prices for agricultural produce. With these three critical areas, we have managed to increase our agricultural production. And while many other developing countries are succumbing to famine and drought as we see in Africa today, India, due to its proper management, is able to send food to Africa today.

"We have paid very special attention to the small farmers, the poor. Our rural development programmes and our anti-poverty programmes have been effective. We, today, are going to see how we can make them more efficient and more effective. To achieve these ends, we need a dynamic industry. And we have tried to develop this during the past plans.

"One of our foremost targets has been self-reliance of the public sector. The public sector is the core of India's industrial development and we use it as a tool for opening up backward and non-industrialised areas to industry and to development. Today our industry is wide-basod and it extends from simple consumer products to very high technology areas of nuclear engineering, space and military technology.

"We have a mixed economy, the public sector and the private sector, both function together for the benefit, for the maximum benefit of the country and for their own faster expansions. Both have grown and gained strength and the best companies in both spheres are equal to any in the world. The development role of our public sector has been very critical in the development of India. And we must keep this in mind when we criticise the public sector for their inefficiency or their lower productivity, because we force them to go into areas where there is no industry, where there is no infrastructure, maybe no roads, no communications, no facilities. So this we must keep in mind before charging them with inefficiency or low productivity. Still, in spite of these positive points, there are certain areas where we find weaknesses in our industrial system. The major weakness is our efficiency. Our industries are not as efficient as other industries in the world and certainly not as efficient as we would like them to be. Their productivity is low, quality standards are not up to those in the rest of the world. The cost of production is still very high and in many areas there is technological stagnation. These are the challenges that we face today.

"The steps that we have taken are just a few of those that we are about to take to invigorate our industry, to get a new thrust into our whole corporate sector. We have restructured the direct tax system to make it easier, smoother and more profitable to work, more efficiently. We are in the process of looking it how to restructure our indirect tax system.

"We have introduced a new import-export policy. Government procedures, in control, are being nationalised, so that there are fewer time delays. We are trying to have one window operations, as far as possible. We are basically opening up our industry to competitive pressures so that they may perform better. I am confident of the competence of our industry and I know that they will respond positively and show a new dynamism. We expect that we cannot do this entirely on our own. We will need help from industries, from friends in other countries. We see this really as a support role for our own industries because self-reliance, self-sufficiency is one of our primary goals. We would like foreign business to help us in this goal, in building a new dynamic, self-reliant economy in our country. At this stage of our development, it is not feasible to open up our industries to free competition from all industries abroad. It would not be fair to our industries. But at the same time, we are, in certain areas, opening up to foreign competition so that our industries might face the pressure and perform under that pressure.

"We look for self-reliance, not autarchy. We in India today need to interact with the world market, with world industry and we realise that too much protection can be damaging to our industries. We look for improved technology, for domestic requirements, for better competitiveness, for better quality in our products, and above all, for a more efficient production process.

"Foreign investment is strictly regulated by our laws. But once an investment is cleared, there are no further restrictions and the same laws apply to all companies—Indian or foreign. We have introduced special terms for high-technology in special areas where we feel that we need more thrust. India offers a massive market of 750 million people. We have a growing per capita income and the strength of the market is much more than our statistics make us believe. We have seen this on various occasions when we have opened up various areas. The roof has suddenly gone off the market. We offer political stability, consistent policies, wide industrial base, a very large trained manpower, access to various markets and a very good past record of dealing with foreign companies. India looks ahead as a developing country, challenging the development economics in the coming years. We hope we will be able to work together for our mutual benefit."

QUESTION: What, Mr. Prime Minister, do you consider as the three most pressing economic problems of your government? What specific actions and what time-table do you have for bringing them under control?

PRIME MINISTER: "The first must be population. Because anything we do, is diluted by our population growth. The second has to be poverty and how to remove it. I suppose really that is where we come to our real problems, which is agricultural development, industrial development. We have tackled population control on a war-footing. Our growth rate for the first time is below two per cent. And we hope to continue this trend to reduce our population growth and to make it manageable in the coming years. To really understand some of our social programmes, one must understand the poverty level in some of our areas. In the West, one talks of free enterprise, one talks of allowing people to go ahead on their own scheme giving them the opportunity and letting their initiatives take over. But when one looksat some areas in India, very large areas in India, one sees people at a poverty level where they do not have the capability to go ahead, even if they have the initiative.

"And for this group we have very large anti-poverty programmes, which help them come up above, just above that level, so that they can then take off on their own, on their own steam. We have found these programmes very good, we have helped a very large number of people but of course whenever you have such programmes when you lift large people up above a certain level, immediately their aspirations, their demands go up even high. So when we have these anti-poverty programmes, we have to match them with infrastructure development so that these people can then make full use of having been lifted up above the poverty levels. We have steadily been reducing the percentage of people below the poverty line since independence. This has been a tremendous achievement, if you match it with the population growth that has taken place. Our population is more than double what it was at the time of independence and the poverty levels have come down very gradually.

"On agricultural and industrial development, I have already given you some areas, some ideas what we are going to do. We are now looking at how we can progress even faster. We are looking at how to select certain areas and concentrate in those directions and make our country equal in those areas of technology anywhere in the world. Once we achieved that, we will find broaden those areas so that we can cover the full spectrums. This is roughly what we have in mind."

QUESTION: Mr. Prime Minister, you spoke already about the role of the public and the private sector. I have one question which is related to this issue. How do you see the role of the entrepreneur in the development of your country's economy? What could and what should be done to facilitate entrepreneurial activities?

PRIME MINISTER: The entrepreneur very definitely carries very high priority with us. This can be seen from our tax laws, from our industrial licensing policies. And in the recent policies we have again given a special thrust, more benefits to entrepreneurs. A very large section of our industry is based on small scale industries, which are really entrepreneurs. We are trying to broaden this into the agricultural areas with rural industries, with agro-industries, and with very very small-scale village industries. We feel that entrepreneurs are really the core of our future industries. And we must give them full scope to develop the entrepreneurship.

QUESTION: Mr. Prime Minister, you spoke about the Indian economy towards its objective, of course in equity. Now the question of the contribution of foreign business collaboration in achieving those objectives, and here a more specific question, Which areas would you single out to be particularly open for foreign collaboration?

PRIME MINISTER: This is a very difficult question, because there are so many areas that we have opened up. But without spending time on the non-essential areas, really the basic infrastructural areas are, where we need most help, which is energy, whether it is power, or fossil energy, communications and transport and in agriculture, Agricultural methods, technology right from the development, the bio-technology required for the seeds to other larger technologies required for maximum output in production from our views. These are the really core areas where we look for more help, but of course, we are open across a very wide pan and I am sure you will know more about it in your discussions this afternoon, when you talk about specific subjects and specific areas of co-operation.

QUESTION: Mr. Prime Minister, I have a still related question which has to do with the issue of the consistency and continuity. And the question is: Can an efficient transfer of technology take place in such a limited period of a time as defined today?

PRIME MINISTER: Well, the short answer of course is, Yes. We have seen this, the Indian industrialist, the Indian mind is very receptive to quick change, to absorbing technologies and, I think, you will also find this when you talk to our industrialist, then you talk to our people. We are able to absorb things much faster than many peoples of the world and use them productively, economically and, may be sometimes in manners which other people could never have envisaged.

QUESTION: Mr. Prime Minister, the key factor for international competitveness are industrial relations. What initiatives will you take in order to improve those relations?

PRIME MINISTER: On the whole, our industrial relations have been fairly good. But that doesn't mean that we can rest at that position. We are looking at various laws to see how we can make them better, better for industry and better for labour as well. We will have these ready shortly and you will see that there will be tremendous improvement in productivity and in work-out.

QUESTION: Mr. Prime Minister, how do you define the aspirations of the young people in your country? To what extent, do they identify themselves with the policies, the values which you represent?

PRIME MINISTER: The aspirations are very very high, and how should I say how they look at our Government. I think the best answer is to see the result of the last election, that they give the support, shows the support that they have given to our Government. But there is one more thing I would like to add, which I should have said earlier in... The real problems that we are facing and I missed out one which is education. Because education really goes to the root of every process of development and in our family planning programme, our population control programme. We are looking at the whole gamut of our education system and seeing how we can change it to make it more dynamic and more productive for the youth of our country and make them come out with more initiative and more drive.

QUESTION: Mr. Prime Minister, a related question: How does your Government reconcile modernisation and materialise which goes with it and its traditional values of society. Do you see here any contradiction and implications for social and political stability of your country?

PRIME MINISTER: I don't see it as a danger to our political stability. We have demonstrated over the past 37 years, since our independence, that India is stable. We have had a number of major changes of Government. Our country has gone through times of very severe trauma but we have still come our every time stronger than we were before. Our democratic structure, our system is now very deeply ingrained and I don't think there is any question of instability coming into it. But the challenges are very real, and we can see the tension between the old strength of India, the spirituality, the inner strength that really defined India, that has kept India as India. In spite of many foreign conquests India has not changed, it is the conqueror that has become Indian. This strength we cannot afford to lose. We have to blend this in which modern technology, hopefully, not with modern materialism but with Indian spirituality.

QUESTION: Mr. Prime Minister, the mobilisation of human resources seems to be the key for progress. This concerns particularly human resources employed by the Government. Would you care to comment on those issues and in this context on democracy and I may add another question which is similar: the world's mood is focussing on India to the excellent policies you are implementing. But there is a fear that in our daily context the changes which are announced by the Government are not going to come to action. Please comment on this.

PRIME MINISTER: Well, I will start with the bureaucracy. I suppose we must start there because you will end there. Our bureaucracy is much maligned. It is true that sometimes they are too bureaucratic, sometimes they are entangled totally in their own red tape. But we see the positive side, they have helped keep India together, they have helped keep India united, they have helped keep India democracy which many other countries in the world would have liked to have seen in their countries. We just have a look around our neighbourhood to see the difference that there is in the systems. At the same time, we must make them more dynamic, we must make them more forward-looking and we are doing this. I cannot claim that this is going to happen in a matter of days or weeks or months. This really goes down to the basic training that the bureaucracy is given in their training institutes and that is where we are starting. At the same time, we are seeing how to make it more dynamic at all levels and I think you can already see a difference. This will become more and better as time goes by.

QUESTION: We have the admiration for your policy but what will you do in order that it is implemented inside, the Government hierarchy?

PRIME MINISTER: Well, it will be implemented. We are already taking a lot of steps for it. And I think you, too, will see that the effects flow right down to the lowest level in a very short period of time.

QUESTION: Mr. Prime Minister, how do you see at a political picture emerging in India in the next decade also in the context of the host of regional parties?

PRIME MINISTER: Well, I have already answered part of that. The political system has been established for about 37 years now. It has proved its strength during various periods of tension, trauma, hardship that our country has gone through. We have shown the world that the system is stronger than any pressure that can be put upon it. I don't see any change in this system coming about in the country. Regional parties have a role but by definition, we have a narrow outlook. And this is not good for the greater good of our country. We have now really only one effective regional party. And that too is looking towards a national outlook. We hope that they can have a national outlook. Of course, as a party, our party will be fighting them all the way but we would like more parties with the national outlook and I see that this is a tendency which is developing.

QUESTION: One question which is related to it. Previously all major decisions were taken by the Prime Minister and Central Government. Now we understand decisions will be decentralised. When and how?

PRIME MINISTER: We have already decentralised substantially. We have pushed the decision-making down to lower levels in almost every area. And this is not when but it is now.

QUESTION: Mr. Prime Minister, we are very happy in India with your dynamic approach and practical budget and a very practical import-export policy, and for these we congratulate you. We run a few industries in the part of Karnataka, may be that the electronic industry is feeling relieved today because of your very dynamic and constructive approach. Sir, whether you could do or you could consider, perhaps, to the power problems at ease, it is only you who could do it?

PRIME MINISTER: Well, it is very difficult for me to talk about power problems in Karnataka specifically, as the hon'ble gentleman is aware that Karnataka is a State run by an opposition party and power is a State subject. It doesn't come under the Centre as such. But power is one of our major problems. But then isn't that by definition a problem of the developing country? Once we have enough energy, we have, by definition, got over the problems of development. And we are looking at this problem, we are trying to see how we can help from the Central sector. In fact, in this year's budget power is the one sector which has had an increase in outlay by almost every single other factor we have had to cut back upon.

QUESTION: My question would be in the high technology and electronic sector. India will be competing the world markets with exports from the Far-East. High effective duty rates provide no incentives for local component manufacturers to become efficient and therefore, their products to be cost competitive. Is the Government prepared to bring duty rate down progressively and expeditiously in order to encourage efficiency in the private sector?

PRIME MINISTER: Well, you have taken the one industry that we have done tremendous work on during the past few months. We have completely revised the whole electronics policy. We have revised the duty rates; tax rates right from the starting point of raw-material and components to the finished products and I am sure during your later discussions when you talk specifically about this area, you will find out how much we have done for electronics. And I would like to add that in electronics, specially in consumer electronics, where the Far-East is mostly competitive, our markets are not necessarily targeted to exports. We have a very very large market in India. And I think the best example of our market, the size of our market can be demonstrated by the two months or three months of customs relief we gave during the Asian Games for import of television sets. I am told that we mocked up almost every single television set that was available in the world right up to Los Angeles. I was told no sets were available. This is the strength of the consumer market in India and we do not only look outside, we also look at our own market.

QUESTION: We are very heartened that the Prime Minister started with population problem. Related to that is the problem of the environment and the ecology. And India has set a very good example already but the problem is so vast for us and is linked with education also. It will be very interesting to request the Prime Minister to please also reassure us again on this great occasion.

PRIME MINISTER: We are fully aware of this problem and this is going to be one of our major thrust-areas in not only in locating industry, in licensing industry, in seeing industry does not upset the ecology and local environment but also in our new education system. So, it is ingrained into our people right from the earliest age and it is not a problem at a later date. We are actively attacking those areas where it has already caused us problems, where it has already become serious. But the policy is really to see that we preserve our ecology, we don't damage it further. We repair it where we have already damaged it. Sometimes this is the constraint to industrial growth. Sometimes, it is more expensive but if we look at the longer term picture, it is essential and it repays many times the investments that we put into it.

QUESTION: Mr. Prime Minister, I was very much impressed by your remark regarding the public sector and reference to private sector. One thought, which has been worrying me a lot, is that we have not sufficiently exploited a joint sector to the extent we should. There is a certain amount of animus between, whether you like it or not, the two and there could be a great scope for both of them together. Small experiment was made years ago on Air India International. And if that pattern could be repeated where the private sector start with 51 per cent and the government put in or contribute 49 per cent with a proviso that the government has the right at any time to take over two per cent automatically when the private sector has misbehaved or not performed well. Now that would take care of a number of capital-intensive industries when today there is dearth of capital and the private sector will supplement the kind of entrepreneurship plus the efficiency that is put in. And between the two of them we have a scope which could be put into our Company Law Act as an instrument which we can show to the world that both together in a mixed economy can progress together without any animus and competition between them, and India can profit a lot. I would like to know your reaction. If we could give greater momentum to a thought which is already there and we have already done that in the past and like to hear little more about it.

PRIME MINISTER: I think, this is an area that we must look into, and see how we can build this co-operation here, and we will be doing this. It is not always that co-operation leads to better results. Sometimes a little bit of conflict is required to push people to perform a little better. But we will definitely look into this.

QUESTION: Mr. Prime Minister, before concluding this session, I have still three very short questions left. The first one is: What concrete advice would you give to the foreign businessmen here? The second one: What concrete advice would you give to the Indian businessmen here to tackle the medium term future of the country? And the last question: What are—maybe a little bit private question—the key personal values that strike you, as a politician, as a human being, and as a leader of your country?

PRIME MINISTER: Very difficult to answer these questions at the time that is left. To answer the second question first: It's really a question of seeing where one wants India to go. When one goes around the country, meets the people, tries to understand their problems, their aspirations, then one realises the tremendous energies that are available, the tremendous potential that is there in our country. At the same time, one sees the inability of a very large section of the people to make use of that because of their poverty level, because of their conditions. We have to see how to bring them out of this. Like I said earlier, without removing what is their intrinsic strength which is an inherent, a depth, a spirituality, something much deeper than modern materialism or consumerism, a strength which will serve not only India but, if we can project positively, will definitely help the world face the 21st century as we go into it. The values that India has built upon can really be summed up into what Gandhiji said many many years ago; 'Truth and non-violence' amongst a lot of other things but the core would be truth and non-violence. Truth in everything. In a way if you translate truth into a world scenario, it really can be projected as being a true democracy where truth is allowed to come up in surface, where every country is allowed to speak its mind freely. Non-violence in a similar way is much deeper than what the West conceived as non-violence. Gandhiji's description of non-violence was not just that you do not hit back, it was just that you do not even feel like hitting back. It is that conditioning which we require today, not only in India, we require it in the whole world, in a world where we are arming up to the teeth, we are only talking about annihilating the other party as a check for violence and we in India feel that this is a ridiculous state of affairs. If we have to progress, we must think positively and not negatively. We from India try to project this in our foreign policy and we have tried to build this into the non-aligned movement, both these things. And it is continuing in this process that we would like a co-operation with others that we are exploiting anybody else. We stand for freedom in every sphere. And the co-operation between our industrialists and industrialists from other countries.

V

THE CONTOURS OF PROGRESS

To ensure gains of economic development are reaped by the people it is necessary to control population by adopting family planning programme but Prime Minister Rajiv Gandhi emphasised that the family planning programme should not be politicised and reduced to a parochial level. Politicians must have only one view on the problem and that should be to bring down the size of population to manageable proportions.

Mr. Gandhi, who inaugurated the second National Conference of Parliamentarians on Population and Development, said whatever successes India had achieved in its family planning programme was through dedication and voluntary efforts, with no element of coercion. "We are proud of this", he said.

Inaugurating the second National Conference of Parliamentarians on Population and Development, the Prime Minister, Mr Rajiv Gandhi, said on May 13, 1985, in New Delhi:

"Four years ago, Indiraji inaugurated a similar conference in this very hall. Indiraji really laid the foundations of our Population Control Programme. She realised the importance the population explosion has for India, for the whole world. And for her work in reducing India's population growth, she was honoured as the first Awardee of the UN Award for population.

"The issue is a very crucial issue not just for India but to the whole world. In India, it is more important to us because we see the rate at which we are growing, we see the way it is affecting our economic growth. We, every year, produce an Australia—44 babies a minute. This is a challenge that is in front of us in India today. Our programme has been fairly successful. We have reduced our birth rate significantly. Our growth rate is now below 2 per cent after a very long time. Our target must be a birth rate of about 20 per thousand towards the end of the century that is when our Net Reproduction Rate becomes one and things will start coming under control.

"Fortunately, we have been able to increase our GNP at a faster rate than our population. For the first time, we are now getting ahead of the real challenges that are facing us. We have achieved this voluntarily in a democratic set-up without coercion and without compulsions. This is something that we in India are extremely proud of.

"Family planning/population control cannot be seen just as a cut and dry family planning process. It must be linked with every other facet for development of our society. The problems of population control are different in different countries. There are many countries where they have reversed the problem. It is not just a question of family planning, it is a question of really planning your society so that it develops as your country grows, as your people become better off and it is in this way that we must look it. Today we are trying to see how we can attack this problem from all sides. We have taken very major steps in direct family planning. It has been successful to an extent. But the real success is where education comes in, where social reforms come in, where women start getting equal rights in society. This is where we must concentrate now.

"We are undertaking a major programme for education. This has to be the basis of any family planning programme. But it is a long-term process. It will take time. And we must see how we can use other methods, methods of folk-lore, all modern media methods to get the message home to the people. We have expanded our television network and we are covering a very large proportion of our people today. With over 180 transmitters, our TV system has a very long range and it must form the basis of education for family planning. I believe we have taken this up in one or two programmes that are being produced by Doordarshan and are becoming extremely popular. I hope this trend continues and the effect is seen in our population figures, in our growth rate.

"The real difference will only be where there is an economic change in our rural areas, where there is a substantial economic change and this, I am very happy to say, is coming about at a rapid rate with more economic activity, with the better standard of living, better education and specially for women we hope that this programme will have an effect which will be directly visible in this statistics that we present.

"The programme is a challenge to the whole world. With the developing countries bearing the brunt, the weight of the population, many developing countries falling behind in their GNP growth. We will have tremendous social tensions in the world, when we look for a peaceful, progressive world. We have to see that the population in every part of the world is under control, is balanced. And this is a challenge which faces all parliamentarians today.

"I am glad that today we have members from every corner of India representing very diverse people. The problem is a social problem and equally a political problem. We must see that politics has only one view of the population problem that is of reducing. It must not be dragged into our political battles, reduced to a parochial level, it is a national challenge, it is a world challenge and I am sure, parliamentarians all over the world will meet this challenge, and will overcome this tremendous problem that is facing all of us today."

Prime Minister Rajiv Gandhi has said his Government will accord top priority to strengthening the country's unity and integrity and frustrate the designs of divisive forces.

In an interview to Soviet news agency Tass, Mr. Gandhi who had gone to the Soviet Union for a six-day visit on May 21, said: "As regards political and social objectives, my first and foremost task is to strengthen the unity and solidarity of our people and fight divisive elements."

Turning to the country's foreign policy, Mr. Gandhi reiterated India's commitment to non-alignment, disarmament, international peace and detente.

Stating the country's economic priorities, Mr. Gandhi said India's foremost task was to continue the process of modernisation and emancipation of the downtrodden.

"Our nation builders—Mahatma Gandhi, Jawaharlal Nehru and Indira Gandhi—have laid down the path as to how to achieve this. We shall pursue the objective of self-reliance, we are determined to enlarge our agricultural and industrial production and we will ensure that best results out of investments already made are secured.

"We shall strengthen our infrastructure, and the public sector, which has a crucial role in our development, will be given the fullest support in fulfilling its role. However, at the same time it is our duty to release the productive forces of our country."

Mr. Gandhi said he was looking forward to his visit to the Soviet Union and expressed the hope that his talks with Soviet President and Communist Party leader Mikhail Gorbachov and other Soviet leaders would be "detailed, comprehensive and fruitful", leading to further strengthening of relations.

He said that in the last 30 years Indo-Soviet relations had grown in all directions—political, economic, scientific and cultural.

"The economic and commercial relations between our two countries have registered spectacular growth in recent years. India attaches great importance of them", Mr Gandhi said.

He added that "in a growing and expanding relationship we must always search for new areas of working together, and there is vast scope for diversification in the trade and economic co-operation between our two countries."

Mr. Gandhi said the economies of the two countries were "complementary", we must work out new areas of production co-operation and transfer of technology.

"In fact it is necessary to view bilateral co-operation in a large time frame. The recent meeting of the Joint Commission was a very useful exercise in this regard and the two sides have identified and agreed upon new areas of co-operation."

Mr. Gandhi said Jawaharlal Nehru, who visited the Soviet Union for the first time in 1955, was rightly remembered for his part in laying the firm foundations of Indo-Soviet co-operation, which had been a factor of stability and peace.

On nuclear disarmament and the six-nation Delhi Declaration, Mr. Gandhi said the six-nation proposal for disarmament was an important initiative. It carried forward the declaration adopted by the seventh summit of the non-aligned nations.

"We greatly appreciate the fact that the Soviet Union promptly welcomed the initiative," he said.

Stating that India had always been a strong champion of peace and the pursuit of peace was one of the cardinal principles of India's philosophy and policy, Mr. Gandhi said, "We welcome the peace-loving policies of the Soviet Union and the initiative taken by the

Soviet Union to re-start discussions on disarmament with a view to reaching meaningful agreements."

Replying to a question on the United Nations, Mr. Gandhi said the UN must be preserved and strengthened. "The world needs a forum where peaceful solutions of differences can be worked out in an atmosphere of fellowship and belonging," he said.

"I do hope the 40th anniversary of the United Nations (this year) at which several world leaders will be present, including, I hope, Mr. Gorbachov, will be the starting point of new effort to reach understandings and improve the prospects for peace," he said.

On the 40th anniversary of the victory over fascism, Mr. Gandhi said the defeat of fascism was a signal event in history.

"I offer my congratulations to the people of the Soviet Union in their years of remembrance," he said.

On May 29, the Prime Minister plainly told public sector executives that these undertakings would have to be competitive and the government could not afford to subsidise them.

He wished to entrust more responsibility to the executives, but they would be accountable for their performance. In fact, they would have to prove themselves by performance.

Mr. Gandhi, who was inaugurating the third conference of chief executives of public enterprises, asked "When will we stand on our feet and compete as equals. You have to do this and you have to do it fast."

In this connection, he indicated that the duty structure might be examined.

He said a new work culture should be created among labour so that they learnt how to produce more efficiently.

He related an anecdote which enlivened the proceedings: "A man had secured a job after a long time in a China shop. The first day he dropped a very expensive jar and the owner of the shop was furious. He told the worker that the cost would be deducted from his salary. The worker did not seem to be bothered. The shopowner then remarked that the price of the jar was very high, in fact running into thousands. On hearing this, the worker seemed to be very happy instead of being downcast. This surprised the owner who asked 'Why are you happy?' The worker replied: 'You see, now I have got a permanent job."

The Prime Minister reminded the executives that the public sector had a major role in augmenting resources. But this should not be achieved through artificial pricing. The prices should stand campari-son with the production costs of similar items elsewhere in the world, taking into account labour and energy costs. The public sector had to be competitive. The country could not afford to subsidise it.

The Prime Minister informed the participants that the report of the Arjun Sen Gupta Committee on the question of giving more responsibility to the heads of public sector enterprises had been received and said he was looking into it. While he wished to give such responsibility to them, he would also hold them much more accountable for their performance.

Although the latest provisional figures of public sector performance were good, with the gross profit around 11 per cent, the net profit was only one to two per cent, "which is not heartening."

He wanted the public sector to make an all-out drive to high productivity.

On training management cadres, he said it was very minimal. In his view, every single person in management must go through a course at least once a year and become up todate on the latest thinking and the latest technology. Only through training could there be improvement in the public sector.

On June 5, 1985, Prime Minister Rajiv Gandhi emphasised the need for "preserving and passing on to the coming generations an environment purer than that which we have inherited."

In a message to the people on the World Environment Day, the Prime Minister said that it was greatly encouraging that "large number of people across the world, particularly the young, have dedicated themselves to restoring the environment. This is an affirmation of faith in life."

Mr. Gandhi spoke of the threat to the earth's environment from a growing population and modern instruments of earth's exploitation "delivered by science into mankind's possession."

"Pollution of air and water, large scale denudation of forests, the extinction of ecosystems, have become the standard bearers of the apocalypse," Mr. Gandhi said.

"We have only one earth. It has generously supported life through millions of years of evolution. Its remarkable powers of regeneration have kept it rich and bountiful even in the face of human green," the Prime Minister recalled in the message.

Mr. Rajiv Gandhi had taken keen interest in the IX Asian Games held in Delhi. Releasing the Official Report of the IX Asian Games the Prime Minister, Mr. Rajiv Gandhi, said on June 26, 1985, in New Delhi:

"I see so many familiar faces, friendly faces, from just three years ago in front of me today but I am feeling extremely moved.

"As has already been said, the real force behind the Asian Games was Indiraji. It was her courage to take a decision in late '80's to hold the Games exactly two years later in 1982. That enables us to have the Asian Games. I am sure, Mr. Cho realises the problems that are faced when Games have to be organised and when that has to be done in two years, you can imagine the efforts that had to be made.

"It would be absolutely incorrect for any one person to take credit for what happened. This was the effort by every single person that was involved—from the labourer to the highest Cabinet Minister. And it was because there was total cooperation that everything worked out so well. May be, if we had been given seven or eight years to prepare everything it would not have worked out so well. But for that we have to thank the indecision of the previous Government.

"During these Games, people from 32 countries got together and what made us proud was the camaraderie that was displayed in the Village. The Games are important, winning and losing is important but there can be no meaning to an international sports event if the youth doesn't get together and make friends with each other and make bonds that not only binds the youth but binds the countries for greater friendship and greater co-operation in our individual endeavours.

"The Asian Games was a window for the world to see what India is capable of doing when we really mean business. Like Indiraji said, 'we showed to world that India can do it'. And this is what we have to do in every task that we undertake today.

"Today, we will release the report on the IX Asian Games and bring an end to this particular part of the Asian Games. Mr. Cho will be holding the X Asian Games and he will take over from us today. I hope that he has all the good luck that we had, all the co-operation that we got from our people, and that the Games in Seoul are even more successful than the Games in Delhi.

"Everybody put in tremendous effort but I most specially thank Sardar Buta Singh as Chairman of the SOC. It is difficult for me to say how much work he put in. He said a lot I did but the fact is he did most of it and as an example I will only like to remind him that, I think, all of you know that Sardar Buta Singhji is a strict vegetarian and during the Asian Games working late at night after almost two years of work he discovered that he had been living on Chicken Patties.

"I once again thank everyone that participated in the Games and everyone's effort that made it possible. I would like to end with just reminding everyone of the slogan of the Asian Games—friendship, fraternity forever."

Addressing the valedictory session of the meeting of Voluntary Organisations on Women Welfare, the Prime Minister, Mr. Rajiv Gandhi, said on July 1, 1985.

"Women may be the largest disadvantaged class in our country today, although much is said about backward classes and scheduled castes and tribals but if we put everything together ultimately it is women who need the most help. At the same time this help must come in a manner that it does not compromise the self-respect, the dignity of women. Government can do a lot of things. We have tried to do a lot of things, we made a lot of laws. **Our Constitution has given equal** rights to women but much of it has not flowed down to women themselves. And the fact is that a social problem cannot be tackled in a Governmental or administrative manner, it has to be tackled at its own level and it must be tackled... well it really can be tackled best by Voluntary Agencies, by highly motivated people working in society. Government can have highly motivated people but we have seen from experience that the number doesn't tend to be very large and this is where your agencies must come in.

"The points that you have made I have noted some. We will look into them and see what can be done but many of them are again not really getting down to the root cause. These are just symptoms that we seem to be tackling. Let the women grow trees but is that the answer. It has to go much deeper than that and it requires much more thought. I don't know I can really put a positive contribution into this but you will have to sit together for some brainstorming session and then really come out with how we have to tackle this problem.

"I was told some other questions that have come up, why are we giving such high priority to women? It doesn't really need an answer but let me give a quotation from Gandhiji. Gandhiji said that 'woman is the companion of man gifted with equal mental capacities. She has the right to participate in the very minute detail in the activities of man. And she has an equal right or freedom and liberty with him. Unfortunately, Gandhiji had also related it to man. This is what we have got to get out of it. The idea is absolutely right but we men, that includes me also, we tend to really put women in a separate category. The fact is we are not. We are all human beings, we are all the same. And everything must be based on that thinking.

"Our Constitution gives some fundamental rights. Discrimination is prohibted. Women's education, again, is a key indicator of economic growth. But really I feel the reason we want to help women to come out and participate more is that in many ways they are the conscience keepers of the nation. I feel India's greater strength is its spirituality, its inner strength and this comes out much more in Indian women than it does in Indian men. And if in this race for progress and for modernisation, we have to maintain our sanity and not get carried away into another stream of civilisation then we must give this strength to our women, so that they are able to come out and see that this is not swept in what we call, or what we tend to call, progress and development today.

"Another question that is being put is how exactly do we view the problem of the status of women in our society ? This is very difficult to answer because it is not just a question of how we view it, it is a question of what we want to achieve, the problems that we see and we face today and finding a method of going from one to the other. The discrimination against the women, the cruelty, all the problems related with dowry, your basic rights, are all related to this. And we have to see that women are able to truly become equal in every sense and they should not need help and assistance and quotas of component plans or other things that we might think of, which we might need today, but we should think in a manner that these are removed and are not necessary at some future date. And anything we do today should be such that it keeps that in mind. I say that specially because many of the programmes that we have for under-privileged groups don't keep this in mind and in their very system they perpetuate that the problem that we set out to solve. We mustn't get into a trap like this when we try to do something for women.

"The special problems of women need to be tackled in that very way. Child birth, child care, special assistance, education, there are so many areas, I don't want to go into all of them, but one of our biggest problems today is population. And I don't want to plug family planning to you because I feel that we have come to a stage where the only thing that is really going to make a dent in family planning is women's education and for this. we must do everything.

"You have raised the question of focussing on general development programmes and several specific suggestions were given—the organic links between education, training, health awareness, female literacy, university education. I was talking to Mrs. Chandrashekhar earlier about women coming out into public life and.... Well at least in U.P. I have found that they are very very independent and are not easy to push down and they are outspoken but she tells me that in the South we have different problems. We must encourage this, not just as a special sort of incentive but because that is how we will be able to carry out our programmes for women much better, if there are more women involved at different levels in our various systems. And we must try and see how this can come about more and in a better way and not only in areas that are related to women's welfare. It is nice to see a woman in women welfare and in health or in something but why not in defence or something else. I think the French have a woman as their Defence Secretary.

"Education problems, well I have mentioned the main things, but one of the key factors will be in keeping girls in schools. There are too many dropouts. They go but they don't have the sustenance to carry on. And we have to see how we can do better in this area. And of course, we will have to look deeper to see why they don't stay in school and get to the root of that. And again it brings us back to our basic social problems, problems of our societies. Resources, vocational training, again it can be very very helpful, for the family, for her own standing in the family and if necessary for her independence if required. Teaching is something that women are good at and we are short of but of course unless they are educated, we will never get enough teachers. And this is an area that I think we must concentrate on specially for primary schools and middle education will be better. I am sure they will attend school more and well they will take an active part in building society.

"You have identified the problem of women gaining access to this system, so to say, to getting the benefits from our various programmes, although the programmes are designed to be totally impartial on sexual basis but the fact is that they don't get projected in that manner, they don't get implemented in that manner. And we have to see that this is adjusted so that women get what they need. We will explore in Government what we can do and we would also like inputs from you on how these programmes can be modified to benefit women. Of course, certain programmes are more amenable for women's participation, things that they can do at home without leaving their families and maybe we need to develop a marketing system which can help women, who don't want to get out of their homes, to be productive, to be self-reliant.

"You have suggested various programmes of preference in distribution of Government assets, in registration of land, social forestry, other supportive services, like I said, this cannot be a full answer. This is only a very short-term help. We will try to improve on this but we need to think much deeper.

"On women's employment, one area we are looking at is the age problem specially for widows and we will try and see what we can do in Government jobs to make it easier and more convenient for women to get involved.

"Component plans have been mentioned and I think it is a very good idea, we will definitely look into it and see what we can do, how we could modify existing programmes and how we could identify special programmes which could be made more effective.

"Dowry is one of our most serious social problems and it is an area where you can come in a big way as voluntary agencies. We can make the laws, we can do many things from Government and we have done them, we have passed some laws, we have put up family courts. If there are certain flaws, which I believe there are, we are willing to change and adjust that and the faster we are given what you feel the deficiencies, the quicker we can correct them. But ultimately it comes down to what the people living in that area actually feel, what they believe, how they react. And there is no law which can cut across that. It is an awareness which you as social workers have to build into our society. We are willing to help you on whatever way we can but this requires lot of leg work and really only voluntary agencies can do this. I don't want to go into the details of dowry and what we have done, etc. I think everybody is aware of that.

"I had mentioned earlier that I feel that women must be more active in politics and at all levels and more especially at the very grass root Panchayat level. In my own constituency I find that they are very active, not only active but they do very good work. This is something that we must try and build up in other areas. Again it is only social awareness which will allow this to happen and you as voluntary agencies must play a big role in this. Gandhiji had said that 'the difference between a hireling lies in the fact that whereas the hireling gives his service to whosoever pays his price a national voluntary worker gives his service to the nation for the cause he believes in'. Today, sometimes,they don't even give their work for the price.

"There are certain problems relating to the information that is available to the average woman. Information on what programmes are available to her, what laws are available to her, what rights she has and this we must try to bridge. We must get across to every woman what she should be fighting, it is only then that she will be able to come out and fight for those things. The procedural difficulties in doing this are not insurmountable and I am sure that together we can overcome them and bring about an awareness which will overcome this hesitation to come about. We have got a very large number of departments dealing with helping women. And again here, I think, we do need some coordination. We are forming a Cabinet Committee for human resources development and this could be a point from which we could start working. We have been working furiously at economic development. Unfortunately, we have not paid enough attention to human development and I feel this is very much an important part but it is very difficult to convince people like the Planning Commission that there is a return from human development and it is not money worth down, they said, but may be they will understand.

"Another area where, I think, we have not been active enough but I think it is time that we really got involved is the drug scene. And this is the time when it is not very big in India and we can try and do something from the Government. We are taking action to see that proper steps are taken but they will be more sort of hard steps—legal systems to stop it, catch it, identify it but what is much more important is to see that the need for drug does not arise amongst the youngsters and that can happen only with the proper environment in the family, with proper advice and instruction, training, again the voluntary agencies really are the key in bringing this about.

"I hope you will look at this and see how you can be more involved in trying to stop the drug business before it really gets down to our system.

"A problem which women really face and which is very serious is old age. And again it is less of a problem as long as our old family system continues but more and more in the urban areas we find that this is not happening and women are finding it a tremendous problem. We have to see what scheme we can devise and how we can help these women in their predicaments.

"Mentally handicapped, well, it is not different from any other mentally handicapped and we should try and see what we can do about it.

"Child labour is another very serious area for us to consider and it is not something that we can just pretend, doesn't exist or legislate away. Again the economic standing, the social standing has to be such that we come out of this as fast as possible. And during that period we should try and see what we can do to make it easiest for the children to see that they get an education, they get proper care, they are not exploited and they are not used in areas which spoils their eyesights, their limbs or make them handicapped in any way.

"But really coming back to the main point is that these are not problems that the Government on its own can tackle. These will only be tackled if Government action is helped by the voluntary agencies and by social change. And this is where you really come in a very big way and I hope that you will accept this as a joint task and we will consult together, work together to see that this problem is alleviated as soon as possible."

The Prime Minister, Mr. Rajiv Gandhi, urged the Directors of the Council of Scientific and Industrial Research laboratories to carry forward the original functions assigned to the CSIR of providing the thrust of scientific knowledge to national development and inculcating a scientific temper in the country.

Addressing a three-day Conference of Directors of CSIR on July 3, 1985, the Prime Minister said that "the vision of Shri Jawaharlal Nehru in giving his full support to the Council of Scientific and Industrial Research had led India to economic and technological self-sufficiency. Shrimati Indira Gandhi had taken scientific research to new heights and her endeavours had put the nation in a strong position especially in agriculture, nuclear science and space. We should take the greatest care to ensure that this spirit did not in any way wane."

Asking "What is research?" Mr. Rajiv Gandhi said that research consisted in going beyond what was already known and bringing about change in any branch of knowledge.

The Prime Minister also emphasised the importance of linking research with users. It was essential that scientists should come up with right ideas and the right processes at the right time. He said that instead of waiting for industry or Government to go to the laboratories, the laboratories should tell industry what they were capable of. He added that research need not be always glamorous or esoteric, but concern itself with the mundane needs of the nation. Electronics, computers, new advances in energy had all to be taken care of, but the main emphasis should be on agriculture. Mr. Rajiv Gandhi said it was not enough to do what was being done elsewhere but do what others were thinking of doing. Anticipating the future was the only way in which we could catch up. "We cannot be chasing other countries all the time", he said. "That might have been adequate when the CSIR was born. But now we should choose some areas and aim at being the foremost in the world".

Our scientists had shown that they were among the best. It was up to the nation to get the best out of them.

In conclusion the Prime Minister told the scientists: "We want to increase your challenges and not reduce them."

The Prime Minister, Mr. Rajiv Gandhi, said on July 4, 1985, that the Government was set on fighting corruption with all the strength it could muster.

He told a joint conference of the Central Bureau of Investigation (CBI) and State Anti-Corruption Officers that they should concentrate on big fish and see that they are punished rather than spend too much time on chasing petty offences.

The Prime Minister said that while not letting any criminal escape, investigating officials must be fair minded and must have a sense of proportion. The basic strategy in fighting corruption was—(a) prevention, (b) actual detection; and (c) seeing that the proper punishment was awarded where due.

Referring to procedural and legal difficulties he said that the Government would see how the legal process could be smoothed without removing the basic rights of citizens.

He further stressed the need for training in service. He wanted a system where at least once a year, everyone got together at all levels so that there was interaction and the difficulties faced in one region, the methods that were worked out to solve problems, could be fed to others. He stressed the need for refresher courses once a year for about a week where these exchanges could take place.

Referring to hindrances in their day-to-day working, the Prime Minister said that the political interference should be reduced to the minimum.

Prime Minister Rajiv Gandhi urged the youth to raise voice for peace, solidarity and humanity in the world on July 6, 1985.

Inaugurating the National Festival of Youth and Students jointly organised by the World Federation of Democratic Youth and the International Union of Students at the Talkatora Indoor Stadium in New Delhi, Mr. Gandhi said the time had come for the youth to speak out collectively against nuclear arms race which had brought the world to the brink of destruction.

The two-day all-party festival is a prelude to the XII World Festival of Youth and Students to be held in Moscow where India will be represented by 500 delegates.

Mr. Gandhi said it was a matter of great concern that when people were dying of hunger in Africa, at other places nations were involved in an arms race so that a situation was arising when things were slipping out of the hands of man to a computer.

He said India had shown time and again that it could do what others could not. The nation had come a long way from 20 years ago when foodgrains were imported from the United States. Today India was supplying wheat to Africa. "The youth have shown that at times of struggle, as about seven months ago, it never backs out", he said.

The Prime Minister said the country was preparing to march into the 21st century on the ideals of truth and non-violence as shown to us by our great leaders. "The way is long and difficult but we will prevail. A new feeling of awareness will be created in our struggle against poverty, population explosion and for emancipation of women", he said. He later formally opened the festival by lighting a lamp.

Prime Minister Rajiv Gandhi addressing at least one-third of the three lakh population of the Union Territory of Pondicherry called the "window of the French culture" by his grandfather Pandit Jawaharlal Nehru, hinted at new programmes shortly for the youth of this country to channelise their energy productively...

The Prime Minister also said that his Government would soon formulate a new education policy for implementation from the next year.

The Uppalam Ground, where Mr. Rajiv Gandhi addressed a cross-section of the people from different parts of India residing in this former French settlement in the spiritual seat of the late Aurobindo

Ghose, was filled to capacity by the time he arrived from Madras in a helicopter

The Prime Minister, who spoke for about 40 minutes, pointed out that the Government's concentration of efforts would not only be on the economic development but also on the nurturing of spiritual and human values.

Referring to the rapid strides the country has made in the past five years during Mrs. Indira Gandhi's leadership Mr. Gandhi felt that this quantum of growth was better than what the UK and USA had achieved during these years.

In the field of agriculture, the Prime Minister said not only steps were being taken to improve production but an agricultural cost commission was also being set up. Similarly Mr. Gandhi said steps would be taken to end discrimination against women and other backward classes.

Emphasising the need for morality in politics, Mr. Gandhi referred to the Anti-Defection Bill and said that stringent steps would be taken to end the shortcomings in administration.

Mr. Gandhi said a perspective programme would be launched for the uplift of the farmers by providing better and more remunerative prices for their produce. He said a big scheme was in the offing in this connection. He said earnest efforts would be made to provide jobs to all.

He said laws aimed at ending the harassment of women would be strengthened and the rights of Harijans and the minorities safeguarded.

Prime Minister Rajiv Gandhi strongly favoured "good people" joining politics, as it was the "most important thing" in the country he told a group of teenage students in the course of a 45-minute televised interview.

"Good people should come forward to join politics, since ultimately function of everything comes back to it," he said. He did not agree with the students who asked him why politicians had "a bad image."

Asked whether he would "influence" his children, Rahul and Priyanka, to join politics, the Prime Minister said he would not like to "influence" them. So far, they had not shown any leaning towards politics.

The interview was unique in that the interviewers were all students ranging from Class V to Class X. The questions were put to the Prime Minister with utter ease and confidence. They were quite unusual and on more than one occasion, Mr. Gandhi described a question as "difficult."

At the same time, the students did not leave out topics of current affairs, putting questions of the like the Prime Minister would be used to answering. Here it was Mr. Gandhi who tried to put across his answer in simple language.

Replying to a question, Mr. Gandhi said dedication, commitment to the nation, non-partisan attitude towards religion and caste and ability to carry the people together were the qualities of a good leader.

For an interview conducted by students, the questions were well prepared and framed and the children did not appear to be overawed by the presence of a Prime Minister.

There were curious queries like how often the Prime Minister played with his children, games like Ludo and Scrabbket "like other good daddies". The children wanted to know how many hours Mr. Gandhi spent doing his work and how did he divide the available time for various activities.

Mr. Gandhi told them that he spent close to 18 hours a day working. He had the "inputs" in the form of discussions with Ministers, officials and others. A child was quick to ask him about the "output"—how the decision-making was done in the Government.

The Prime Minister explained at length how he discussed with the Ministers or the officials concerned before taking a decision. His wife and children did not help him to take any decision.

He also explained at length the working of the various Cabinet committees on political affairs and economic affairs and how all major decisions were taken by the Cabinet.

He told a teenager why he was opposed to the Star Wars programme of President Reagan. It would open an entirely new vista in warfare and make the space a dangerous place.

He spoke at length on how modern technology did not mean only electronics and computers but also knowhow that would help the country's development at all levels. The crucial question was of applying the modern technology for the greatest good of the society.

To a question what was common between piloting a plane and leading a nation, Mr. Gandhi said both required discipline, without which everything could go wrong.

Asked what he learnt from his parents, the Prime Minister made a telling remark that it was basically the character acquired from parents on which all future training and knowledge were built. Lack of character could leave even the most educated and the advanced with a void.

He admitted to be a "very shy boy" as a student, never having participated in debating. He also admitted that he missed his flying "sometimes", but said that once in politics, there was no going back, losing interest or running away from responsibility.

Prime Minister Rajiv Gandhi said that he would "certainly take the country into confidence before taking a decision on the nuclear weapons programme on July 15, 1985.

Addressing a Press conference after attending the Congress(I) centenary celebrations, the Prime Minister said India had to be concerned about Pakistan's attempts to develop capability for a nuclear bomb as the country had attacked us several times. As such there was no parallel between the Indo-Pak situation and that of China. Though China too attacked India once, there was not much of a tension since then between that and our country.

Referring to Sri Lanka's Tamils' issue, Mr. Gandhi said "what we are doing is to bring the Tamil groups and the Sri Lankan Government together" for evolving a solution to their problems.

Mr. Gandhi said that he was optimistic about the peace talks at Thimpu between the Sri Lankan Tamils and the island Government.

Answering a question, Mr. Gandhi said there was no shift in the Indian Government's stand on the Tamil issue. While the Government wanted the ethnic groups in the island to live in peace, it was for the Tamils and the Government there to iron out the differences.

Mr.Gandhi said the Indian Government did not want to interfere in the talks between the Tamils and the Sri Lanka Government.

Referring to the price rise, the Prime Minister said the actual increase in prices was less this year than the previous year. Though the price was sharper during certain periods, the net increase in prices was merely 3.1 per cent during the last three months.

On the question of river water disputes, Mr. Gandhi felt that rivers should be treated as national assets. He said the Government had not yet decided on the Ganga-Cauveri project. On the Telugu Ganga controversy, Mr. Gandhi said that he would talk to the Chief Ministers of Karnataka and Andhra Pradesh and others. He said that the decision about the Telugu Ganga was taken by all the four Chief

Ministers and as such he did not see why there should be a problem on that issue now.

The Prime Minister, Mr. Rajiv Gandhi, released a book, "Indira Reader" on July 19, 1985. Speaking on the occasion he said:

"One of our biggest shortcomings since Independence has been a lack of material on the Independence Struggle, on the people who participated in it, a lack of material for our younger generation on construction and building up of our nation after independence. And when we remember that the young are a very high proportion of our country, then this inadequacy becomes very large. It is appropriate that you have produced this book which will present Indiraji as she was, to the new generation in India. It will present them the struggle of a leader. More than that, it is also the story of India in the past 16 or 17 years, giving an insight into the difficult times through which Indiraji piloted India. Her Prime Ministership was during one of the most turbulent periods in the world and in post-freedom India. She faced every challenge courageously and undauntedly. There was no compromise on basic issues of principles. If she felt something was right and correct, she stood up and she fought for it. It is a quality which we must all build in India today.

"Strength of character is what we are lacking in India. People are not outspoken enough, questioning enough. Part of this comes from the educational system. When you go to school, small children in India do not ask questions, they accept what is handed out to them. This is the beginning of a subservient attitude. And this is what we must get rid of right from the primary school stage. This was developed to a very high degree in Indiraji. She was able to project what India stood for in the world. India today is in a strong position economically and politically in the world. The development work that we have done is very substantial. The latest figures on the anti-poverty measures are just out and they indicate that in the four years from 1980 to 1984 the poverty level has dropped from 51 per cent in 1980 to 37 per cent in 1984—a very substantial drop of 14 per cent in four years. So this is the type of struggle that Indiraji waged. And this happened during a phase when the world economy was in tremendous turmoil. When every major country was going through difficulties, India was able to forge ahead, because she had the courage of conviction to carry out what she stood for and what the Congress had stood for a hundred years. It is this that we must develop in every individual in India. I think it is epitomised in her favourite song—Rabindranath's 'Ekla Chalo Re'—'Walk alone even if nobody is willing to walk with you, if you feel that your path is the path of truth.'

At another gathering, where he released a commemorative volume "Shukul Ank" brought out in connection with the birth centenary of Acharya Ram Chandra Shukul, the Prime Minister said his Government was against the imposition of Hindi on non-Hindi speaking people in the country.

Mr. Gandhi said Acharya Shukul was for propagation and enrichment of Hindi although Hindi was understood and spoken by far more people than English in the country. It should not be forced upon the non-Hindi speaking people. Hindi could be further developed and propagated by the Hindi scholars, writers and poets.

Assuring full co-operation for the propagation of Hindi, Mr. Gandhi said other languages had also rich traditions and sentiments of their own. These must be remembered while furthering the cause of Hindi, he said.

vi

REAFFIRMATION OF IME-TESTED FRIENDSHIP

In his first ever State visit abroad, the Prime Minister, Mr. Rajiv Gandhi, visited the USSR from May 21-26, 1985. This visit was in continuation of tradition of exchange of visits at the highest level which have characterised Indo-Soviet relations for the last three decades. During this visit, apart from Moscow, the Prime Minister visited Minsk and Frunze.

On his arrival in Moscow, Mr. Gandhi was given an impressive ceremonial welcome and a large crowd, in spite of rain, came out in the streets to greet him. The CPSU General Secretary, Mr. Mikhail S. Gorbachov, and Mrs. Raisa Gorbachov, were at the steps of the Kremlin's St. Catherine Hall to receive Mr. Rajiv Gandhi and his wife.

Mr. N.C. Menon has presented in nutshell the idea of Mr. Rajiv Gandhi's visit to Moscow. He says: "Prime Minister Rajiv Gandhi made a powerful plea for peace on earth, amity among nations and goodwill among men. Indira Gandhi's assassination, he pointed out, is clear evidence that humanity's major enemy is violence fed by hatred."

Making a strong plea for disarmament, Mr. Gandhi pointed out that in the nuclear age, peace was the basic yearning of all peoples of the world. "The danger comes from the very weapons that have been developed in the name of security", he pointed out. The stockpiles are growing—and the onus of disarmament is that of the nuclear-weapon powers."

Other nations, however, could not remain unconcerned because there could be no greater leveller and decimator than a nuclear war. Mr. Gandhi welcomed the resumption of the USSR-USA negotiations on disarmament in Geneva and the declaration by both nations of their resolve to work for complete elimination of nuclear weapons.

The West, and particularly the USA, which had been complaining that India had not taken a firm stand on Afghanistan had something to cheer about when the Prime Minister categorically stated that "we are opposed to any outside intervention and interference anywhere." At the same time, Mr. Gandhi also deplored efforts to frustrate the functioning of Governments in Latin America, thereby proving that as Indira Gandhi had once said, India leans neither left nor right, but is "upright". The Prime Minister warned that world peace and regional tranquillity were closely intertwined. Regional conflicts could turn global with surprising speed.

Earlier, during a two-hour-45-minute discussion the Indian and Soviet delegations reaffirmed their desire to raise bilateral economic and trade relations to new levels of expansion and co-operation.

During more than an hour of talks on disarmament, Mr. Gandhi welcomed the initiative taken by Mr. Gorbachov. The Soviet leader, in turn, appreciated the initiatives taken by India by the six-nation conference and by the non-aligned summit. We hoped such strong support would create a world opinion which would put pressure on the USA and others.

The Indian Ocean, China, Pakistan and the problems of Asia were the other subjects discussed.

Mr. Gandhi explained India's fears and concerns, particularly about militarisation of the Indian Ocean and of its neighbourhood. Mr. Gorbachov welcomed the declaration of the Indian Ocean as a zone of peace. He suggested that India work much harder to influence international opinion to hold a conference on the Indian Ocean, as had been agreed by the UN, without delay.

Each side briefed the other on the negotiations that had been going on with China. Mr. Gandhi explained that though India had been talking to China, the problem of territory remained a major one. Mr. Gorbachov pointed out that China had made territorial claims on the Soviet Union too. Both sides agreed, however, that it was important to improve relations with China.

Mr. Gandhi pointed to India's worry over the induction of sophisticated arms into Pakistan as well as that country's nuclear programme, which seemed to have support from some quarters. In this connection, it was taken note of that Pakistan had been trying to use the Afghanistan issue to get more arms. The Soviet side fully appreciated India's fears and apprehensions in the matter.

Prime Minister Rajiv Gandhi in his reply to the banquet speech of General Secretary Gorbachov of the USSR, said that "Peace is the shining star which guides our two peoples who have given so much to civilization. Both our countries want mankind to be assured of a brighter tomorrow. We do not wish the spirit of any people anywhere to be gnawed by fear and anxiety. Every ideal demands faith, labour and sacrifice. The world knows the enormous sacrifices the Soviet people made in building up their new State, and later, in defending their independence from Fascist invaders. You have just celebrated the 40th anniversary of the victory over fascism. In two years more, you will observe the 70th anniversary of the October Revolution. In India, we are this year celebrating the 100th anniversary of the Indian National Congress which led the struggle for our freedom. In your epic battles, your nation produced countless heroes and heroines. So did we in India when we fought against imperialism through our weapon of non-violent civil resistance. Out people have borne immeasurable hardships in building a new India and in consolidating our unity.

"I am moved by the references you have made to Shrimati Indira Gandhi. She lived and toiled for the people of India. But she reached out to the people of other lands as well. Her aim was to mould an India which would realise its potential and play a role in the making of a better world. Millions adored her, but a few were unreconciled. Her death is a reminder that humanity's major enemy is violence fed by hatred. It also underlines the threats that the new order faces from old prejudices and ways of thought.

"The Soviet people's commitment to peace springs from their ideals as well as from the fact that no people have suffered more from war. We in India are also deeply committed to peace because all our hopes for a better life hinge on it. Under the inspiration of Mahatma Gandhi, Jawaharlal Nehru and Indira Gandhi, we have been engaged in the endeavour of lifting the burdens which centuries of feudalism and imperialist rule had placed on the backs of our people. We are committed to socialism and an equitable social order. Since independence, the Indian economy has impressive achievements to its credit. We have become self-sufficient in grain production and laid the foundation of a modern industrial society. We are proud of the work of our scientists and technologists in many frontier areas and sophisticated fields of application. We are on the threshold of much faster all-round development.

"The path of national development charted for us by Shri Jawaharlal Nehru and Shrimati Indira Gandhi is best suited for our social conditions. Its correctness has been proved by the test of results We shall continue along the path of building self-reliant strength assigning a key role in development to the public sector and keeping the people's needs above all. We have taken up massive programmes of enlarging and strengthening agriculture, power, transport and communication, creating new employment for our rural masses, and providing fuller outlets for the productive capacities of our people. In the vital field of human and social development, we are paying increasing attention to education and health care.

"The overwhelming part of the endeavour has been our own people's. But friends have certainly helped. We deeply appreciate the substantial and principled support which the Soviet Union has given to our economic development. We look forward to a rapid enlargement of this co-operation. We are interested in stable and long-term expansion of trade and economic relations which takes cognisance of the needs, constraints and potentialities of our two national economies. New areas and mechanisms of co-operation must be evolved. The scope for economic, scientific and cultural co-operation is immense. The Soviet and Indian cosmonauts who went into space have been heralds of a new era in our peoples working together.

"Friendship and co-operation with the Soviet Union are an integral element of our foreign policy. Our people regard the Soviet people as friends who have stood by them in times of need. The splendid record of Indo-Soviet relations owes much to the vision and exertions of the leaders of both our countries over the last three decades. I am here to continue the tradition set for us by Shri

Jawaharlal Nehru and practised by successive Governments of India of sharing assessments and perceptions so that our two countries can work together for a better world. The Treaty of Peace, Friendship and Cooperation of 1971 reflects our high regard for each other and has served the cause of peace. I had the privilege of meeting you, Excellency, when you assumed your present high office at a crucial phase of world history. I vividly recall the feeling reference you made to India and to the importance you personally attach to Indo-Soviet relations. We had a fruitful exchange of views this afternoon. I look forward to continuing the conversation tomorrow. We hope that you will soon give us the opportunity to welcome you in India.

"In this nuclear age, peace is the basic yearning of all peoples of the world. Yet at no time in history has the danger to peace been greater. This danger comes from the very weapons that have been developed in the name of security. The stockpiles are growing. It is a good sign that there is repeated public expression of a desire to reduce and eliminate nuclear weapons. The onus of disarmament is that of the nuclear-weapon powers. But can any other nation remain unconcerned? There can be no greater leveller and decimator than a nuclear war. Nuclear death will not inspect people's passports. It will not care for nationality as it will not care for life. There are no winnable nuclear wars, nor any impregnable defences against nuclear weapons.

"India and the rest of the non-aligned community have been assiduous in urging all States to ban the use or threat of use of nuclear weapons, suspend all weapons tests, seek a comprehensive weapon test ban treaty, freeze production of nuclear weapons and fissionable material for weapons purpose, and prevent the testing, production and deployment of chemical, biological and space weapons. We issued this call at the Non-Aligned Summit which met under Shrimati Indira Gandhi's Chairmanship in Delhi in 1983. More recently the Heads of State and Government of six nations from five continents reiterated this appeal through the Delhi Declaration.

"We are glad that the Soviet Union has responded promptly and positively to the appeal. We have welcomed the various initiatives that you have personally taken. We sincerely wish success to your efforts. We welcome the resumption of the USSR-USA negotiations on disarmament in Geneva and the Declaration by both nations of their resolve to work for the complete elimination of nuclear weapons. World peace and regional tranquillity are closely intertwined. Regional conflicts can turn global with surprising speed.

We in India are greatly concerned at the increasing militarisation across our border and the entire Indian Ocean. We are opposed to any outside intervention and interference anywhere.

"We have initiated discussions with out neighbours to improve the total environment of regional peace and co-operation. We desire South Asian Regional Co-operation to make a contribution to better, mutually beneficial relations among the countries of our region. There are tensions in other regions about which we must all be greatly concerned: the continued denial of the legitimate rights of Palestinians, the blatant practice of aparthied and aggression in South Africa against African peoples, the denial of the rights of the Namibians, the efforts to frustrate the functioning of Governments in Latin America and the continuing armed conflicts in South-West and South-East Asia.

"None of us, while safeguarding the interests of our nations, can overlook our duty to the human race. The prism of geography may colour our peoples differently, but in the white light, we are one humanity. It is to the service of that humanity that Indo-Soviet friendship is dedicated."

In Moscow the Prime Minister had two long sessions of talks with the General Secretary of the Communist Party of the Soviet Union. The two leaders expressed deep satisfaction at the successful development of relations of close friendship and multifaceted co-operation between the two countries. They discussed further bi-lateral co-operation in the economic, trade, scientific and technological spheres. They also exchanged views on a number of international, political and economic issues. In their banquet speeches, both the leaders reaffirmed that relations between the two countries were based on equality and mutual respect. Saying that the record of Indo-Soviet relations owed much to the visions of the leaders of both countries, Mr. Gandhi added that he would continue the traditions set by India's first Prime Minister Jawaharlal Nehru.

On May 22, after laying wreaths at the Mausoleum of Lenin and the Tomb of the Unknown Soldier, the P.M. held exclusive talks with the Soviet leader. The latter broke all protocol and arrived at the PM's Kremlin residence 10 minutes before their scheduled meeting, and suggested they walk together to his office. As they strolled along the Kremlim lawns, Mr. Gorbachov plucked some tulips and lilacs and presented them to the P.M. The General Secretary of the Communist Party of the Soviet Union told Mr. Gandhi, "this is not in the protocol books but you and I can take care of the protocol boys."

After the exclusive talks the Prime Minister, Mr. Rajiv Gandhi, and the General Secretary of the Soviet Communist Party, Mr. Mikhail Gorbachov, also signed two long-term agreements. Under the first the Soviet Union agreed to give India credit worth one billion roubles to bolster bilateral economic co-operation. The agreement provides for greater Soviet co-operation in key sectors of the Indian economy like steel, power, drilling for oil and mining.

The second agreement pertained to economic, trade and scientific and technical co-operation between India and the USSR for the period up to 2000 A.D. The main sectors covered by the agreement will be power, petroleum, the coal industry, ferrous and non-ferrous metallurgy, mechine building and co-operation in science and technology.

In the afternoon the P.M. inaugurated the "Indira Gandhi Square" at the naming ceremony. The Square is situated near the picturesque botanical gardens of Moscow University. He also laid flowers at the "Jawaharlal Nehru Square."

At the civic reception in the Hall of Columns that evening, Mr. Gandhi received the Lenin Peace Prize on behalf of his mother, the late Smt. Indira Gandhi on May 22, 1985. Speaking on the occasion Mr. Gandhi said:

"My great grandfather Motilal Nehru, and my grandfather Jawaharlal Nehru, both of whom were in the front rank of India's struggle for freedom, visited the Soviet Union in 1927 on the tenth anniversary of the Great October Revolution. Both were keenly interested in studying at first hand the new social system that was being built in the Soviet Union. Jawaharlal Nehru said at that time:

"To understand the great drama of the Russian revolution and the inner changes that shaped and brought the great change about, a study of cold theory is of little use. The October Revolution was undoubtedly one of the great events of world history... and its story is more absorbing from the human and the dramatic point of view, than any tale of fantasy.'

"India's fight for independence received outspoken support from the Soviet people. We in turn were concerned at the conflicts that were developing in Europe in the twenties and thirties, especially the ominous rise of Fascism. Jawaharlal Nehru kept warning the world of the danger to come. He was distressed at the attitude of some European Governments towards Hitler. We in India, although not free, were ranged unequivocally against Fascism. We admired the heroic resistance of the Soviet People. You demonstrated that no price is too high to pay for principles, for honour, for the independence and integrity of one's motherland. This year you celebrate the 40th anniversary of that victory over Fascism. We join in your rejoicing. We salute your brave.

"India's freedom struggle was a saga of the resistance of an unarmed people against the world's biggest empire. On gaining freedom we adopted a multi-party parliamentary system. The Indian nation is built on the principles of democracy, secularism and socialism. We have adopted the method of planned development and we have concentrated all our energies on overcoming mass poverty which was the legacy of two centuries of colonialism.

"We have scored notable success. In grain production we have become self-sufficient and are able to export cereals to others. A country which had virtually no industry has now become a major industrial nation. The work of our research laboratories in finding solutions to several deep-seated problems commands the respect of the international scientific community.

In this vast undertaking of modernisation we have received invaluable understanding and co-operation from the Soviet Union. Your contribution has been particularly crucial to us in building up our mineral, metallurgical and machine-building industries. We warmly appreciate this help.

"We have, during my visit, discussed plans for production, co-operation and diversification of trade as well as industrial and technological co-operation in a perspective of fifteen years. The scope is immense. As India's industry, science and technology grow, we shall need to have greater exchange with the Soviet Union and other great industrial countries. Our joint efforts will benefit both economies.

"Soviet support has not been confined to the economic field. You have stood by us in our difficulties. It is adversity that tests friendships. The Indian people regard the Soviet people as reliable friends.

"Indo-Soviet friendship demonstrates how two peoples with different social systems can establish a firm relationship of understanding and work for a larger common cause. The largest common cause is peace. Our friendship is not against any other nation, but actuated solely by the desire to strengthen our own peoples and to further the cause of global peace and international cooperation. We both long for peace because of our memories of the past and our dreams for the future. Only the tree of peace can yield life sustaining fruit to humanity.

"We in India have believed that we serve peace best by staying out of military alliances. The Soviet Union has recognised that this policy of non-alignment has contributed solidly to strengthening the world-wide environment in favour of peace. Late Prime Minister Indira Gandhi, when she presided over the Seventh Conference of Non-aligned Nations in New Delhi two years ago, reiterated the Movement's total commitment to peace. That Conference also appealed to the nuclear powers to take positive steps for disarmament so that in the foreseeable future the world would be rid of all weapons which had the power to destroy life on earth. At a time when peace is perched precariously on nuclear stockpiles, I reaffirm the Non-Aligned Movement's and India's resolve to work for peace and disarmament. The land of Gautam Buddha and Mahatma Gandhi will always be on the side of peace. We welcome the initiative taken by the Soviet Union to resume negotiations on disarmament.

"You have honoured Indira Gandhi with the Lenin Peace Prize. It is a gesture which the people of India deeply appreciate. Vladimir Ilyich Lenin, after whom the Prize is named, is one of the mankind's immortals whose name will forever be linked with struggle against oppression and exploitation. As time passes, he grows greater, as Jawaharlal Nehru pointed out. While commemorating Lenin, the Prize also honours peace and those who work for peace. I am touched by your eloquent tributes to Indira Gandhi's life and work. This Award is an appreciation not only of her personality, but also of causes dear to her India, namely peace, international co-operation and Indo-Soviet friendship.

"Indira Gandhi belonged to a line of eminent leaders who embodied the best in our heritage in all its depth and diversity. She was profoundly aware of the strength and continuity of India's culture. Yet she regarded all humankind as her kin. A humanity at peace with itself was Indira Gandhi's dream. She was in forefront of the struggle to establish a just and equitable international order. It gives me great pleasure to accept the Lenin Peace Prize given to my mother.

From Moscow, the Prime Minister paid a two-day visit to Minsk, capital of the Byelorussian Soviet Socialist Republic on May 23-24.

Apart from holding talks with senior leaders of the Republic, the Prime Minister acquainted himself with the history and the present achievements in science and industry of the Republic. He also visited World Wan II memorials in the Republic.

The visit to Frunze, the capital of the Kirghiz Soviet Socialist Republic, formed the final leg of Mr. Gandhi's tour to the USSR. In Frunze he was acquainted with the achievements of the Republic by senior political and government leaders of the Republic. The P.M. also had a boat ride on the Issyk-Ku lake near Frunze which is well-known Soviet health resort and witnessed a horse show. He returned to New Delhi on May 26, 1985.

Mr. Rajiv Gandhi's visit was widely covered in both the Soviet and Indian Press. A joint communique was issued at the conclusion of the visit.

The Prime Minister, Mr. Rajiv Gandhi, addressed the Soviet people on TV on May 22, 1985.

"Your and our cinematographers have jointly produced a film on Shri Jawaharlal Nehru. It brought out how Shri Jawaharlal Nehru hailed the Great October Revolution as one of the most significant events in the history of man. Even before he became the first Prime Minister of free India he was keen that the peoples of India and the Soviet Union must know each other well and work together. He was the architect, from our side, of Indo-Soviet friendship. He believed as you might know, in the doctrine of Non-Alignment and of keeping out of military pacts. Soviet statesmen have consistently befriended India and have respected our non-alignment.

"Indo-Soviet co-operation has grown steadily in the last 30 years. You have helped in setting up many of our large industries in our effort to build a modern economy. Plants built by your engineers dot our landscape, and places like Bhilai and Bokaro have become household names, symbolising the relationship between our two countries. Thousands of our technicians have been trained in your country, and they now run the projects which were originally set up in collaboration with you. More joint ventures are being planned. Last year there was a dramatic, heart-warming demonstration of scientific co-operation between our peoples. A young Indian aviator went aboard the Soviet space vessel Soyuz T-11 with your cosmonauts. Millions of our people sat up night and day to watch their progress in space. This voyage evoked great admiration among our people for Soviet technology and achievement.

"The story of India dates back thousands of years. We were one of the early cradles of civilisation. In our long history there have been several Golden Ages. One of the earliest was the age of the Buddha, in the sixth century B.C. The Buddha taught us the message of kindliness, of avoidance of hatred and violence. Four centuries ago, the fabled wealth of India brought European traders to our shores. The traders in due course became rulers. By the time we ultimately reasserted our freedom under Mahatma Gandhi's leadership, colonialist exploitation had reduced India to one of the world's poorest nations. The Industrial Revolution had passed us by.

"Our endeavour has been to haul our country over the hump of technological backwardness and shake off mass poverty. We have won half the battle. We have built the inner technological strength with which we can complete the remaining task. Our agricultural production has almost trebled. We have established a variety of basic and heavy industries. We have built centres of research and advanced training. A great deal of the old blight of poverty still remains. But we have the technological capability, the hope, the will to build a new bright age. This is the legacy to us of Smt. Indira Gandhi, who built on the foundations laid by Shri Jawaharlal Nehru.

"Nearly three-fourths of India's people are below 35 years of age. They have no memory of colonial rule. So they will not appreciate the burdens their elders had to bear. They are impatient of getting into the 21st century. It is my task, and that of others whom the nation has elected, to take them there. In doing so our endeavour will be to preserve all that is worthwhile in our great heritage while availing ourselves of the new knowledge.

"This dream, this yearning, will be fulfilled only if there is peace— "peace on the earth, peace in the waters, and peace in the skies," to use the perspective works of one of our ancient verses. So it is natural that we should befriend other peoples who are equally devoted to peace. This is one of the great common bonds between the Soviet Union and India.

"We know how greatly your nation has suffered in the wars following the Revolution. We know the sacrifice that every family of your great country has made. Out of the anguish and blood has sprung the rose of your love of peace, even as out of our colonial suffering has grown the lotus of our hope and determination. So let us tend this rose and this lotus.

"Humanity as a whole benefits from Indo-Soviet friendship. We work together for peace. Our friendship is not against anyone. Our relations show how nations with differing social systems coexist, develop trust and work for the mutual good of our people as well as humankind. We the Soviet and Indian peoples will continue to march together towards a golden tomorrow."

In a Press conference in Moscow on May 22, 1985, the Prime Minister, Mr. Rajiv Gandhi, said:

"India and the Soviet Union share close and friendly ties. Our friendship has developed and matured over more than 30 years. The Soviet Union has stood by us through thick and thin. Our relations cover a wide range, commerce, science, technology, culture and so on. More than 70 industrial projects based on Soviet collaborations are working successfully in India. We both have a keen desire to enlarge them and place them in a longer time frame.

"Only a few hours ago the General Secretary and I have signed two major agreements on economic co-operation. Both agreements are significant and will provide the guidelines for the expansion of our multi-faceted economic co-operation on a dynamic and planned basis and with new form and content.

"The first agreement relates to Indo-Soviet co-operation in the construction of a number of major projects in India. It provides for credit by the Soviet Union of one billion roubles for financing the cost of Soviet goods and services in respect of projects in power, oil, coal and machine building sectors.

"As an illustration, in the power sector the credit will cover the Kahalgaon thermal power plant to be located in Bihar with a total capacity of 840 megawatts. In the coal sector the credit covers development of open cast mines and underground collieries in U.P. and Bihar and designing of a coal beneficiation plant. In the oil sector it covers intensive and integrated exploration of hydrocarbons in two areas in two on-shore basins tobe mutually agreed upon. The agreement also provides for the possibility of Soviet participation in some of our plans for modernising machine-building plants which had been set up with Soviet co-operation.

"The second agreement relates to basic directions of economic, trade, scientific and technical co-operation between India and USSR for the period up to the year 2000. It takes into account the evolving pattern of development of technology and capabilities in our two countries.

"The main sectors concerned by this agreement are power, coal, oil and gas industry, science and technology, ferrous and non-ferrous metallurgy, machine-building, production co-operation, medicine and public health. It also covers the participation of Indian organizations in civil and industrial projects in the Soviet Union in areas that may be mutually agreed on as well as joint participation in construction of industrial and other projects in third countries. Special attention has been devoted to long-term trade. Both countries have agreed to maintain the tempo of growth of trade and provide for diversifications.

"Indo-Soviet co-operation should be seen in longer context of our solid commitment to peace. We are both opposed to the escalation of nuclear arms race. We desire to eliminate the growing menace of nuclear war.

The Soviet Union and India have found common ground on many current international issues such as the situation in the Middle East, Namibia and South Africa, on steps to be taken for implementing the UN Resolution declaring the Indian Ocean as a Zone of Peace, the important role which the United Nations has to play in preserving world peace.

Mr Gandhi invited questions from the Press:

QUESTION (B.B.C.): Are there any commitments that the Soviet Union asked you to make which you felt you could not? am thinking particularly of a certain amount of speculation here that they may feel that you may be coming closer to the West than perhaps previous Indian Governments?

PRIME MINISTER: There were no such commitments.

QUESTION (KUWAIT NEWS AGENCY): We are well aware of the sincere efforts exerted by India as a State and as Chairman of the Non-Aligned Movement to solving the Iran-Iraq war. We all also know that the Soviet Union is deeply concerned with this conflict. Was there any discussion on the ways to end this conflict during your talks with the Soviet leaders?

PRIME MINISTER: It has been a part of our discussions, yes. As you know many people have been trying to end this terrible war, but there are certain positions that the two countries have taken and it might still take some time.

QUESTION (EXCELSIOR OF MEXICO): What do you think of the embargo declared against Nicaragua by President Reagan? Did you discuss this with Gorbachov as also the situation in Central America?

PRIME MINISTER: We did not talk in very much detail about

this, but it did come up in the talks. Our position on the embargo is very clear. We think there should not be an embargo and we are against it.

QUESTION (DAN AGENCY, ARGENTINA): (a) How does your Government see the recent opening by U.K. on Malvinas, sovereignty of which belongs to Argentina, of a naval-cum-air base placed at the service of NATO, in order to facilitate receiving large aeroplanes to conventional and nuclear weapons at the same time as the USA has declared its intention to use the Easter Islands as a landing base for its space ships?

(b) Do you consider this will prevent turning South America into a genuine Nuclear Free Zone and will South America be drawn into U.S. plans for Star Wars?

PRIME MINISTER: We are against this proliferation in the arms race wherever it is, and we are not for the major powers moving into any of the Oceans.

QUESTION (TASS, B. CHEKHONIN): As Chairman of NAM and as one of the sponsors of the Six-Nation Summit on Disarmament, what in your opinion can be done in the immediate future by the non-aligned countries in order to attain, as a first step, an agreement on a freeze at the present level of nuclear weapons? What in your opinion can the developing countries do for averting a world-wide nuclear catastrophe?

PRIME MINISTER: Regarding the freeze, this really has to be done by nuclear weapon countries. There is very little that the non-weapon countries can do to freeze this apart from building up public opinion. The nuclear weapon countries must realise the responsibility that lies on them today and must take more initiatives in this direction. The developing countries can help build an atmosphere, help build public opinion against armaments, against spreading of the arms race into new dimensions and bring home to everyone that a nuclear war today will not be limited just to those countries with nuclear weapons but will damage, even destroy everyone, on this earth.

QUESTION (BALTIMORE SUN): You have a major gas pipeline project under way in India. In your conversations with the Soviet General Secretary did you arrive at any kind of agreement that might allow Soviet participation in the construction of this pipeline?

PRIME MINISTER: It was not one of the items that we discussed at our level.

QUESTION (SWEDISH RADIO): Just before leaving your country you concluded a deal on receiving high technology from the USA. How do you look upon the fact that you seem to get what Mr. Gorbachov is being denied—high technology from the USA? Could that be a problem?

PRIME MINISTER: A problem for whom? For us? No, it is not a problem for us.

QUESTION (N.H.K. TV and RADIO, JAPAN): Did you talk with Mr. Gorbachov about your forthcoming visit to the USA and if you did, did you get any message from Mr. Gorbachov to tell President Reagan?

PRIME MINISTER: We did discuss my visit to the USA. No, I have not got a message for President Reagan.

QUESTION (FOREIGN TRADE NEWS, FRG): By what means do you want to promote Indian exports to the Soviet Union? I read that in the past two years trade balance was pleasant for India in relation with the Soviet Union.

PRIME MINISTER: Our trade has increased over the years, but it has not increased as much as we would have liked it to have increased and as much as it could increase. There are many areas where we can co-operate and the agreements we are signing now will look after some of these. I am sure there are many more areas of technical development where we can co-operate even more, and we will be looking into these areas in the near future.

QUESTION (MOSCOW NEWS): India is one of the countries from where man has gone into space. Right now man is facing the dilemma whether space should be militarised or be peaceful. What can you say in this regard? What is your reaction to the Soviet proposal that outer space should not be an arena for star wars?

PRIME MINISTER: Our stand on this is very very clear. We are against any new dimensions being brought into the arms race, and that includes outer space. We feel that every time a new technology has been brought into the arms race, it has only increased the arms race and not reduced it. There has never been a stage where something new has been brought in that has not been countered by something of equal destruction or of equal technological levels, and this will be the same for space weapons. We feel that S.D.I. is only increasing the arms race and will further endanger humankind. We feel that it should not be undertaken.

QUESTION (SOTSIALISTICHESKAYA INDUSTRIA, MOS-

COW): Mr. Prime Minister, what measures does your Government plan to take for the economic development of your country in the immediate future and what will be the role assigned to the public sector in this regard? And in this connection what role will be assigned to Soviet-Indian economic co-operation?

PRIME MINISTER: Well, that is a very wide question. In the time available I will only answer it partially. India looks forward to a very rapid industrial development. We are in a position where we have established a substantial technological, management and engineering base, and we can progress very rapidly. The public sector will remain the core of our development—it has to. The prime need today in India is for infrastructure and the public sector is almost entirely responsible for this and will be handling this task in the future.

There will be substantial participation with the Soviet Union in developing these areas as there has been in the past. We look forward to more co-operation, more help and new technology from the Soviet Union. As was earlier mentioned we have signed an agreement to look into these very areas.

QUESTION (WARSAW DAILY ZYCIE WARCZAWY): (a) Mr. Prime Minister, last year leaders of six non-aligned countries met in Delhi to join their efforts to push the world situation towards more co-operation and less armaments. Are there any new details about this initiative? Is it at all alive?

(b) And a bit personal question, if you would permit. How do you describe the main characteristics of the Indian way to the future?

PRIME MINISTER: Firstly, the six leaders that met in Delhi in January were not from six non-aligned countries. They were from five different continents, some from major alignments. There were some non-aligned, they were from every colour—Sweden, Greece, Argentina, Tanzania, India and Mexico. So it is a very wide spectrum that was covered by the six leaders. The initiative is still on—we are in touch with each other. We had decided in January that we would meet other world leaders to discuss the intiative and keep in contact with each other, and we are doing just that.

India looks ahead to a very dynamic development. Like I said in answer to another question, we have developed a very strong base in the past 35 years, and today we can look ahead to a very bright future. I can see that India has the will and India will do it.

QUESTION (RIZOSPASTIS, GREECE): Mr. Prime Minister,

was the problem of Cyprus discussed in your talks in Moscow? As chairman of NAM what do you think the Non-Aligned Movement can do to decide this problem of one of the non-aligned countries?

PRIME MINISTER: Cyprus was not a part of the discussions that we had in Moscow. There are many problems like this among the non-aligned and we are looking into it. We are in touch with the leaders and when something is ripe we will come out with it.

QUESTION (CHRISTIAN SCIENCE MONITOR): Mr. Prime Minister, would you comment on the possibility of some sort of Asian Security conference?

PRIME MINISTER: Asian Security is an old concept and we are really for countries not interfering or intervening in areas outside their own. We ourselves have put forward the proposal for the Indian Ocean to be a nuclear-free zone. Other countries have put forward other proposals for peace and nuclear-free areas within Asia, and there is a growing feeling among Asian nations that we do not want Asia to become another hot-bed of tension. We would not like nuclear weapons, nuclear-carrying ships to be stationed near our shores and in our areas.

QUESTION (NEWSWEEK): Do you detect any changes, however subtle, in Soviet foreign policy under the new leadership of Mikhail Gorbachov? And why did you decide to come to the Soviet Union for your first trip overseas as Prime Minister?

PRIME MINISTER: I think their foreign policy has been very consistent and steady and I do not see change in the foreign policy. Why did I come to the Soviet Union first? You have to go somewhere first. The Soviet Union has been an old friend over 30 years and we have stood together in times of trial—we recognise that. And also, may be most important they were the first to invite me here.

QUESTION (A.B.C. NEWS, U.S.A.): Regarding your forthcoming visit to Washington and your talks with President Reagan, keeping in view there response and warm welcome you have received here in Moscow, how would you define your relationship and that of your Government with the President and with the United States?

PRIME MINISTER: Our relationship with President Reagan, our relationship with the USA has been good. Our trade has increased and today the USA is our largest trading partner. We look to the USA for technology, better and deeper cultural exchanges and more trade. I personally have only met President Reagan once for a very short while. So it is difficult for me to have had a relationship with him. But I look forward to meeting him and maybe developing such a relationship.

QUESTION (GUARDIAN): Did the topic of Afghanistan come up in your talks with Mr. Gorbachov and do you have any hopes that perhaps the level of Soviet troops deployment there might be reduced in the near future?

PRIME MINISTER: The topic did come up and we discussed and put forward our own point of view on Afghanistan. Our position on Afghanistan is very clear—we are not for any country interfering or intervening in the internal affairs of another country.

QUESTION (NEWS AGENCY OF NIGERIA): Mr. Prime Minister, as Chairman of NAM do you have any future or immediate plans for the Movement to put pressure on the world powers to stop the arms race?

PRIME MINISTER: Well, like I said earlier, there is very little that we can, in fact, do to stop the arms race in hard means. We can build up public opinion. We can raise our voice and we can try and pressurise them in that manner. But there is nothing by which, any method by which, we can force them to disarm or to stop arming further.

QUESTION (NEWS AGENCY OF KUWAIT): How do you react to the Pakistani attempts to obtain a nuclear weapon? How will your country meet this threat? Was this theme a part of your discussions with Gorbachov?

PRIME MINISTER: We are extremely worried about Pakistan's nuclear programme. We feel that they are very close to developing a nuclear weapon. It did come up during our discussions and this is also being debated in India. We are especially worried about the programme, because we feel that the USA could do more to stop them developing a nuclear weapon and they are not doing so. We have seen recently a Pakistani national trying to smuggle out of the USA certain triggering devices for nuclear weapons. Although he was apprehended by the Customs, there were some changes made in the charges that were put and he was allowed to go to Pakistan and that was the end of the case. Pakistan also has been the only exemption to the Symington amendment which again indicates that the USA wants to turn a blind eye to Pakistan's nuclear programme. We feel that this is extremely serious.

QUESTION (C.B.S. NEWS, USA): Mr. Prime Minister, you have discussed your own up-coming visit to the USA and talks with

President Reagan. Did you discuss the prospect of a similar visit by Mr. Gorbachov? Did he describe to you or did you have any sense as to whether he was in fact contemplating such a trip?

PRIME MINISTER: We did not discuss this but we have invited him to visit India.

QUESTION (PHILADELPHIA ENQUIRER, USA): You have said in your statement that India and the Soviet Union will always stand together in the quest for peace. I was wondering, in your opinion if you feel, as the Soviets here put it, that Soviet foreign policy is essentially peace-loving and that the United States represents a greater threat to world peace than the Soviet Union; or do you find fault in some aspects of Soviet policy as well?

PRIME MINISTER: Well, I will just give you one example. Recently we had the Six-Nation Summit in New Delhi and six nations from every continent, nations that were members of NATO, European nations, American nations, Asian nations, were all represented. The Soviet Union is the only nuclear weapon power that accepted the Delhi Declaration. The USA did not even bother to pick up the Declaration.

QUESTION: At the time of the tragic assassination of your mother, Mrs. Gandhi, the Soviet commentators linked directly that tragic assassination with what is described here as the policy of state terrorism as conducted by the USA. Have the enquiries which have been conducted by your Government in India found any evidence whatsoever to support that suggestion?

PRIME MINISTER: The commission of enquiry that we set up to look into this has not given a report yet. It will be premature for me to say anything.

QUESTION (ABC NEWS): You have said that when you visit with Mr. Reagan you hope to develop a relationship and that you look to the USA for technological assistance. Do you find it reasonable to presume that the President would expect a little more enthusiasm regarding his foreign policy in return for that assistance?

PRIME MINISTER: We do not compromise our position in return for anything.

QUESTION (N. RAM, THE HINDU): Mr. Prime Minister, could you give us an up-dated assessment of the role that the Indo-Soviet Friendship Treaty has played? What is their emphasis on it and what is our emphasis at this point?

PRIME MINISTER: I think the Indo-Soviet Friendship Treaty

has played a very major role in Indo-Soviet relations. With the Treaty we have developed economic, cultural and other relations—they have developed much stronger—and we see the future even brighter on these relations. We have now signed another agreement up to the year 2000 for technical and other collaborations.

QUESTION (N. RAM, HINDU): What concrete progress has been made, not necessarily during this visit, but during your time as Prime Minister with respect to our defence requirements? Where does the Soviet Union come in, particularly in qualitative terms? What are the major areas where they could strengthen our defence capability and potential? What specifically is the progress made during your period as Prime Minister?

PRIME MINISTER: As you are aware our Defence Minister had conversation with the Soviet Ministries. Our co-operation in that field is improving substantially.

QUESTION (SAEED NAQVI): Mr. Prime Minister, has there been any revival of the concept of Asian security in your conversation with the Soviet leadership?

PRIME MINISTER: It was discussed but so specific finite proposal came up.

QUESTION (MAINICHI, JAPAN): Regarding your next visit to the USA, will you discuss with President Reagan the alleged American back-up to Punjabi terrorists?

PRIME MINISTER: Yes, we will.

QUESTION (N.C. MENON, HINDUSTAN TIMES): IDA and other multilateral aid has come down quite a bit. Do you think the agreement signed here in Moscow will assist you in some way, make it less of a burden because you do not get the other thing?

PRIME MINISTER: Of course, it will. But it is not a *quid pro quo* for anything. We would like that aid as well and I think we need that aid.

QUESTION (Ms. P. SUMEET SINGH, PREET LARI): In the year 2000 will we be any nearer to socialism?

PRIME MINISTER: I think India is very much on the way to socialism, and we will be moving towards that target in the coming years.

QUESTION (R. SAREEN, POT): When you discussed Afghanistan with the General Secretary did he inform you about the extent and magnitude of the insurgency in Afghanistan operating from Pakistan?

PRIME MINISTER: Well, he gave us some idea of how much interference was going on and what sort of assistance was being given to the insurgents.

QUESTION (R. SAREEN, POT): Recently there have been some instances of execution of Russian soldiers and in the past few months there have been incidents involving Afghan aircraft in Pakistan territory. Did anything about that come up?

PRIME MINISTER: Well we did discuss it, yes.

QUESTION (PRENSA LATINA, CUBA): Fidel Castro of Cuba has said that the external debt of the Third World is very large—it is impossible to be paid. What is your position about this opinion?

PRIME MINISTER: Most of this debt is concentrated in the Americas, in Central and Latin America and this is really a problem that is better looked at by the Contadora Group. We would like that President Castro and other countries in that area first come to some provisional conclusion before we get involved in that.

QUESTION: What is the role of branches of big Western companies in India in Soviet-Indian trade? Can you describe the role of these branches in the future of Soviet-Indian trade, and can you give some examples in what fields these branches of Western firms can take part in Soviet-Indian projects?

PRIME MINISTER: How can multi-national firms operating in India take advantage of Indo-Soviet trade? Well, we have no special rules or laws regulating this. We have our trade agreements with the Soviet Union, some for trade at Government level with public sector companies, some where the Soviet Union trades with the private sector in India. They are a part of this. They can compete and be involved. This is an operation directly between them and the Soviet Union.

QUESTION (INDERJIT, INFA):. In the course of your discussions with the Soviet leader did the question of China come up? Did Mr. Gorbachov give any indication of the progress achieved in their effort to build bridges with China? And if so, the likely effect on Chinese-Indian relations.

PRIME MINISTER: It did come up in our discussions, and he informed us of the talks they have had with Chinese, some of the questions that have been raised. There are three basic demands the Chinese have projected—pre-conditions, demands whatever you may call them—that are still there and they are a drawback for any real progress on that line.

QUESTION (P.T.I.): The Chinese border claim on both countries—Soviet Union and India, is this one of these three?

PRIME MINISTER: No, it is not part of the three.

QUESTION (INDERJIT, INFA): When India resumed its talks with China, the Soviet leaders seemed to be very concerned and wanted to be assured that it would not affect our relations with them. Now what is their attitude vis-a-vis India in the course of their talks with the Chinese?

PRIME MINISTER: We have been in touch with them about our talks and they have been in touch with us regarding their talks. There is no problem here.

QUESTION (NAQVI): What is the Soviet appreciation of the moderating role that India has played in the affairs of Sri Lanka and what is their assessment of the situation there?

PRIME MINISTER: This point did come up and we explained in fairly great detail what we had done and what progress has been made with Sri Lanka. I think they appreciated our position and the role that we have played in trying to bring about some sort of agreement in that area. The position in Sri Lanka is sensitive and it will need the Sri Lankan Government to take some initiatives to try and come to a solution. We believe that there can be no military solution and there can only be a political solution. We hope that the Sri Lanka Government will come forward with such a solution.

QUESTION (D.R. GOYAL, NATIONAL HERALD): Under your leadership a new initiative has been taken for a new relationship with India's neighbours. Did you discuss the new initiative and what was the response?

PRIME MINISTER: Yes, we did talk about and explain how we are trying to improve relations in all South Asian countries, what steps we had taken to try to defuse tensions and how during the past months the relations between the countries have, in fact, improved, tensions have been reduced and there is much more exchange between us.

QUESTION (MORNING STAR): Did you exchange opinions with Mr. Gorbachov about the question of Indian national unity? Is your country's relations with the U.K. affected by the fact that at the moment certain Sikh extremist groups are organising from Britain?

PRIME MINISTER: Yes, we did explain the problem we are having with some Sikh extremists and terrorists, and I think he appreciates the situation.

Our relations with the U.K. are not affected by the terrorists there, but we do feel that the U.K. Government could take more steps and tougher steps to deal with the actions that the terrorists are taking and the type of publicity they are getting in the U.K.

On May 23, Prime Minister Rajiv Gandhi flew in to Minsk, the capital of the Byelorussian Soviet Socialist Republic, for a more relaxed day after two days of tight scheduled official functions in Moscow.

His arrival at the airport was greeted by even more rain than in Moscow, but the inclement weather was more than made up by the warmth of the welcome. Pretty young girls, wearing traditional costume, presented bouquets to the Prime Minister and other members of the delegation. A mixed group of local and Indian residents stood in line, waving the national flags of the two countries. The Byelorussians rent the air with enthusiastic slogans of "Mirdhruzba" (peace and friendship).

The only "official" function for the Prime Minister was talks with the Chairman of the Presidium of the Byelorussian Supreme Soviet, Mr. I.E. Polyakov, and his Council of Ministers.

Mr. Gandhi laid a wreath at the Victory Square and visited the Museum of History of the Great Patriotic War.

Soon after his arrival in Minsk, Mr. Rajiv Gandhi met the Prime Minister of the Byelorussian Republic, Mr. V. Brovikov, and deliberated on bilateral issues.

One of the highlights of the visit was a trip to the Khatyn Memorial, where the Prime Minister laid some flowers amidst the sepulcharal tolling of bells in memory of war martyrs

Meanwhile, Mrs. Sonia Gandhi, no mean linguist herself, visited the Minsk Institute of Foreign Languages.

The Prime Minister left on May 24, 1985, for Frunze in Kirghizia.

vii

VOYAGE OF DISCOVERY

Prime Minister Rajiv Gandhi could not have picked a better moment to visit the United States. This was indeed a period when interest in India was at a peak, fortuitously and by design.

Rajiv Gandhi went to the USA not only as the youngest Indian Prime Minister, but also as the youngest-ever chairman of the Non-Aligned Movement. The changes in India's economic policy, as evidenced in the Union Budget for 1985-86, have caused merriment in the liberal West. The Wall Street Journal had sought to label the young Prime Minister as Rajiv Gandhi Reagan after the budget. According to reports emanating from Washington, Rajiv Gandhi's visit has received the top billing in the politico-social circuit in the American capital if invitations to important events in the U.S. capital are considered a yardstick to measure social status. There had been a mad rush since February to seek invitations to Rajiv Gandhi's functions among the American elite.

Even before the Prime Minister of India left for his two great journeys of courage and friendship, he had made his and his country's point of view on domestic and world affairs crytsal clear to the famous American TV journalist, Mr. David Hartman, in the two-part interview in the famous programme "Good Morning America" telecast by the American Broadcasting Company (ABC). David Hartman had flown all the way to New Delhi to interview Mr. Gandhi and asked brutally frank questions for which he received equally clear and frank answers from Rajiv.

The young Prime Minister of India told Hartman in his simple and smiling manner that he was not going to America with the aim of specially asking for something. He said, "We are economically stronger than most developing countries. We do not have to depend on food aid any more. Our industries, our human development, have progressed to a level where we are self-sufficient in most of them."

Rajiv made it clear, "If we could get better understanding between India and the Unites States, everything else will flow from that."

Superficially the tour may appear to be no different from similar other goodwill visits by Indian Prime Ministers. But Mr. Rajiv Gandhi's activities, as Prime Minister of India and also as the current Chairman of the Non-Aligned Movement, had many aspects, each one of them warranting independent appraisal. An important dimension of the Prime Minister's tour was that within the short space of a mere three weeks, he came in close personal touch with the two important world leaders—Mr. Gorbachov in Moscow and President Reagan in Washington—who between them hold the key to war and peace on earth, and also in outer space now. The Prime Minister's five-nation tour, taken in juxtaposition with his visit to the Soviet Union only a few days earlier, was his first foray into the highly delicate summit level international diplomacy—and he acquitted himself so well that even his critics could not help being impressed.

The Prime Minister visited Egypt, France, Algeria, the United States of America and Switzerland. With all of them India has close and friendly relations. Egypt, which was Mr. Rajiv Gandhi's first stop, is a civilisation as old as India's own. India and Egypt supported the Palestinians' struggle for a homeland and called for Israel's withdrawal from occupied Arab territories.

This was among the major international issues on which Prime Minister Rajiv Gandhi and President Hosni Mubarak were in agreement at the talks they held soon after the Indian Prime Minister's arrival at Cairo on a two-day official visit on the first leg of his four-nation tour.

Speaking later at an Iftar banquet hosted by President Mubarak, Mr. Gandhi said: "We have consistently and uncompromisingly supported the Arab cause. We support the struggle of the Palestinian people led by the Palestine Liberation Organisation as their sole representative."

The Palestinian people "cannot be denied a homeland of their own", Mr. Gandhi said, adding that Israel must withdraw from all occupied Arab territories.

Mr. Mubarak, in his banquet speach, dwelt largely on bilateral relations and expressed confidence that Mr. Gandhi's visit would contribute to consolidation of Indo-Egyptian ties.

He said his talks with Mr. Gandhi showed a "closeness of viewpoints and a similarity of our priorities".

Mr. Gandhi said peace could be preserved only by peaceful coexistence among equal and sovereign countries and not through unstable balance of terror.

He said "our methodology is not confrontation but consensus, not domination, but dialogue."

Referring to the tragic 57-month-old Iran-Iraq conflict, he said it had resulted in untold suffering to their peoples and caused "us deep anguish."

He said India was in close contact with the leaders of Iran and Iraq and "our efforts to restore the peace are complementary to the initiatives being taken by others to the same end."

Mr. Gandhi said "India and Egypt both abhor racialism and apartheid. South Africa and Namibia must be rid of both."

Mr. Gandhi renewed calls for nuclear arms to be banned from space. He said the non-aligned movement saw war "as an anachronism" adding "we call on nuclear weapon States to reverse the arms race and to prevent an arms race in outer space."

Mr. Gandhi apprised Mr. Mubarak of the problems of the sub-continent especially arising out of Pakistan's nuclear programme and reports that it might make a nuclear bomb.

Mr. Mubarak spoke about the Palestinian issue and apprised Mr. Gandhi of his country's relations with neighbours—Libya and Syria.

Acquainting Mr. Mubarak with the talks with Sri Lankan President J. R. Jayewardene and their joint visit to cyclone-ravaged Bangladesh, Mr. Gandhi said he had reasons to believe that a solution could be found to the ethnic problem on the island republic.

From Cairo Rajiv Gandhi went to France, which is solidly within the Western Alliance, yet it does not prevent French from expressing views on certain issues which are very close to the non-aligned nations position. It is more keen to expand co-operation with India than perhaps any other prosperous and technologically advanced Western country.

Prime Minister Rajiv Gandhi said on June 7, 1985, at Paris that India would like to continue with its policy of using atmoic energy for peaceful purposes but warned that it would have to take proper measures if Pakistan made a nuclear bomb. There would be "problems" between India and France if the French helped Pakistan in its efforts to make nuclear weapons, he said.

In an interview to French political weekly Le Nouvel Observateur, Mr. Gandhi said if Pakistan did not have the atomic bomb now, it was near to having one. On the other hand India did not have a nuclear weapon. Mr. Gandhi added in case Pakistan acquired the bomb, it would be used against India.

Mr. Gandhi said he had raised the question of Pakistan's nuclear capability with French President Francois Mitterrand during the one-hour discussions.

Mr. Gandhi said he did not think that inspection of nuclear facilities by New Delhi and Islamabad would work, as had been agreed by some South American countries, because it would not be "foolproof". "Much better understanding between our countries is the way to create less distrust", Mr. Gandhi said. Over the last six months he had twice met Pakistani President Zia-ul-Haq and both Foreign Secretaries had held talks to that end, he added.

He said India would not sign the nuclear non-proliferation treaty, which is due for renewal in September, if it had two categories dividing nuclear and non-nuclear powers.

Mr. Gandhi said his six days in the United States were intended "to increase understanding" between New Delhi and Washington. "Star wars (the U.S. space based defence project) will only add to tension without materially adding to any peace", he said.

India had need of U.S. technology to aid its economy, he said, in particular advanced meteorological equipment to predict more accurately the arrival of the monsoons, which could be a major economic factor.

India would also be seeking U.S. technology to improve agriculture.

Turning to the home front, Mr. Gandhi said population was the "main problem" for India. The Government "will go into population control in a big way, without any rewards or penalties. Ultimately the real answer is education, especially for women", he said.

Mr. Gandhi said he did not intend to turn India into a consumer society, "but there are large sections of our society which have progressed far enough to be demanding certain products", he said.

If they were not available officially they would be smuggled in. "Our task is to raise the standards of living of all our society," he said.

India would like to balance its trade deficit with France, but was also interested in further arms purchases, including helicopters, Exocet missiles and 150-mm artillery pieces. Several major contracts were pending and could be decided in the coming weeks, he said.

Mr. Gandhi pledged India's support to any constructive effort which would resolve UNESCO's dilemma. Talking about the problems faced by UNESCO, Mr. Gandhi regretted that almost all international organisations were under pressure today because the strong nations had tried to bend them to their purpose.

There was an unfortunate retreat from multilateralism and internationalism, the Prime Minister said. There was no human institution which could work better than UNESCO. To turn away from UNESCO was to turn away from universal co-operation and to reject democracy in world bodies.

During his first round of talks with President Mitterrand soon after his arrival Mr. Gandhi discussed the regional situation and other topics of mutual interest. He is understood to have given the French leader an assessment of the situation in South Asian region and heard from Mr. Mitterrand about the situation in Europe.

Bilateral issues and French help in project to clean Ganga water were among a wide range of issues discussed by Mr. Rajiv Gandhi and his French counterpart Laurent Fabius.

Leaders of important French political parties called on Mr. Rajiv Gandhi on the second day of his five-day visit to France. Former Prime Minister Raymond Barre also had a meeting with Mr. Gandhi. The Prime Minister also had a meeting with about 20 prominent journalists and publishers.

Prime Minister Rajiv Gandhi delivered an address at UNESCO in Paris on June 7, 1985: "It is an honour to be in UNESCO, which Jawaharlal Nehru called the conscience of the world community. The purpose of UNESCO, in the words of Dr. Radhakrishnan, the philosopher who became our President, is to foster liberality, understanding and freedom, the truths of the spirit.

" UNESCO deals with education, science and culture. It is possible for a person to have gone to school and yet be uncultured, it is also possible to be uneducated in the formal sense, yet cultured, as millions of people who are bored on orally transmitted wisdom are. One may be so exclusively immersed in a highly specialised discipline as to be impervious to larger impulses. A few years ago we used to hear a great deal about the two cultures and their mutual exclusiveness. The very deabte led to the introduction of humanities and social sciences in science courses. The rigid categorisations of yesterday are giving way to broader-based scientific disciplines.

"We are becoming increasingly aware of the inter-relationship of various branches of knowledge and of various phenomena sages with insight have always known and proclaimed.

"The wholeness of life and of knowledge, but lesser people, as in the story of the blind men and the elephant claim that only their own perception is valid. Science has begun to obliterate the dividing line between matter and energy, between mind and matter, between the living and the non-living.

"Education has a key role to play in understanding the world, in coping with life, in adding savour to existence. There is practically no country in the world which is satisfied with its educational system. For centuries education was the preserve of the few. But all societies now are casting aside old hierarchies, castes and vested interests. Education has come to be regarded as a basic human right.

"True education, Ruskin said, is training which makes people happiest in themselves and also most serviceable to others. One of the basic functions of education is evidently to make a person productive. But it is more important to enlarge his total personality. Excessive emphasis on the utilitarian has led to the materialism that bedevils modern life. In fact, it is not even very practical. The acquisition of today's vocational skills will not suffice when technologies are changing fast. The silicon chip has already joined the wheel, steampower and the internal combustion engine as a major turning point in the development of technology. The technological revolution, which is upon us, is changing types of occupation, patterns of employment, levels of productivity and techniques of training. What serves is not just a skill to imbibe new skills, a mind that can cope with new situations and challenges, a temperament that is confident, co-operative and creative.

"Education has made impressive quantitative progress in India. We have about 120 million children at school. Our universities have grown. But a large number of our young do not know what to do with themselves. They are ill-equipped to deal with today's problems, not to speak of tomorrow's challenges. We have taken up the task of educational restructuring. New advances in communication and transfer of knowledge provide us an opportunity to overcome some of the limitations of conventional ideas that will help people overcome social and economic handicaps and also give them access to the best by way of quality and authenticity.

"That does not mean we are neglecting institutionalised education. We are emphasising the schooling of girls. We are working on strategies to reduce the rate of dropouts. We are redesigning the linkages between the world of learning and the world of work. We are establishing open universities and centres of excellence.

"All this is a gigantic task. It needs vast resources. Even more, it needs the best available intellectual talent and dedication Non-formal education calls for considerably greater imagination and the innovative use of information technology.

"It is not enough if we set out to do what has been done in the more affluent countries. The answer to the educational problems of developing countries is not imitation. Conventional indices do not lead to great wisdom or less of convention indices do not tell the full story. Total literacy need not lead to great wisdom or less of violence and venality. The educational challenges of the so-called advanced are no less daunting than those in supposedly backward countries. Both must join hands in the endeavour of moulding better minds and better hearts.

"Civilisations such as India's which stretch back into antiquity, have a special responsibility to ensure that they modernize themselves without losing the inner core of their spirituality and traditions. Traditions, said Indira Gandhi, who represented India on UNESCO's Executive Board for several years, is not just the past. It is that part of the past which lives on in the present and enables the people to face the challenges of the future.

"UNESCO has done notable work in helping to preserve some of such priceless treasures of the human heritage as Abu Simbel, Mohenjo-Daro, the Acropolis, Bamiyan and Borobodur. India is seeking the organisation's support in preserving our monuments at Ajanta, Ellora, Mahabalipuram, Konarak and that marvel in marble, the Taj Mahal at Agra. Besides ensuring that archaeological monuments withstand the ravages of the elements, societies must also be helped to conserve their songs and stories. Inculcation of an instinct of conservation is the best antidote to the exploitative tendency.

"In science, the emphasis has been too much on utility and not so much on the joy of discovering the laws that govern natural phenomena, on casting aside prejudice, on being ready to give up what is not tenable. Science has been so submissive to the purpose of the State that the globe is today burdened with a destructive power which can extinguish all life and reduce us to a planet of gray ash and silence. Martin Luther King bemoaned that we have guided missiles and misguided men. Working for peace is one of the functions assigned to UNESCO by its very Charter.

"The peoples of the world must know more about one another; modern communications, it is said, have made the world a global village, we in India are indeed using satellite technology to take the world to everyone's doorstep. But people are very often at the mercy of the media. More information must lead to greater strength for the individual and not greater manipulation of his mind by image builders and propagators of prejudice. Excessive power over the means of communication on the part of a handful of countries is not conducive to real freedom as it affects the right to inform and the right to be informed of people in the less developed countries. UNESCO's constitution asks it to promote communication in order to foster understanding. In doing so, it is not our desire to put information in any straitjacket or to suborn the institutions of others. We support UNESCO's new world information and communication order in order to ensure the participation of all peoples in life enhancing knowledge.

"UNESCO has problems We know that almost all international organisations are under pressure today because strong nations have tried to bend them to their purposes. There is an unfortunate retreat from multilateralism and internationalism. All who care for a saner and more equitable world order must come to the help of UNESCO in its hour of trial. India will support any constructive effort which will resolve UNESCO's dilemmas. There is no human institution which cannot work better than it is doing. But to turn away from UNESCO is to turn away from universal co-operation and to reject the democracy of international relations in world bodies. Human history is a story of bondage and freedom, of strife and harmony, of rivalry and co-operation, of aggression and accommodation.

"As the great Indian saint, Guru Nanak, proclaimed, a man is born to be free. For beauty to be free, History is basically the record of man's search for freedom for beauty, for meaning and fulfilment. It is only through acceptance of coexistence, through a willingness to preserve the wonderful diversity of the earth, through seeking the new and fusing it with the old, that civilisation built with the bricks of education, science and culture can be preserved and enriched.

"I shall tell you a great secret, my friend,' wrote Albert Camus: 'Do not wait for the last Judgement. It takes place every day. It is inner strength and repose that help us to survive that judgement. 'UNESCO must build not only defence against war in the minds of men and women, but defences against dehumanisation."

The Prime Minister, Mr. Rajiv Gandhi, spoke at the civic reception in Paris on June 8, 1985:

"I am grateful to you, Mr. Mayor, and to the Council of Paris for having invited me to this most beautiful civic centre of your magnificent city. I am delighted to be in your midst.

"Yesterday, President Mitterrand and I inaugurated the Year of India. There was a tremendous public response. Thousands of Parisians, milling around the Mela on the Trocadero, made India their home for an evening. My grateful thanks to you for having made this area available for such a Festival for the first time in over half a century. I thank you also for all the help, co-operation and personal interest you have taken. Over the next 12 months, Paris will see performances of traditional folk art, classical dances and music, exhibitions of contemporary modern art, photography, textiles, architecture and cinema from India. Our 700 artists and performers will not only project to you the culture of India but also benefit immensly from the cultural life of Paris.

"Mr. Mayor, Paris is a city of extraordinary charm. The splendid monuments and museums of this city treasure some of the first creations of mankind. Paris adroitly combines a rich heritage of bygone centuries with all that is modern. The skilful manner in which the city has adapted to the needs of a fast changing world, without losing its moorings in the past, is a lesson for us who are coping with rapid urbanisation, with the change from yesterday to today.

"Mr. Mayor, we recall your visit to India in January 1976, when important steps were taken towards development of mutually beneficial co-operation between our two countries. We have built on that. We look forward to further developing and diversifying India's already excellent relations with France."

The Prime Ministers of India and France affirmed that they had reached a broad convergence of views on major international issues and that Indo-French relations had been placed on a strong footing.

Summing up the five-day official visit of Mr. Rajiv Gandhi his French counterpart, Mr. Laurent Fabius, declared that the visit has been "fairly positive and very effective." New and strong bilateral cooperation will follow as a result of this visit, he said.

At the joint Press conference the two Prime Ministers stresssed that the close relations between the two countries had been further strengthened following their talks which covered a very wide range of subjects.

Mr. Gandhi said that while he had not come to France to sign any agreement, many were in the pipeline. He hoped that the discussions on these would conclude in a few weeks.

Mr. Gandhi said that he had not signed any agreement about the purchases of French helicopters and Airbus planes because it was not his department.

Mr. Gandhi emphasised that his talks with President Mitterrand and Mr. Fabius had resulted in much more improved understanding. This puts relations between the two countries on a strong footing from which more trade and cooperation would flow, he said.

Mr. Gandhi said that the views of India and France were slightly different on the issue of "Star Wars" but in essence both the countries were opposed to it.

About Middle East, Mr. Gandhi said the situation there was complicated, "We felt nothing could be achieved immediately."

Mr. Gandhi rejected reports that India would be prepared to sign the nuclear non-proliferation treaty (NPT) if Pakistan agrees not to make nuclear bomb.

"I said it very clearly that India is unwilling to sign the NPT because it is biased," in favour of nuclear power States.

Mr. Gandhi noted with satisfaction the signing of two agreements during his visit to France. The first related to the establishment of an Indo-French Centre for advanced research in Delhi and second for cleaning of the Ganges.

On June 10, 1985, Mr. Rajiv Gandhi reached Algeria.

In a rare gesture, the Algerian President had come personally to the airport to welcome Mr. Gandhi, symbolising the high esteem in which India is held by the Algerian people.

Mr. Gandhi praised Algeria's role in the non-aligned movement. He noted that India and Algeria have been working closely to resolve differences among members of NAM. He said it is important that the non-aligned nations should sink their differences. Mr. Gandhi referred to the unfortunate war between Iran and Iraq and the stalemate over the Palestinian issue.

About the relations between Algeria and India Mr. Gandhi said that our people have much in common and both the countries are engaged in building a new life for their people.

The Prime Minister's visit had generated a great deal of interest among the Algerian people, even though it is a short visit. All Algerian newspapers have published the news of the visit on the front page and have carried special articles on India and its leaders. A photographic exhibition of Mrs. Indira Gandhi was inaugurated in Algiers before the Prime Minister's arrival. The exhibition is entitled 'Priyadarshini'. The exhibition depicts the former Prime Minister's life and work and her leadership of the Non-Aligned Movement.

On June 11, 1985, Mr Rajiv Gandhi reached the USA. The significance of his visit to the USA hardly needs to be stressed, especially in the present-day international context.

Amidst the pomp and protocol of the official welcome President Reagan greeted Prime Minister Rajiv Gandhi, linking the latter's trip to "the voyage of discovery" made by Jawaharlal Nehru in 1949.

"We put great value on India's friendship. Our sharing of domocratic ideals serves as a bridge between us," President Reagan said in his address to a select audience.

"Our mutual commitment to the freedom and dignity of man set us on a different road, a higher road, than Governments that deny human right so cherished by our two peoples.

"You will sense", the President told Mr. Gandhi, "the deep admiration" Americans have for India's ability to overcome adversity. And with loud slogan-shouting by Sikhs protesting "human rights abuse of Sikhs in India" renting the air in the background, Mr. Reagan assured the Indian Prime Minister that he would discover that "the United States remains steadfastly dedicated to India's unity."

In his welcoming speech, the U.S. President declared his "respect" for India's non-alignment, praised the "pivotal role it (India) plays in South Asia", and lauded the Indian Government's "efforts" to "invigorate the Indian economy". "In much of the developing world people are moving away from redistribution and State Control", he said, and described these methods as "having brought only scarcity and suffering."

Mr Gandhi acknowledged policy divergencies. "Yes there are differences", he said. "But rising above them are the beliefs we share in common in the supremacy of freedom, in the necessity of equality, in the sovereignty of the people's will.

Alluding to the "strife-torn, hate-filled violence-prone world ot ours," he talked about the "inevitability of coexistence (which) must propel us towards the imperative of co-operation.

"The best minds of our age tell us", he asserted in the most eloquent part of his speech, "that a world divided against itself cannot long endure."

The Prime Minister referring to the "tradition" of India and the United States working together said that "if my visit strengthens the tradition, I shall feel that it has been worthwhile."

The dicussions that followed the White House ceremony stretched over an hour and were understood to have been held in a "pleasant and constructive" environment. While no meeting of minds seems to have taken place on the most important issues dividing the two countries, the talks, said an official Indian spokesman, did reflect the willingness of the two sides to pursue a consensus.

It was agreed, for instance, that officials of the two Governments would meet soon (whether in the next few days or later is not clear) to try to reach some kind of an agreement on a negotiated settlement to the Afghanistan problem.

The Prime Minister told President Reagan that the success of India's efforts in reducing tensions in South Asia depended very much upon "what the Big Powers do in our region in pursuit of their interests."

"A stable united peaceful India, I think, is in everybody's interest", he said, replying to a toast proposed at a White House banquet given in his honour by President Reagan.

Mr. Gandhi stressed the urgent need for disarmament and said India was "appalled" at the destructive power men had built over the years and concerned at the new dimensions of the arms race.

The Prime Minister welcomed the arms negotiations between the

United States and the Soviet Union at Geneva and expressed the hope that their deliberations "will lead to positive results."

In an apparent reference to U.S. apprehensions about India's close ties with the Soviet Union, Mr. Gandhi said one friendship need not be at the cost of another.

"We want to enlarge the co-operation between our two countries in numerous fields," he said.

Mr. Gandhi said non-alignment had been a positive force for peace. It stood for friendship and co-operation with all. Any nation's independence must include the option to steer clear of bloc identification.

The Prime Minister's concern over the nuclear arms race was evident throughout in the banquet speech. He said the very survival of mankind rested in the hands of a very few countries.

"The world waits in fear and hope," he told President Reagan.

Mr. Gandhi referred to the disarmament appeal by the six-nation meet in New Delhi in January this year and said any positive step taken towards disarmament would be acclaimed and supported by India, the non-aligned community and by all the people.

Keeping the date made two years ago by his late mother, Mr. Gandhi was scheduled to inaugurate on June 13, 1985, the Festival of India, an extravaganza of Indian arts, folklore, music, dance and theatre being staged across the United States during the next 18 months.

"Mr. Gandhi and Mr. Reagan's talks are expected to be wide-ranging and frank. There will be no effort to submerge our differences," one senior U.S. official said.

Prime Minister Rajiv Gandhi told President Reagan to put greater pressure on Pakistan to give up its nuclear programme. He is also supposed to have complained about the transfer of sophisticated weapons to Pakistan, like the Harpoon sea skimming missile, which forces India to go in for equally advanced counter weapon instead of husbanding the scarce resources for development purposes.

The most interesting exchange, however, took place reportedly on the subject of nuclear proliferation in South Asia. To the American suggestion that India sign the nuclear non-proliferation treaty, the Prime Minister is supposed to have reacted by saying that India would consider doing so if the "basically discriminatory" nature of the treaty were to be changed.

Mr. Gandhi said the arms being supplied to Pakistan like sea-skimming missiles were not the kind which could be used in the mountains in Afghanistan.

"We are very keen not to embark on an arms race with Pakistan. Our object is to reduce the arms in the region," he said.

Mr. Reagan, on his part, said the USA was also concerned about Pakistan's nuclear programme and it was doing all it could to discourage Islamabad.

Secretary of State George Shultz, explaining America's point of view in the supply of armaments to Pakistan, said it was motivated by the objective that this would render Pakistan's nuclear programme unnecessary.

Mr. Reagan said his country was keen on non-proliferation and would like to co-operate with India in this regard.

Mr. Gandhi also referred to America's initiatives in Lebanon and West Asia and reiterated that it was necessary for all concerned to be involved in the discussions to promote peace in the region.

He hoped the disarmament talks between the two Super Powers would lead to arms limitation, especially as the range and scope of the arms race had assumed alarming proportions.

Mr. Gandhi also apprised the U.S. leaders of the initiatives taken by him to strengthen India's relations with its neighbours and his talks with Sri Lankan President J.R. Jayewardene on the ethnic crisis in the island nation.

He indicated that after his return to New Delhi, there would be some more intensive discussions on the Tamil problem in Sri Lanka. He was hopeful that this issue would be resolved soon.

Comparisons between Prime Minister Rajiv Gandhi's visits to the Soviet Union and the United States have been well brought out by noted journalist N.C Menon. He writes: As the Prime Minister flew into Andrews Air Force base and later during the official reception on the green and colourful expanse of the south lawns of the White House, the weather in Washington was certainly as different from what was encountered in the Soviet Union as the political climate in the two countries. In the Soviet Union, wherever Mr. Gandhi went, it rained. In Washington, it was bright sunshine, with a cool breeze. For the reception in the White House, official America had pulled out all the steps: the 21-gun salute, full contingents of all Services in full dress uniform, a contingent in colonial uniform with the celebrated pipes and drums, over a thousand guests, hundreds of representatives of the media, and a welcome speech by President Reagan which vied with the weather in warmth.

It is quite obvious that the U.S. administration is determined to make the most of the Rajiv Gandhi visit to improve Indo-U.S. relations, to emphasise the basic commonalities of democratic principles, and, in the process, perhaps to draw India a little away from a perceived over-dependence on the Soviet Union. It was not without significance that President Reagan expressed his gratification and admiration at India's having moved economically from controls to incentives, a system which the United States had also adopted for maximum egalitarian benefit.

Prime Minister Rajiv Gandhi too struck a responsivechord, pointing out that the United States and India had a tradition of working together and that "the inevitability of co-existence must propel us towards the imperative of co-operation". From the initial speeches and considering the imperatives of the two countries' perceptions, it is clear that a great deal of stress will be laid on collaboration in the economic and related fields: trade, scientific co-operation, hi-tech transfer, American investment in India and the rest. The visit is not likely to have any great political fallout except perhaps to bring about among U.S. officials and legislators a greater appreciation of the compulsions of India's view and policies. But that itself will be no mean achievement since changing perceptions among those responsible for American policies and strategies are sure to bring about a gradual alteration of attitudes.

Mr Rajiv Gandhi's fifth, and last, stop—Switzerland—was in a different category as it was not a bilateral visit. He only went to Geneva, the headquarters of a number of U.N. bodies, and his main engagement there was to address the current session of the International Labour Organisation.

According to Mr. Trakru since this tour came quickly on the heels of his visit to the Soviet Union where he had extensive talks with Mr. Gorbachov and his colleagues, the Prime Minister was admirably equipped to disscuss the wide range of international developments with his hosts. In the regional sphere he briefed his hosts about developments in India's own neighbourhood. He expressed New Delhi's apprehensions and fears over the likelihood of Pakistan as a nuclear weapon power. On another important question vis-a-vis Pakistan, namely the supply of highly sophisticated arms to that country, the Prime Minister told his hosts of the heavy burden it means on India. At meetings with the leaders of the countries he visited, he emphasised that India does not want to embark upon an arms race with Pakistan. But to ensure its security in the face of the supply of large quantities of sophisticated arms to Pakistan, India has to divert its resources from its economic programmes. From all accounts, the Prime Minister's private meeting with President Reagan went off well and both of them, on later occasions, expressed sentiments to the effect that they had "hit it off well". President Reagan was pleased with his quest, a youthful Prime Minister of an ancient country, and even quipped that there was only a few years difference between their ages. Mr Rajiv Gandhi is forty while his host is around seventyfive. That did not prevent them from gaining a better understanding of each other's positions and, what is more, from establishing a personal rapport which is going to be of immense benefit in fostering closer relations between India and United States. Certain differences in the approaches of the two countries are inevitable given their respective economic strength and their positions on various international issues. India takes these as fact of life and the Prime Minister emphasised the need to build up mutual confidence. The net gain has been that differences of perception have been narrowed down and the two are able to talk to each other with great understanding. Following the meeting between the Prime Minister and President Reagan, the two sides got down to sorting out how to expand their co-operation in different areas. Among these areas primacy is to be given to high technology, which is a priority programme in Mr Rajiv Gandhi's development plans for India. But he emphasised when he met American scientists and businessmen that "we want to acquire only that technology which will make a real dent on our poverty and help the man in the street. The same applies to U.S. investment and co-operation in other areas." On its part the U.S. side was quite pleased at the prospect of greater co-operation with India, especially after the dynamic liberalisation of some of the old regulations in this country, and the facilities of which they have been assured. All the same, it is too early to expect tangible results at once. There are a great many questions which have no instant answers. But a process has been set in motion and there is no doubt that a great deal will be achieved, especially in more trade, with the United States, and in the acquisition of new technology.

Mr Rajiv Gandhi also met the representatives of the U.S. Chamber of Commerce. He told them of India's plans for accelerated growth and welcomed their co-operation in the economy as a whole. His discussions with them were followed by a meeting they had with the representatives of Indian business and industry.

Mr. Rajiv Gandhi had the opportunity, which was afforded only once before to an Indian Prime Minister—Jawaharlal Nehru in 1949—to address the joint meeting of the U.S. Congress to make friends among the American legislators, inform them about the economic progress made by India in the last three and a half decades, and to seek co-operation in realising his dream, which he described as making "India strong, independent, self-reliant, and in the front rank of nations of the world in the service of mankind. He extolled the peculiar relationship between the people of India and the United States, saying that they "are not allies in security strategies, but they are friends in larger human causes—freedom, justice and peace".

He also reminded them how Mahatma Gandhi was influenced by the American philosopher Henry David Thoreau, and whose lessons in the moral power of non-violence came back to America when the black leader, Martin Luther King, picked them up to promote the cause of civil rights for minorities here.

On the subject of Afghanistan, Mr. Gandhi said that "Afghanistan and South West Asia are all on our minds. Outside interference and intervention have put in jeopardy the stability, security and programmes of the region. We are opposed to both foreign presences and pressures. The one is advanced as a justification for the other". And the second stands for a political settlement in Afghanistan that ensures sovereignty, integrity, independence and non-aligned status and enables the refugees to return to their homes in safety and honour. He cautioned against the "militarisation of outer space" and advocated "disarmament under effective international supervision".

A major outcome of Mr. Rajiv Gandhi's visit is the setting up of an independent Indo-U.S. study group to study the scope of technology co-operation for telecommunications, transport and energy.

During this Voyage of Discovery Mr. Rajiv Gandhi gave the pride of place to the issues that are of prime concern to the non-aligned nations. He discussed both with President Reagan and with President Mitterrand the elusive question of the urgent need for steps towards a more just international economic order. He emphasised the total unfairness of ever increasing trade barriers and impressed upon his two rich hosts the urgency to get the dialogue going in this connection. While the French President's sympathetic attitude was in line with his policy in this regard and was therefore wholly expected, the United States also indicated that it would adopt a more positive approach to this entire issue.

Mr. Gandhi discussed in details, particularly with President Reagan, the question of disarmament. He brought to their notice once again the six-nation appeal by Argentina, Mexico, Sweden, Greece and Tanzania, besides India, which called upon the nuclear powers to halt testing their weapons and work towards their total elimination. While discussing with President Reagan the question of the so-called "Star Wars", he explained his view that there can be no totally defensive system and the adversary will always come up with an antidote. The "Star Wars" concept minimises the role of man and leaves the decision, more or less, to electronic gadgets, which is hardly advisable.

Both Mr. Gandhi and Mr. Reagan stressed the importance of nuclear disarmament and welcomed the resumption of arms control negotiations between the USA and USSR as a step towards the elimination of nuclear weapons.

The two leaders agreed that the initiative on science and technology, begun after Prime Minister Indira Gandhi's visit in 1982, has been highly successful in fostering productive collaboration in the field between the two countries.

It was agreed that the programme would be extended for an additional three-year period beginning in October, 1985.

Encouraged by the success of science and technology collaboration to date, Mr. Reagan and the Prime Minister decided to initiate two new efforts.

The first is an action programme to develop and produce new and improved vaccines against major communicable diseases.

The second is a long-term research and technology development programme covering activities in agriculture and forestry, health and nutrition, family welfare and biomedical research and industrial research and development.

President Reagan stated that the USA would share with India its experience in reducing pollution of large river systems.

A start has already been made with the recent discussion between pollution control specialists of the two countries on the possibilities of Indo-U.S. collaboration in the Ganga action plan.

On June 14, 1985, Prime Minister Rajiv Gandhi said in Washington that India was not concerned about Pakistan acquiring equipment for its defence but was opposed to supply of sophisticated

equipment to Pakistan meant certainly not for defensive purposes.

"We have to counter it by buying weapons by diverting our scarce resources which otherwise could have been used for the development of the people and not for arms race," the Prime Minister said.

Mr. Gandhi was replying to a volley of questions at the luncheon Press conference at the National Press Club.

Mr. Gandhi replied to a wide range of questions covering the Indo-U.S. relations vis-a-vis India's relations with the USSR, arms supply to Pakistan, the situation in Sri Lanka, Afghan issue and the U.S. Star Wars programme.

On the Punjab issue, Mr. Gandhi expressed confidence that the problem "can be solved and will be solved."

There had been a positive response from the Akali Dal, though not to the extent expected to the recent measures announced by the Government, he said.

"We must realise that there are probiems that the Akali Dal feels they are facing.

"We are willing to discuss anything within our Constitution and within the limitation of a united integral India" he said.

He also pointed out to the American audience that there was absolutely no discrimination against Sikhs in India.

When a correspondent asked about the possibility of an independent Khalistan in future, Mr. Gandhi shot back: "I don't think there will be an independent Khalistan in India." As loud laughter and cheers greeted the remarks, Mr. Gandhi added: "I see some Sikh friends in the corner. I would like to remind them when there was a kingdom of Maharaja Ranjit Singh, his capital was Lahore." (renewed laughter).

On the question of Star Wars programme, Mr. Gandhi said: "We do have reservations about the Star Wars project. In spite of the briefing this morning (about the utility of project), we are not convinced about its suitability in the present-day world." The Prime Minister said there could not be a defensive system since it was bound to be countered by an offensive system which would complicate the matter.

Mr. Gandhi observed that the development of the Star Wars system was a very complicated one. Referring to the tremendous task involved, he said it was humanly impossible to identify more than 12,000 missiles decoys and warheads which would need a massive computer. It would require another massive computer to check the programme. "We do not have any human being to check the programme. The human being is removed from the chain. This is dangerous as slowly the point of human decision is being handed over to machines. Every single machine is capable of mistake and there is no time to correct the mistake," he observed.

The Prime Minister replied to questions in a forthright manner and drew repeated cheers from the capacity gathering when he reiterated India was against any escalation of the arms race.

Mr. Gandhi said Pakistan had substantial uranium enrichment facilities. There was no way to use this enriched uranium as their power plants used natural uranium, he said and wondered where it was going.

To a query as to where was it going, Mr.Gandhi retorted: "We can all guess".

In reply to another question, Mr.Gandhi said India was not at all afraid of supply of American F-16 to Pakistan. India's problem, he said, was that it had to divert scarce resources to weapons.

The Prime Minister said India's policy on the Nuclear Non-Proliferation Treaty (NPT) was very clear and there was no intention of changing it. NPT treated nuclear weapon powers and non-nuclear States differently. This, India felt, was blatantly unfair and "we will not sign it," Mr. Gandhi said categorically.

On Sri Lanka, Mr. Gandhi said both he and Sri Lanka President Junius Jayewardene were confident of finding a solution to the ethnic problem in the island state.

"India would not involve itself politically or militarily (in the Sri Lankan internal problem), though it has involved itself diplomatically for the past two years to help Sri Lanka solve the Tamil problem," he said.

Asked if India should request the United States to suspend aid to Sri Lanka, Mr. Gandhi said, the Sri Lanka President was taking some positive steps and India would watch before precipitating any action.

Replying to a question on the Afghanistan issue, the Prime Minister suggested that the United States and the Soviet Union should "get together and sort it out."

Mr. Gandhi said that "any compromise that comes about must include both a stoppage of the intervention and the interference that is taking place at the moment. Neither can be used as a precondition.... There must be some talks to bring about a position from which a solution can be found."

Mr. Gandhi said the issue had figured in his discussions with the U.S. leaders and added: "We think they are very keen on a solution. We believe the Soviets are also keen to come to some sort of conclusion on this. If both countries could get together and sort it out, it will be for all of us in our region and our world, a very great favour".

Mr.Gandhi described his talks with President Reagan as "very warm and open without any strain" and said: "I think we will get along very well together."

"I found him (President Reagan) very forthright, easy to talk to and most of all very humane. And I think that is the type of relationship we look forward to with the United States", he said.

The Prime Minister noted that the United States as a major power and India as a developing country had different perspectives on certain issues.

"After the conversations and meeting with the US leadership we feel that we can co-operate and reduce the differences and work together for the ideals that both the countries hold dear—of liberty, freedom and democracy," he added.

The President of the National Press Club, Mr. David Hess, told Mr. Gandhi that he could not remember a time when the visit of a Head of State had evoked "so much curiosity, interest, sympathy, affection and hope."

The New York Times said that Mr. Gandhi had in the eyes of American officials quietly and firmly removed the shadow they felt had been cast over the relationship with the United States by his mother, Mrs. Indira Gandhi.

The paper quoted an Administration official as saying: "There is a night and day contrast between Rajiv and his mother. It is a whole new generation and the irony is that Reagan has far more rapport with Rajiv than he had with Mrs. Gandhi."

According to U.S. officials, the differences on such issues as American military aid to Pakistan were voiced without prickliness that they felt often marked the comments of Mrs. Gandhi.

An unnamed veteran American diplomat was quoted by the Times as saying: "I don't think Rajiv Gandhi has an ideological perspective. He relates to modern American. Whatever India's policy may be, I think it is easier, more direct."

In the view of one Administration official, despite the warm series of meetings held by Mr. Gandhi, questions remained about the path he would follow.

The Washington Post quoted a State Department official as saying Mr. Gandhi came across as "a very thoughtful and excellent listener" and "very much his own man."

Even hardened U.S. newsmen wondered how the Prime Minister managed to remain so unruffled and fresh in spite of the gruelling pace. Perhaps it was because he implicitly believed in what he had been saying, that is perhaps because he believes he had done a good job in Washington and achieved all that he had set out to do:

The joint communique issued at the conclusion of Prime Minister Rajiv Gandhi's U.S. visit is cleverly and diplomatically worded. It spells out what India and the United States can jointly accomplish but is silent on their differences. Come to think of it, why should differences be highlighted when the imperative need is for intense co-operation? The communique is undoubtedly a confirmation of the welcome turn which Indo-U.S. relations have taken in the wake of Rajiv Gandhi's visit. The frank exchange of views between him and President Reagan has been beneficial to both; their adherence to the democratic path has enabled them to appreciate each other's point of view on a variety of issues relating to freedom, peace and prosperity.

The non-mention of Afghanistan and the supply of sophisticated weaponry to Pakistan by the United States in the communique clearly shows that Washington and New Delhi do not think identically on these two major issues. But the Indian Prime Minister's utterances from various forums must have provided ample food for thought for the Reagan Administration on the danger of creating a military imbalance in South Asia. A major test of Washington's sincerity to India is whether it will refrain from recklessly arming Pakistan with the latest weapons and thereby hindering India's development process, writes Hindustan Times in an editorial entitled Indo-U.S. Relations and adds that it is significant that India and the United States will maintain close co-operation to combat "the international dimensions of terrorist violence against India". The problem of terrorist violence against India has not been diluted by making it a part of international terrorism. The fool-proof security arrangements provided for the Prime Minister in the United States were a clear indication of Washington's realisation of the potential of the sort of terrorism which the advocates of Khalistan are capable of unleashing. It is hoped that these misguided elements will not be allowed to plot and act against India from U.S. soil. These terrorists will find themselves ineffective if Britain and Canada also take steps to foil their sinister designs.

The main fields in which Indo-U.S. co-operation can fructify most are economic, scientific and technological and there is ample indication that a firm base has been laid for such co-operation. The communique refers to two programmes; one is to develop and produce new and improved vaccines against major communicable diseases; the other is a long-term research and technology development programme covering activities in agriculture and forestry, health and nutrition, family welfare and biomedical research and industrial research. Another direction in which U.S. assistance has been assured is towards reducing pollution of the river systems. Agreement has also been reached on sharing commercial technology which "promises to provide important links between Indian and American firms in scientific and technical and research development areas."

What has been accomplished by Rajiv Gandhi's visit, however, needs to be followed up by frequent contacts and exchange of views by the Governments of the two countries. Even if New Delhi and Washington do not share the same views and play identical political tunes, they can remain friends helping each other and in the process promoting international peace. This, in fact, is the gist of Mr. Rajiv Gandhi's message to the United States and it appears that the Reagan Administration has accepted it in the right spirit.

In a leading editorial entitled "Washington's Calculated Response" published in Hindustan Times the editor has tried to assess the USA's response to India.

According to him Mr. Rajiv Gandhi has evoked considerable curiosity in the United States. Now that he has been seen watched and listened to, the Americans must have gained an idea of the direction in which the young leader is eager to take his country, the problems he faces and the support he needs. He has unmistakably provided food for thought for his hosts. Exchange of views between top leaders is one way to clear misunderstanding and to promote friendship. When friends disagree it is not necessary that they should spoil their relations. Instead of deepening their differences, the two countries seem to be eager to promote co-operation in as many fields as possible, which is a major outcome of Mr. Rajiv Gandhi's current visit.

The Festival of India which the Prime Minister has inaugurated in Washington provides the Americans with an unprecedented opportunity to have a glimpse of India's hoary past and to study its fascinating cultural mosaic. Who will not be enamoured by the long uninterrupted chain of history linking the ancient world to the modern?

The purpose of Mr. Rajiv Gandhi's visit, however, has not been merely to expose himself and his country to the U.S. public. Major political, scientific and military questions have figured in his deliberations with the U.S. leaders and Washington's response has been quite calculated.

Washington judges India by the distance that it keeps from the two super-powers. It continues to turn whatever step it takes into a device to draw India away from its "Soviet-tilted" non-alignment. And there lies the rub.

In fact Washington's keen interest in Mr. Rajiv Gandhi is largely due to its hope that his administration provides an opportunity to check the drift in Indo-U.S. relations. This is understandable but Washington should realise that Indo-Soviet friendship does not stand in the way of Indo-U.S. friendship. International relations cannot be built upon narrow, selfish motives. Rajiv Gandhi has made this clear to the high and the low in the United States.

India's non-aligned foreign policy is not designed to put up one super-power against the other or to achieve equidistance between the two. The policy is meant to judge each international issue on merit. Explaining India's stand on Afghanistan. Mr. Rajiv Gandhi has underlined the need for the withdrawal of Soviet troops from that country but at the same time spelt out the conditions for bringing about the withdrawal.

Washington is still reluctant to see the danger in supplying highly sophisticated weapons to Pakistan. The U.S. fear is that some sort of American military involvement is inevitable in the context of growing tensions on the Pakistan-Afghanistan border. That explains the U.S. dumping of arms in Pakistan but it has not yet dawned on the U.S. leaders that Pakistan has used its arms only against India.

When the current U.S.-Pakistan $ 1.5 billion arms aid agreement expires next year, will another agreement be signed to enable Pakistan to become militarily still stronger? Has Washington realised the disaster which can befall the Indian subcontinent in case Pakistan is encouraged to go ahead with its nuclear programme to produce the bomb? It is yet to be seen whether the Reagan Administration will modify its Pakistan policy in the context of the hard facts presented by Mr. Rajiv Gandhi.

The most important outcome of the Prime Minister's U.S. visit, however, is the improvement of the prospects for greater economic, scientific and technological co-operation between the two countries. There is a welcome realisation among the Americans that India's progress will be faster if it gets high technology from the U.S.A. It would be no mean achievement if the way has been cleared for the flow of such aid to India.

Prime Minister Rajiv Gandhi said on arrival after his five-nation tour that although American arms supply to Pakistan was a bilateral matter between them, India felt concerned as it had to divert its resources from developmental needs to match Pakistan's weaponry.

The Prime Minister said he was fairly satisfied with his talks with President Ronald Reagan and others and believed that America would do all it could to stop Pakistan from going nuclear. But that did not mean that Pakistan would give up nuclear programme.

Summing up the results of his visits to Egypt, France, Algeria, the United States and Switzerland, Mr. Gandhi said that they had contributed to India's understanding and friendship with all these countries. He had benefited from the views of the non-aligned countries like Algeria and Egypt as well as the industrialised countries like France and the USA.

He assured one questioner that "India will have more than cordial relations with both super-powers and our position will remain non-aligned". India's policy was not one of equi-distance but one of non-alignment, he affirmed.

Mr. Gandhi said he had not during this visit taken any initiative on the Afghanistan question. All wanted the United Nations to take a lead.

The impression gained from his recent visit to the Soviet Union and the United States was that they both would like to come to a conclusion on this issue.

Answering further questions on his discussions in the United States the Prime Minister said "we had very good talks. Our points of view have come closer, without compromising our basic stands and the requirements of developing countries." There were many areas of discussion such as that of establishing a new international economic order that would have to be brought to a conclusion. Tariffs and trade, international institutions too had been discussed. Where there had been differences, these were talked about frankly. "We will meet again to come closer", Mr. Gandhi remarked, indicating that the dialogue on these matters would continue.

Answering a question about prospects of American technology transfer to India on various "high technology" fields, the Prime Minister recalled there ought to be "no serious problem". He recalled that the matter had been sorted out and an agreement signed in New Delhi before he had gone out on his visit to the Soviet Union.

Mr. Rajiv Gandhi's last stop was a 24-hour halt at Geneva where he called upon the International Labour Organisation (ILO) to do some hard thinking on the problems facing the unorganised sectors of labour in developing countries. The ILO held a special sitting to hear him. Dominated as it is numerically by the developing nations, his message that multinationals should have a code of safety for their installations in the poorer countries, went home and he was repeatedly applauded.

The following is the text of the address of the Prime Minister, Mr. Rajiv Gandhi, to the special session of the International Labour Conference at the Palace of Nations, Geneva, on June 17, 1985:

"It is a pleasure to be with you this morning. The International Labour Conference brings together governments, workers and employers. The ILO champions the rights of those who through their labour create wealth for their nations and peoples. I am grateful for the special honour you have done me in asking me to address this Session. I also thank the Canton authorities of Geneva and the Federal Government of Switzerland for their gracious welcome.

"The underprivileged, the poor and the disinherited have won many an important victory, but the struggle must continue. Millions of poverty-stricken people in Asia, in Africa and in Latin America are denied fulfilment of basic human needs. Even today starvation is a stark reality in some parts of the world. The ravaged faces of men, women and children seeking food are an indictment of the existing world order. The great moral paradox of want amidst plenty is yet to be resolved.

"It is in this larger perspective that we have to consider the role of the ILO. What we do here must relate to the major issues of our time, else our work and our achievements will not endure.

"The basic objective of the ILO is to secure social justice and peace through international co-operation. Just as the ILO was the response of the international community to the exploitation of labour, the U.N. system as a whole was a response to the utter futility of the methods devised earlier to preserve peace and to promote a just world order. We had hoped that the hour of international co-operation had come.

"And so it seemed for some time, although armed conflicts did not disappear, and the theme of development did not always have an easy passage, the belief in the positive forces of collective action through multilateral institutions gained strength. The ideals of the U.N. Charter were the source of inspiration for several international organisations and specialised agencies. Many crises were overcome. World opinion was mobilised for a vast co-operative effort to banish the scourges of war and want.

"Today the very idea of joint international endeavour for peace and prosperity is under challenge. We are witnessing a retreat from multilateralism. Doubt, discord and dissension are gnawing at the system. There are pressures for conformity. There is reluctance to consider the wider effects of a policy that small groups of countries theme of interdependence is publicly professed, but diluted in practice. The dialogue to create understanding is encountering serious resistance.

"Forty years after the end of the Second World War, the dark and lengthening shadow of a nuclear holocaust lies across the futures of mankind. The crushing burden of armaments grows. Scarce resources are earmarked for the engines of destruction, while development falters for want of funds.

"Are there no exits?

"We in India believe that the crisis of our age can be resolved only through a renewal of commitment to the principles of the U.N. Charter. The ILO, the oldest representative of international co-operation, is a most appropriate forum for us to reaffirm that faith on which the United Nations was founded. We have to hold fast to the vision of a future for mankind at peace with itself and dedicated to the progress and prosperity of all.

"India, which is a founder member of the ILO, has pursued these objectives in its national policies. We won our independence through a mass movement in which industrial labour and rural workers played a notable part. When we drew up our Constitution, we proclaimed that the State should make 'provision for securing just and humane conditions of work' besides ensuring 'a living wage and a decent standard of life to all workers, agricultural, industrial or other'. These form important articles in the chapter in our constitution outlining the Directive Principles of State Policy.

"Over the last thirty-eight years, we have endeavoured to achieve these objectives through the process of planned development. The concept of planning grew as part of our struggle for freedom. Jawaharlal Nehru roused the Indian social consciousness to recognise that exploitation of labour was inherent in underdevelopment and that underdevelopment itself was the product of colonialism. The struggle against colonialism was simultaneously a struggle against the deep-rooted causes of India's poverty. That is why the protection of the rights of workers has formed an integral part of our design of development. I am glad to say that our trade union movement, which has zealously guarded the rights and interests of the workers, has been an enthusiastic participant in the wider process of development.

"The wider process of development raises a number of issues which demand urgent attention. The ILO's tripartite social contact between organised labour, employers and governments has made a notable contribution in advancing the cause of social justice. However, if the ILO had remained circumscribed by that limited but important gain, it would not have been the focus of aspirations of the developing world that it is today. We know that the ILO has travelled beyond that and now faces the wider challenge of world poverty. The Philadelphia Declaration recognised that 'poverty anywhere constitutes a danger to prosperity everywhere'. This was said in 1944. This noble objective has yet to become an international reality.

"The pioneering work of the ILO in the field of labour legislation has certainly produced impressive results. The basic concepts behind the ILO standards are unquestionable and universally shared. The living and working conditions of labour have improved significantly. But we are still only talking about those who are employed. And only those among the employed who are unorganised, as the vast majority of workers in developing countries are.

"We must remember that in developing countries, organised labour forms a small part of the total labour force. In my country the earnings of organised labour fall within the top decile of all income-earners. Ninety per cent of all Indians earn less than the organised workers. These are the millions spread over our countryside who work as landless labour or as contract labour on building sites, in quarrying, road construction and in service trades, all at low income levels. In addition, there are millions who can find no work or are grossly underemployed. My question is: What more can the ILO do to make these segments of labour a major focus of its activity?

"I should like to tell you what we in India are doing to improve the conditions of unorganised labour. Since the mid-seventies we have implemented a series of special programmes aimed at alleviating acute poverty and increasing rural employment. These include schemes for integrated rural development, for training youth for self-employment, special programmes for hill regions, drought-prone areas, deserts, and schemes for guaranted employment to landless rural labour. We have also paid attention to the specific needs of women workers, the physically handicapped, and the socially disadvantaged sections of society. These anti-poverty programmes have given the poor an opportunity to be productive and have aroused tremendous enthusiasm.

"The results speak for themselves. Fifteen million families below the poverty line have been helped in the last five years under the integrated rural development programmes. More than three hundered million man-days of additional employment are being generated under the rural employment programmes annually.

"We have still a long way to go. But where earlier there was despair, there is now hope for a new life. New skills, assets and incomes have been generated; a valuable base now exists to go forward.

"In the Seventh Plan, which we have just launched, the thrust for social justice will be continued with greater vigour. We have learnt from experience that to achieve a significant reduction of poverty, simultaneous action is needed in several key areas.

"We have to restructure our educational system to relate it meaningfully to employment opportunities. Our youth have to be trained to use new technology in all areas, especially agriculture, where it matters most. Modern advances in genetics and bio-technology have to be brought to the doors of our enterprising and hard.working farmers. The more than five hundred thousand villages of India have to feel the beneficial impact of the new communication and information technologies. New horizons are opening up in the field of non-conventional sources of energy, in the spread of new knowledge to areas of subsistence agriculture and in agro-industry. All this cannot happen without significant, indeed revolutionary, changes in our education systems.

"The economic and social emancipation of women ranks high on our agenda. The totality of their welfare, equal access to education, equal wages, maternity and child benefits, special health care, the ending of socially discriminatory resources will raise their social status.

"Above all, we shall proceed to tackle earnestly and systematically the problem of burgeoning population. This will involve measures to reduce infant mortality, ensure child survival, improve mother and child care, improve health services, and provide education for responsible citizenship.

"Poverty alleviation is the core of our strategy for development. It is not only a function of growth. It also requires conscious State intervention. But in the ultimate analysis it is faster growth that provides us the means of intervention. We have been able to mount anti-poverty programmes precisely because we have struggled hard to build the foundations of a self-reliant and dynamic economy. In the Sixth Plan, the Indian economy grew at an average annual rate of over 5 per cent. For faster growth in the Seventh Plan, technological change will have to be qualitatively higher and swifter. Workers in India can look forward to greater opportunities of contributing to progress and sharing in it.

"We are creating a policy environment conducive to faster growth, to the infusion of modern technology and to higher productivity. This has been a process of evolution. Policy changes were initiated in the early eighties. We are integrating them in a framework consistent with our philosophy of planning. And we are accelerating their pace to galvanise the productive forces of our society for the welfare of the poorest sections.

"These are the issues that will dominate the transition to the twenty-first century. An enormous range and complexity of issues are inherent in the management of the dramatic changes in technology for the welfare of the poor in developing countries. The development process and what it does to those without the protective umbrella of organised action must increasingly claim our attention. I trust that the work that the ILO has initiated for the weak, the unemployed and the unorganised will be further enlarged.

"We should not overlook the danger signals. Some developed countries are trying to solve the problem of unemployment through reducing or shutting our imports from developing countries. Protectionism in the developed world is growing just when developing countries are being enjoined to liberalise their trade regimes. Sometimes the concept of fair-labour standards is invoked for perpetuating protectionism. But protecting employment in this

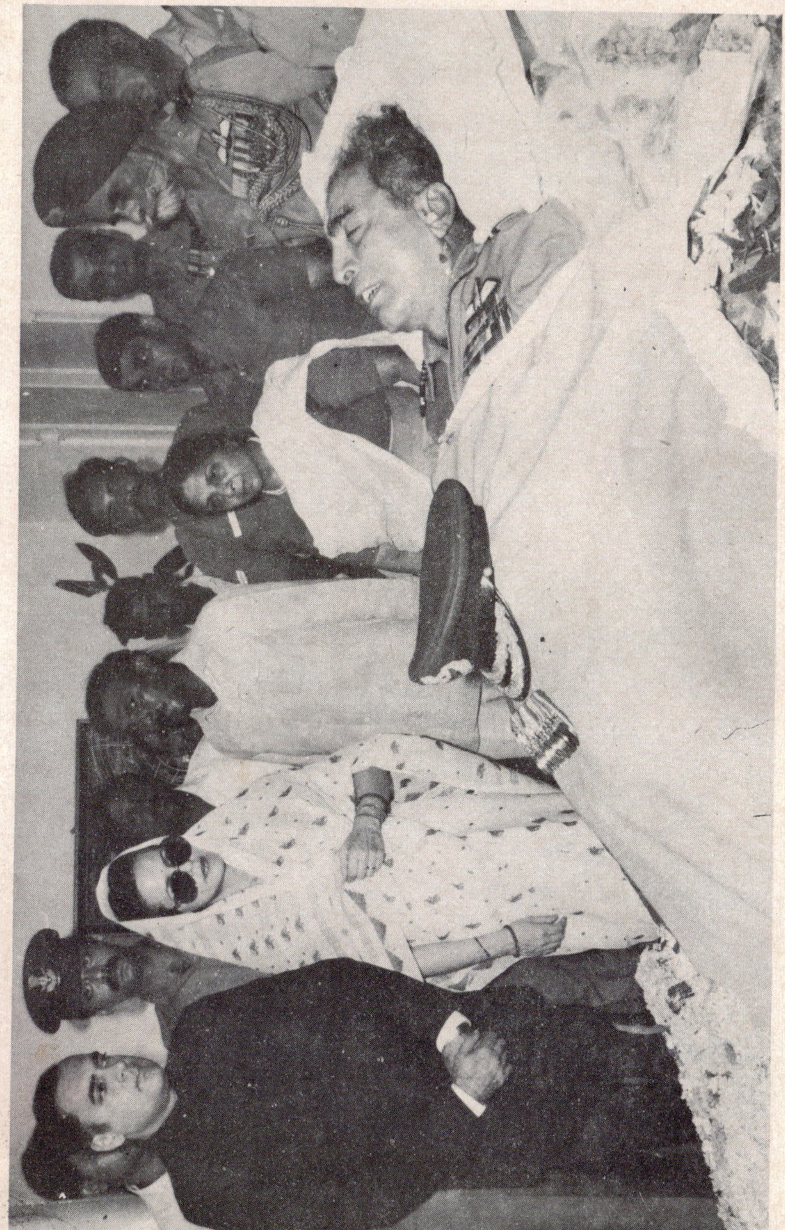

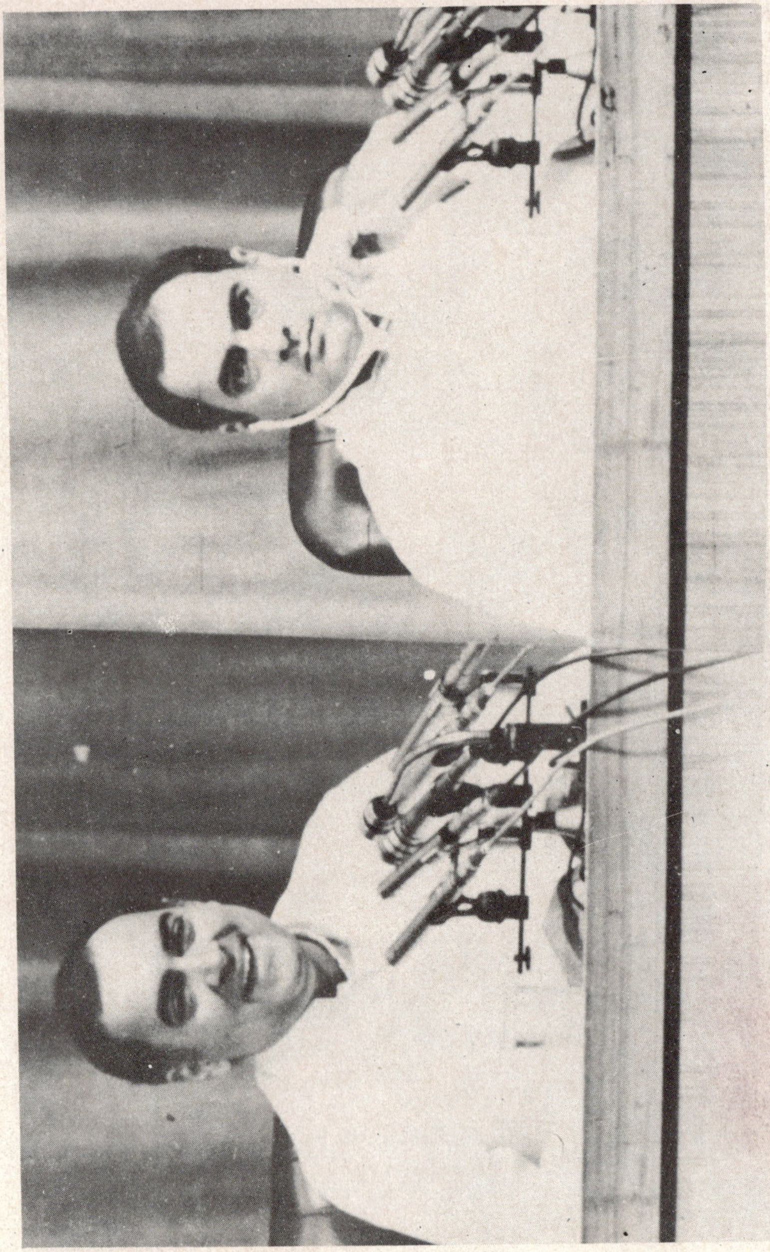

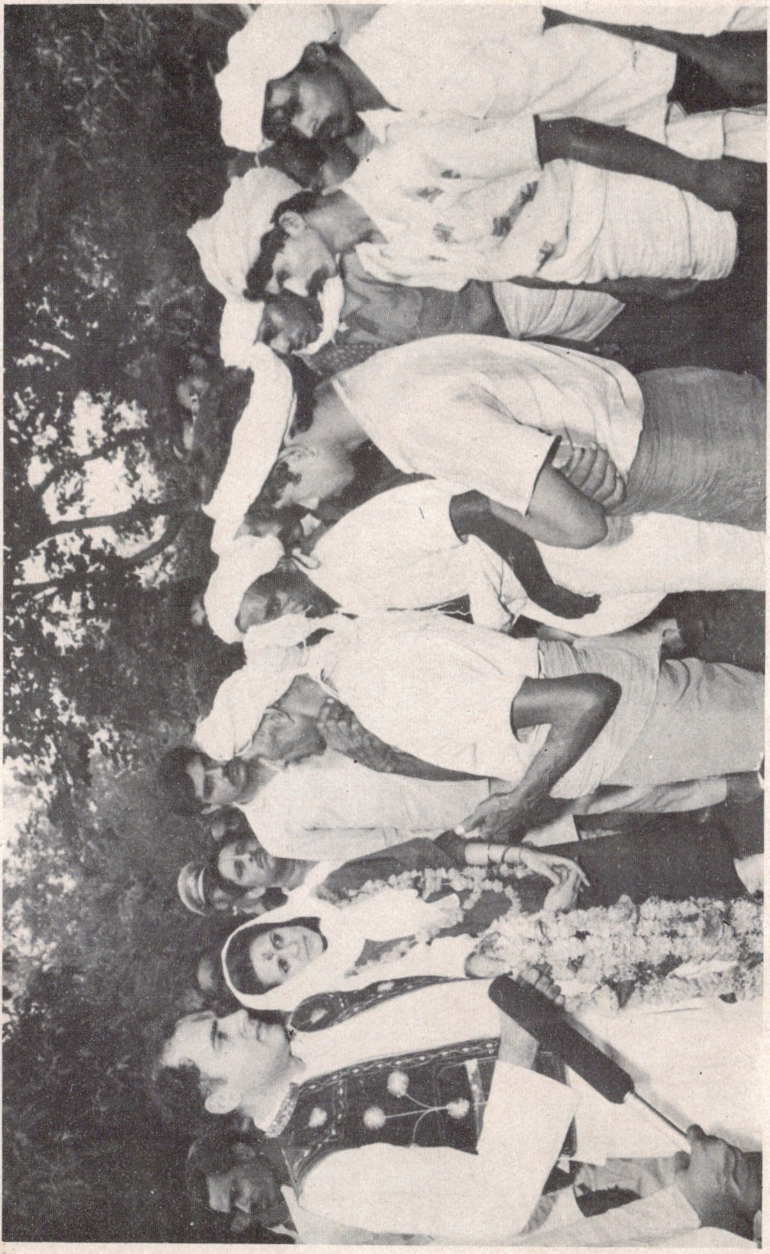

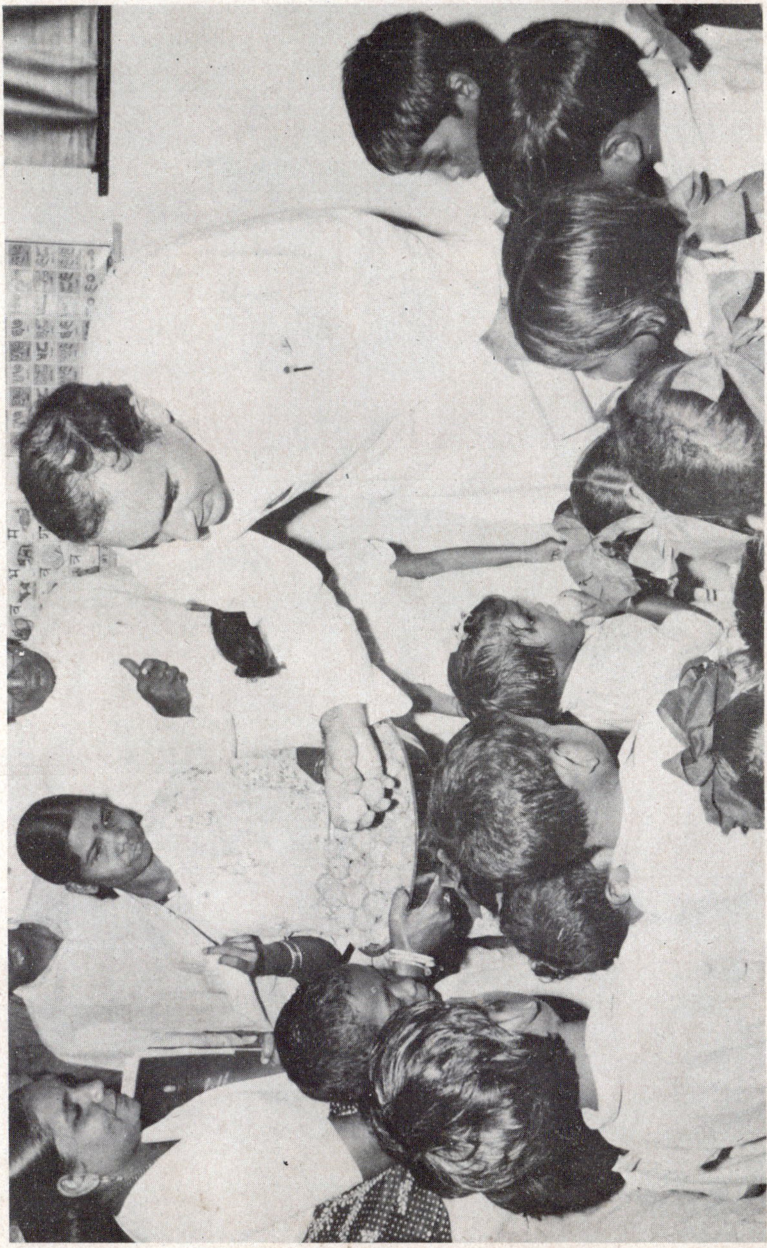

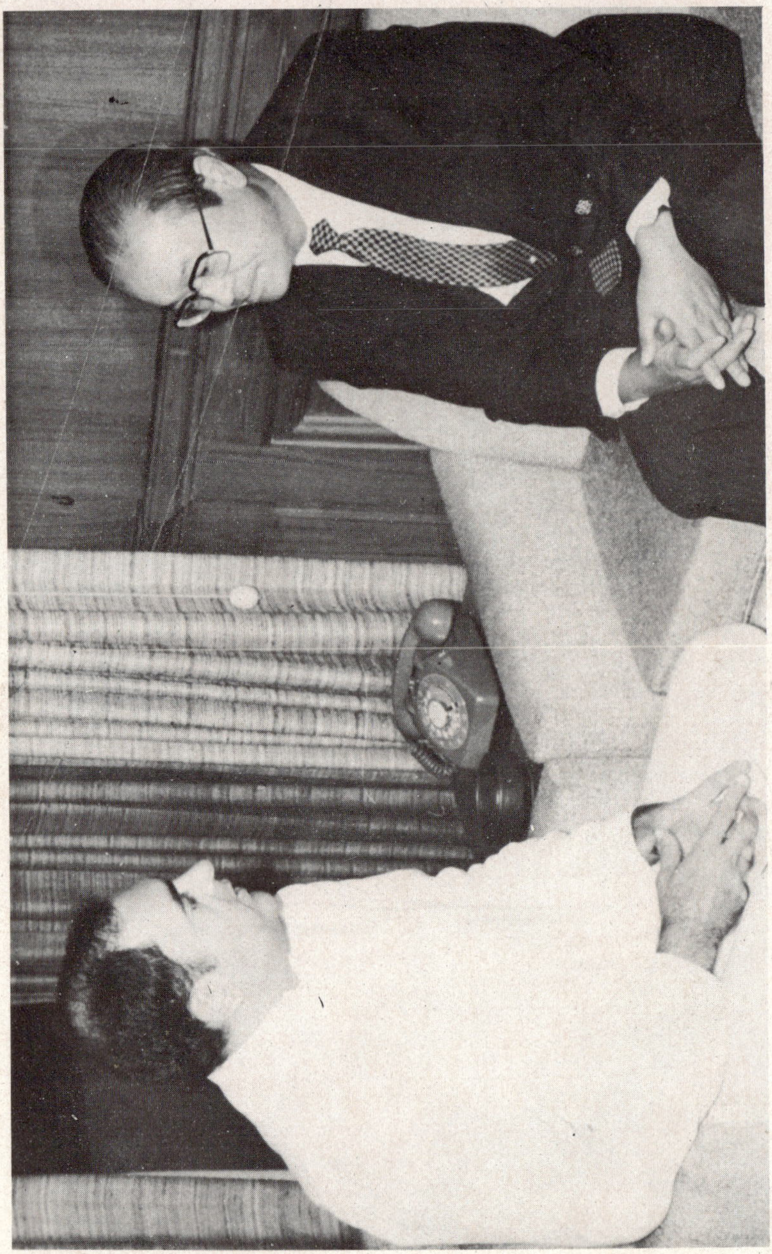

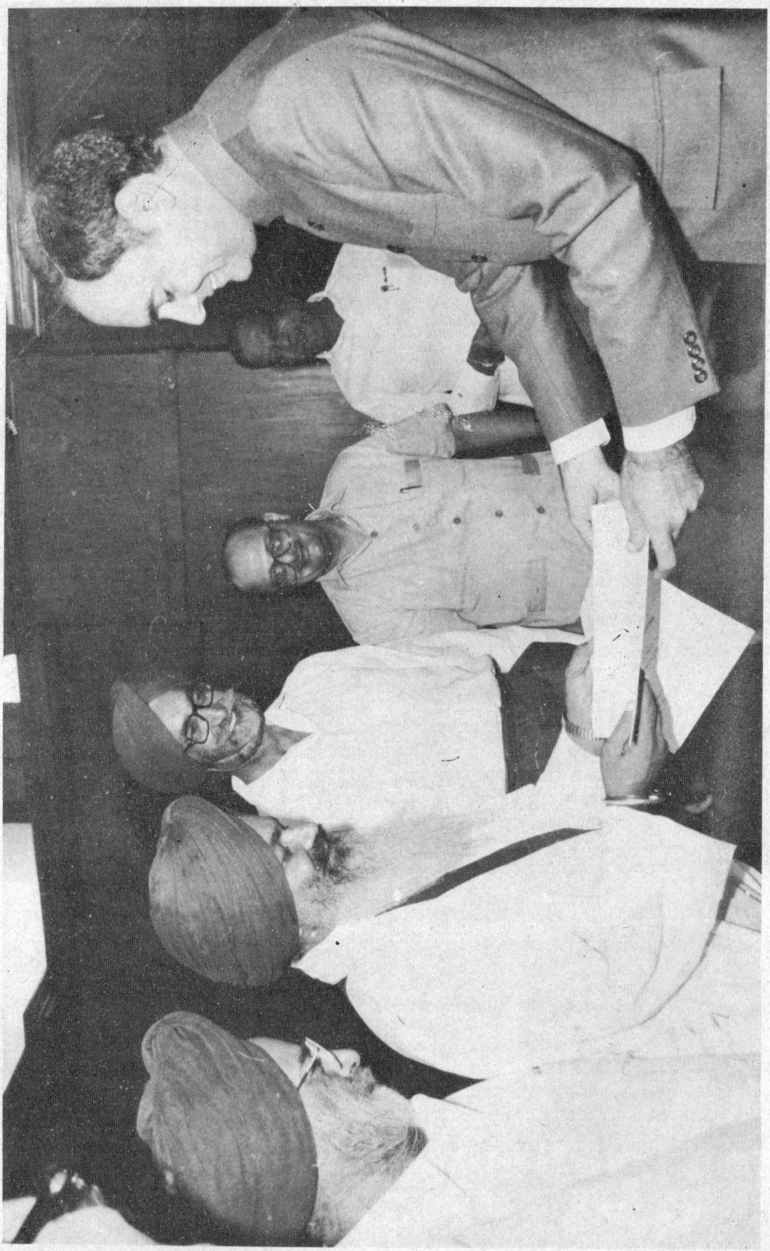

STERIAL MEETING ON
TEM OF TRADE PREFERENCES
ew D
26 July 1985

way is bound to be a shortlived affair. If the developing countries cannot export, they will not be able to import the goods and services produced by the developed countries. And the fastest growing markets are in the developing countries. Thus protectionism has wider ramifications. It concerns not only foreign trade policies, but the basic issue of the livelihood of millions in the poor countries. Therefore, it deserves to be discussed internationally in terms of its long-term impact on employment both in the developed and developing countries.

"The human dimensions of technology compel a reorientation of thinking about the whole set of relationship between developed and developing countries. The agony of Bhopal, the scene of one of the worst industrial disasters, shows the terrible dangers to which workers in high technology industries are exposed. We are taking action to mitigate the direct and indirect effects of that tragedy. But larger questions of the social responsibility of transnational corporations arise and have to be tackled nationally and internationally, in organisations such as the ILO. It is more urgent than ever before that such corporations abide by a well defined code of conduct. The risks facing the developing countries in the area of higher technology have increased manifold, but international procedures of surveillance of policies and practices of transnational corporations have yet to acquire form and content.

"India, which needs sophisticated technology in frontier areas, welcomes collaborations with advanced countries, but we earnestly hope there will be a more open sharing of technological information and more rigorous enforcement of safety standards.

"Friends, we Indians are an ancient people. Out history goes back 5000 years. Our culture has endured through the vicissitudes of time. Always we have shown the capacity to absorb and to synthesise. Different races, cultures and religions have mingled in India to produce the rich diversity of our life. And now, after the end of colonial servitude, our young nation is showing afresh the vitality of endeavour to build a new, fuller life for our people. Our workers and peasants are in the forefront of this struggle, this demanding but very rewarding struggle. And we are struggling not only for ourselves, but for all those who are in chains everywhere else. We must wipe every tear from every eye.

"This can be achieved best when nations pool their efforts and work in unison. The United Nations Charter and the constitutions of

ILO and other international organisations embody a vision of global peace and prosperity. We must prevent the erosion of the United Nations system. As a popular song on the travails of the African people puts it, 'We are the world we are the children'. Mankind is one. Let us not break it up by narrow domestic walls."

In all the places Mr. Rajiv Gandhi went he addressed the Indian communities, updating them on the happenings at home, both on the political and economic fronts. He had a good word for Indian scientists and technologists working in richer countries and pooh-poohed the phrase "brain drain". He would rather call them "brain banks", in the expectation that the nation could beckon them to its service whenever the need arose. No wonder that at some places the slogan was "We Want Rajiv."

The Prime Minister, Mr. Rajiv Gandhi, made the following statement in Parliament on July 23, 1985, on his foreign tours:

"I seek leave to make a statement to the House on my visits abroad since the House last met and to give hon'ble Members a brief assessment of the talks I have held with the leaders of each of the countries I visited.

"I paid an official visit to the Soviet Union from May 21 to 26. I flew to Bangladesh for a day on June 2. From June 5 to 18 I visited Egypt, France, Algeria, the United States of America and Geneva in Switzerland.

"As the House knows, our relations with the Soviet Union have throughout been excellent and my visit helped further to strengthen the friendship and mutually beneficial co-operation that exists between our countries.

"I was accorded an especially warm reception in the Soviet Union. I had several meetings with Mr. Mikhail Gorbachov, General Secretary of the Central Committee of the Communist Party of the Soviet Union, during which he reiterated the importance which the Soviet Union attached to maintaining high-level contacts with India and to enlarging friendship and understanding with India. I, on my part, pointed out the high value which the Government and people of India attach to our ties.

"Our discussions were most cordial and far-ranging, covering bilateral relations and international issues of importance. In regard to bilateral relations we agreed to expand and deepen our existing co-operation in various sectors in a long-term perspective. The international issues discussed included peace and disarmament and the developments in South-East Asia, South-West Asia, West Asia, Iran and Iraq, South Africa and Central America. We also briefed them on the efforts we have been making to develop friendly relations with our neighbours as well as our initiatives as the Chairman of the Non-Aligned Movement. I also met Mr. Nikolai Tikhonov, Chairman of the USSR Council of Ministers, Mr. Andrei Gromyko, who has now become the President of the Soviet Union and was then Foreign Minister, and other leaders.

"The outcome of our discussions has been set out in the Joint Statement which was issued at the end of my visit. Two agreements were signed. The first, Agreement on Economic and Technical Cooperation, provides for Soviet participation in some important projects included in our Seventh Five Year Plan, particularly in the power, coal and petroleum sectors. There is also provision for Soviet participation in the iron and steel and machine-building sectors. Soviet co-operation under this agreement is to be covered by a credit of 1 billion roubles.

"The second agreement signed was on the main directions of economic, trade, scientific and technical co-operation between our countries up to 2000 A.D.

"My programme included visits to Minsk in the Byelorussian Republic and Frunze in the Kirghiz Republic. At a public function in Moscow organised by the Union of Soviet Friendship Societies and the Soviet-India Friendship Society, the Lenin Peace Prize was awarded posthumously to our late Prime Minister, Smt. Indira Gandhi. A square in Moscow was also named after her.

"In my assessment, the visit has been very useful in enabling the leadership of the Soviet Union to get acquainted with our point of view and in taking Indo-Soviet understanding and co-operation to a new level of cordiality.

"The purpose of my visit to Bangladesh on June 2 was to express India's sincere sympathy to the Government and people of that country over the devastation and loss they had suffered as a result of cyclone. President Jayewardene of Sri Lanka, who was in New Delhi for discussions, also went with me to Bangladesh. We had talks with Lt.-General Ershad, President of the People's Republic of Bangladesh. The visit was also an expression of the growing spirit of solidarity among the countries of South Asia.

"Egypt and Algeria have been close colleagues of ours in the Non-Aligned Movement. Smt. Indira Gandhi was to have visited both countries in April 1984 but could not do so. After I assumed office, their invitations were renewed.

"In Cairo, President Hosni Mubarak received me with great warmth and cordiality. We had an in-depth exchange of views both on international and bilateral matters. Egypt was particularly appreciative of our chairmanship of the Non-Aligned movement, our role in promoting disarmament and our efforts to bring about an early end to the Iran-Iraq war. There was agreement on the need to co-operate closely with each other and to remain in touch on the West Asia question. We also were of accord on the need to maximise bilateral, economic and commercial co-operation. It was decided that the possibilities might be explored in a more concrete manner at the first meeting of the Indo-Egyptian Joint Commission, which is likely to be held in October 1985. I also had discussion with Mr. Kamal Hassan Ali, Prime Minister of Egypt.

"In Algeria I had extensive discussions with President Chandli Bednedid, covering the entire range of bilateral issues. There was identity of views on international issues of mutual concern and we have agreed to keep in close touch, particularly on non aligned issues. It was agreed to set up an institutionalised system of annual exchanges between our two Foreign Offices alternatively in Algiers and New Delhi. I also had talks with the Prime Minister, Mr. Abdelhamid Brahimi.

"In order to give a further impetus to our economic and commercial exchanges we agreed to purchase half a million tonnes of Algerian crude. Algeria has indicated its readiness to accord high priority to the award of commercial contracts and projects to India.

"On the question of Western Sahara, our sympathy and support for the Polisario was reiterated. I received Mr. Mahfoud Ali Beiba, Prime Minister of the SADR and Member of the Executive Committee of the Polisario. It was made known to him that, following the SADR's participation at the 20th OAU Summit in November 1984, upgradation of our relations had been under active consideration.

"My visit to France followed a series of high-level exchanges since President Giscard Estaing's visit in January 1980, the late Prime Minister Indira Gandhi's visit to France in November 1981, President Mitterrand's visit to India in November 1982 and Shrimati Indira Gandhi's short transit stop-over in Paris in September, 1983. My visit proved to be very useful and reinforced the foundation for a more dynamic bilateral relationship.

"President Mitterrand and I took stock of the world situation and the imperative need to promote international peace as well as greater co-operation between the developed and developing countries. I also had extensive discussions with the Prime Minister, Mr. Laurent Fabius.

"In my meeting, I stressed the need to develop the political and economic aspects of our bilateral relationship in a balanced manner. The French displayed marked receptivity to our point of view.

"Two accords were signed during the visit: one on the setting up of an Indo-French Centre for Promotion of Advanced Research in India and the other for French assistance in the conversion of urban wastes into energy, and depollution of the Ganga river. Overall Indo-French economic co-operation in a number of fields is expected to be significantly enhanced.

"I inaugurated the Festival of India on June 7. As Members are aware, the Festival will continue until mid-1986, and, already, it has had a marked impact on the French public.

"In Paris I also addressed the UNESCO and reiterated our support to the work which that organistation is doing.

"My visit to the USA from June 11 to 15 was most useful.

"I had an opportunity to exchange views with President Reagan on major international issues and also on matters of immediate concern to India like reports of Pakistan's plans to produce nuclear weapons and the activities of some terrorist elements. The talks were charaterised by warmth and openness.

"I welcomed the desire of the President for close co-operation with us on the international dimensions of terrorist violence against India.

"I found both in the President and his advisers a great deal of interest and understanding in regard to what we are trying to do in India. Even where we have differences in policy or in approach, I got the feeling that we could still discuss the issues and work together. We value these high-level contacts and would like to continue the dialogue. I believe there is good scope for building on these foundations to broaden our understanding and co-operation.

"Hon'ble Members would have seen the text of the joint statement which was issued at the conclusion of my visit to the United States, which lists out some areas of economic, scientific and technological co-operation. We have identified some specific areas of collaboration, like extending the Science and Technology Initiative for another three years, initiating a vaccination programme, and a long-term research and technology development programme and a programme for the advancement of commercial technology.

"India was honoured by the invitation extended to me to address a joint meeting of Congress. I also had meetings with other important members of the Administration as well as prominent scientists, leaders of the Press and the media and the U.S. Chamber of Commerce.

"Both in Washington and in Houston there were functions with the Indian community. Vice-President Bush graciously accompanied us to Houston, where I paid a brief visit to NASA. A major event in my programme was the formal inauguration of the Festival of India, which was dedicated to the memory of Smt. Indira Gandhi. President Reagan has referred to the Festival as "an unprecedented nationwide celebration.'

"Hon'ble Members would have seen reports about President Reagan's recent surgery. I am sure the entire House would join me in conveying to Mr. Reagan and to the American people our best wishes for his full and speedy recovery.

"On the way back from the United States I broke journey for a day in Geneva where I was accorded the privilege of addressing the International Labour Organisation. In my address I reiterated India's commitment to ameliorating the conditions of our workers in both the organised and unorganised sectors and to urge greater action on the part of ILO in the service of unorganised workers all over the world."

viii

OPENING NEW VISTAS

A comprehensive accord was reached between Prime Minister Rajiv Gandhi and Akali Dal president Sant Harchand Singh Longowal on July 24, 1985, on the entire range of issues concerning Punjab, marking a welcome end to the prolonged crisis in the border State that has bedevilled the nation.

The accord on Punjab that brings to an end an era of confrontation is a singular triumph for Prime Minister Rajiv Gandhi's statesmanship and single-minded pursuit of peace and amity. The Prime Minister has now fulfilled his pledge to give the highest priority to the settlement of the Punjab imbroglio. With the signing of the agreement the Prime Minister has proved, if proof were needed, that he has matured into a leader who can and will take India to unprecedented heights of stability, unity and prosperity.

The 11-point Memorandum of Settlement signed at 5.30 p.m. in Parliament House provides for transfer of Chandigarh to Punjab, two high-power commissions to decide on the territorial disputes between Punjab and Haryana and a tribunal on the Ravi-Beas water systems, reference of the controversial Anandpur Sahib resolution to the Sarkaria Commission, widening of the scope of the inquiry into last November's riots, rehabilitation of those discharged from the Army, and compensation to the families of all the innocent people killed in agitation and riots since August 1982.

The memorandum was tabled in the Lok Sabha within 20 minutes of its signing by a beaming Prime Minister, who expressed the hope that this "will bring to an end a very difficult period through which the nation has passed."

The five-page memorandum, signed by the two leaders, itself ends thus: "This settlement brings to an era of amity, goodwill and co-operation, which will promote and strengthen the unity and integrity of India."

The announcement by Mr. Gandhi which had been awaited anxiously by members in both Houses of Parliament, was greeted with loud and prolonged thumping of desks by members on all sides. Two senior Opposition leaders in the Lok Sabha, Prof. Madhu Dandavate (Janata) and Mr. C. Madhava Reddy (Telugu Desam), welcomed it immediately.

On the whole, the agreement is eminently reasonable and fair to all concerned. Efforts should now be made by the parties and the people in Punjab and elsewhere to ensure that it is properly implemented so that peace and progress can return to the strife-torn State.

The transfer of Chandigarh to Punjab, as also of Hindi-speaking areas now in Punjab to Haryana, is to take place simultaneously on the next Republic Day, January 26, 1986. The commission will give its findings by December 31, 1985, which will be binding on both sides.

The agreement provides for the rehabilitation of all those discharged from the Army, through gainful employment.

The jurisdiction of the Justice Ranganath Mishra Commission inquiring into the November 1984 riots that followed the assassination of Mrs. Indira Gandhi will be extended to cover the disturbances in Bokaro (Bihar) and Kanpur.

The Government agreed to consider the formulation of an all-India gurdwara Bill. "The legislation will be brought forward for this purpose in consultation with the Shiromani Akali Dal and others concerned and after fulfilling all relevant constitutional requirements."

Under the accord the Government agreed to withdraw the notification applying the Armed Forces Special Powers Act to Punjab.

The existing special courts will now try only cases relating to the offences of "waging war" and "hijacking". All other cases will be transferred to ordinary courts and enabling legislation, if needed. will be brought forward in the current session of Parliament.

The river water dispute is to be adjudicated by a tribunal headed by a Supreme Court judge. The accord provides that the report of the tribunal will be submitted within six months and will be binding on both Punjab and Haryana.

Mr. Gandhi said that on the Anandpur Sahib resolution, Sant Longowal made it very clear that it was meant to be an exercise for greater autonomy within the Indian Union. Those aspects of the resolution, passed by the Akali Dal first in 1973 and again in 1978, which pertain to Centre-State relations, now stand transferred to the Commission on Centre-State Relations headed by Mr. Justice R.S. Sarkaria.

The accord specifically provides for the promotion of Punjabi language.

The Prime Minister will write to the Chief Ministers on the question of according adequate representation to the minorities in employment and other avenues.

On Chandigarh, the accord provides for the city going to Punjab. The present Union Territory has some adjoining areas included both from Punjab and Haryana. The Hindi-speaking areas will now be transferred to Haryana and the Punjabi-speaking areas to Punjab.

The entire Sukhna lake is to remain part of the capital project and go to Punjab.

The memorandum recalls that the late Mrs. Indira Gandhi had always maintained that when Chandigarh goes to Punjab, the Hindi-speaking territories of Abohar and Fazilka will go to Haryana. The specific areas as per the language spoken, with village as the unit, will be determined by a commission. The principle of contiguity and linguistic affinity will also be adhered to.

While the task of the commission will be confined to division of territories between Punjab and Haryana, the general boundary claims are to be settled by another commission.

The agreement reached between the Centre and the Akali Dal, resolving the vexed Punjab tangle, was widely hailed by political parties and leaders from all walks of life.

Accosted by newsmen just after signing the memorandum of settlment, Akali president Sant Harchand Singh Longowal said that he was fully satisfied with the accord. "The period of confrontation between the Akalis and the Centre is now over." he added.

Punjab Governor Arjun Singh hoped that with the signing of the memorandum "agony of Punjab and anxiety of the country" would come to an end.

Mr. Arjun Singh, who watched the Prime Minister's announcement in the Lok Sabha from the speakers' gallery, told newsmen that "as a servant of the people of Punjab I hope that the statesmanship and compassion shown by the Prime Minister and the courage exhibited by Sant Longowal would bring to an end the agony of Punjab and anxiety of the country."

Mr. Arjun Singh said that he would like to place it on record that this "desire and ambition" was achieved by the good wishes of the Prime Minister.

Janata Parliamentary Party leader Madhu Dandavate said that his party wholeheartedly welcomed the agreement. The accord will further strengthen Hindu-Sikh unity.

Welcoming the agreement the Communist Party of India (Marxist) said that it should have been reached long ago.

Stating that while one might have reservations about specific provisions of the memorandum of settlement between the Prime Minister and Akali Dal chief Sant Harchand Singh Longowal, Mr. L.K. Advani, leader of the BJP Parliamentary Party, said that "the fact that there has been a settlement is in itself a great relief. I am happy about it."

He, however, said that had the Akalis and the Government shown this kind of sagacity at the time of the tripartite conference in January 1983 "the country and Punjab might have been spared a lot of agony and bloodshed."

It was noteworthy, he said, that at the time of the tripartite conference all Opposition parties had opposed any formal reference by the Government to the Anandpur Sahib resolution.

"It is strange", Mr. Advani said, "that the ruling party whose principal election plank was that the Opposition parties were favouring the Anandpur Sahib resolution and it alone was resisting it, has now in an official communique signed by the Prime Minister himself formally recognised it."

Janavadi Party president Chandrajit Yadav said it was the victory of negotiated settlement over the forces of terrorism.

The Telugu Desam leader in the Rajya Sabha, Mr. P. Upendra, said the Prime Minister had displayed statesmanship and sagacity in solving the vexed Punjab problem.

However, disapproving of the accord, former Haryana Chief Minister Devi Lal said injustice had been done to Haryana.

Mr. Devi Lal, who is president of the Haryana Lok Dal, said he would convene a meeting of his party in the State soon to discuss this issue.

Former Punjab Minister Umrao Singh, and Mr. Hanspal, MP, in separate statements said a new chapter begins in the history of Punjab which had witnessed destruction and violence during the past four years.

Dr. Shankar Dayal Sharma, Governor of Andhra Pradesh, welcomed the agreement and said the whole nation rejoiced in the settlement of the long pending dispute.

While congratulating Prime Minister Rajiv Gandhi and Akali leader Sant Longowal, Dr. Sharma said he looked forward to a new era of amity and friendship among all sections of the people in Punjab and prosperity of the State.

Former Union Information Minister Inder Kumar Gujral paid glowing tributes to the "sagacity and sincerity" of Sant Longowal and expressed his "deep appreciation" for the Prime Minister's statesmanship.

Mr. Vishwa Bandhu Gupta, MP and president of the All India Newspaper Editors' Conference, appealed to the Press and media to create an atmosphere of national unity by highlighting the goodwill generated by this historic agreement.

Dr. G.S. Rajhans, Cong (I) MP from Bihar, said the Punjab accord has started a new era of Hindu-Sikh amity. "The dark phase seems to be over. Every patriotic Indian will rejoice on this heartening development."

Mr. Lalit Maken, Cong (I) MP, congratulated the Prime Minister and said that the agreement would be especially welcome to the working class in Punjab which had suffered a great deal because of the agitation.

Sant Harchand Singh Longowal accompanied by two of his aides. Mr. Balwant Singh and Mr. S.S. Barnala, drove straight from Parliament House to Gurdwara Bangla Sahib to offer prayers soon after signing the accord.

Mr. Longowal was profusely garlanded and thousands of Sikhs collected at the gurdwara shouted slogans "Longowal Zindabad, Panth Ki Jeet" (Victory for the Panth). He was also offered 'Saropas' at the gurdwara.

Mr. Longowal said he was returning to Punjab "victorious" as all the Akali demands had been conceded by the Government. There was jubilation at Punjab Bhavan where the Akali leaders were staying and sweets were distributed to mark the occasion.

Delhi Chief Executive Councillor Jag Parvesh Chandra hailed the agreement between the Government and the Akali Dal saying it would go a long way towards bringing back normalcy and amity to Punjab.

Mr. Onkar Singh Thapar, general secretary of the Delhi State Akali Dal (L), welcomed the "package deal". Saying that the long conflict between the Centre and the Akali Dal had now ended, he expressed his hope for peace and amity throughout the country.

On behalf of the Punjabi Cultural Federation, its general secretary, Mr. Avtar Singh Sethi, congratulated the Prime Minister for the "historical decision," adding that he had proved that his Government works faster.

Elections in Punjab now look almost certain. This was the reaction of most of the political leaders to the signing of the agreement between the Centre and Akali Dal president Longowal.

Former Akali Minister Sukhdev Singh Dhindsa, Dr. Gurnam Singh Tir, Akali Dal legal adviser. Mr. S.S. Dhuri, and Giani Arjun Singh, both former Akali MLAs have welcomed the agreement.

Punjab PCC(I) president Rajinder Singh Sparrow, former Haryana Governor H.S. Brar, Mr. Nasib Singh and Mr. Gopal Kishan Chatrath (both Congress (I) MLAs) have also welcomed the agreement. They have said it will help in restoring normalcy.

Punjab CPI secretary Avtar Singh Malhotra said the agreement would pave the way for bringing back normalcy. He said the extremists and terrorists would be completely isolated.

The considered opinion in political circles is that Punjab Governor Arjun Singh proved himself to be an able politician-diplomat and statesman by preparing the ground for the agreement.

It is reliably understood that Mr. Arjun Singh had been in close touch secretly with Sant Longowal, Mr. S.S. Barnala and Mr. Balwant Singh for quite some time and made them agree to negotiate.

These reports say that much before receiving the formal letter from the Prime Minister the modalities of the agreement had been decided.

It is learnt that four days ago, Sant Longowal had come to Chandigarh with the Prime Minister's letter. It was shown to Mr. Badal, Mr. Tohra and some others. The consensus of opinion was that he should write back to Mr. Rajiv Gandhi and stick to the strategy adopted at Anandpur Sahib recently.

People of Amritsar, who have been leading an abnormal life for the past four years, were jubilant over the Akali Dal-Centre accord.

Having remained glued to their transistor sets for the past two days, expecting to hear the cheering news, they danced in the streets soon after the evening bulletin of All India Radio, announcing the accord. Sweets were distributed both by the Sikhs and the Hindus and they embraced one another.

"An era of peace will now be ushered in", said a local Akali leader. He appealed to the other Akali leaders to join hands in bringing normalcy to Punjab.

Mr. Mubarak Singh, president of the local unit of the Janata Party, welcomed the accord and said "Punjab will be back on the rails again." He congratulated the Prime Minister and Sant Longowal for solving the Punjab problem.

In an editorial in Indian Express the accord has been highly acclaimed: "The Punjab accord represents as near a national consensus as might be expected on a matter that aroused such deep passions and all but tore the country apart. It is a triumph for the democratic process and the ultimate maturity of the Indian people. The Prime Minister and his colleagues will be hailed by a grateful nation for moving towards an agreement with determination and despatch and concluding it in what was essentially a single, continuous session round the clock over two days to tie up a neat and fair package. Mr. Harchand Singh Longowal and his advisers have shown great statesmanship, fortitude and courage in rising above the bitterness of the past. Theirs was the more difficult task in a way after the emotional trauma of the past 14 months and the continued sniping from hardliners in their own camp and the pressure of extremists and terrorists. High praise is due to the Punjab Governor, Mr. Arjun Singh, whose patience, tact and sympathy enabled him to build a bridge of understanding. The Opposition by and large has readily acclaimed the accord, thereby ensuring that it is seen as a national solution, above petty partisan controversy. As the signatories, Mr. Rajiv Gandhi and Mr. Longowal, themselves acknowledge, 'the settlement brings to an end a period of confrontation and ushers in an era of amity, goodwill and co-operation, which will promote and strengthen the unity and integrity of India.' This is a victory for all."

The Memorandum of Settlement is comprehensive. Most of the heads of agreement are in terms that were available two or more years ago. This is no time for recrimination but there is a larger lesson in this for everybody in the heavy price in blood paid for past default. Abohar remains with Punjab on the entirely reasonable basis of contiguity, with the village as the unit. This precludes territorial claims based on the dangerous and pernicious corridor principle which should never be entertained. With this red herring out of the way, the territorial question has been resolved by awarding the Chandigarh capital project area to Punjab (where it legitimately belongs) and setting up a commission to award some Hindi-speaking areas of Punjab to Haryana by January 26 by way of compensation. Additionally, Haryana will, by the earlier understanding, be assisted by the Centre to build a new capital which will in the course of time be seen as a tremendous boon, the true value of which has strangely not been recognised by Haryanvis thus far. The sharing of Ravi-Beas water will be referred to a tribunal under a Supreme Court judge, whose award shall be binding. The Anandpur Sahib resolution, which had needlessly been made into a huge bogey, is being referred to the Sarkaria Commission in so far as it relates to Centre-State relations. Mr. Longowal had long back stated that the document was not secessionist and the memorandum says that it is intended to "bring out the true federal characteristics of our unitary Constitution."

The settlement covers a number of collateral issues. Compensation is to be paid to all innocent victims of violence and for loss of property after August 1, 1982; Sikhs have been assured that, like all citizens, they have a right to enrol in the Army and that recruitment will be on merit, as before; the scope of the November riots inquiry has been widened to include Bokaro and Kanpur which were the scene of the worst incidents after Delhi; those discharged from the Army after Operation Bluestar are to be rehabilitated in gainful employment; the notification applying the Armed Forces Special Powers Act to Punjab has been withdrawn and special courts will be abolished except for cases pertaining to offences of waging war and hijacking. By this, the Akali Dal has again distanced itself from past acts of terrorism. Finally, an All-India Gurdwara Act is to be legislated. A few minor issues have not been covered and are presumably not being pressed. Many of them were no more than bargaining counters.

K. Gopal Krishnan has given a pen picture in Sunday of how the accord was arrived at. He wrote: "The normally stringent security checks were waived as Akali Dal president Harchand Singh Longowal entered Parliament House at 9.58 a.m. on July 23. Anticipation and anxiety were writ large on the faces of everyone present. Would the high-level talks between Prime Minister Rajiv Gandhi and the Akali Dal chief for a solution of the Punjab problem be fruitful?

Punjab Governor Arjun Singh escorted Longowal to Rajiv's office. The two were left alone for half an hour. The men, accompanying Longowal, Surjit Singh Barnala and Balwant Singh, simultaneously began discussions with the members of the Cabinet Committee on Political Affairs, P.V. Narasimha Rao, V.P. Singh and S.B. Chavan.

After half an hour Rajiv Gandhi and Longowal came out. "*Achi baath hui*" (the talks were good) was all that they said. At Punjab House, where Longowal was occupying the Chief Minister's suite, newsmen sought more details in vain. By afternoon, it had become clear that the talks were progressing well and a package deal was under discussion. There was hope. And apprehensions too, as Prakash Singh Badal and G.S. Tohra were not in the picture.

Would an agreement reached without the involvement of the two be acceptable to the Akali Dal?

In the first round of talks on July 23 both sides put forward their demands. The talks between Rajiv Gandhi and Longowal were of a general nature and both agreed on the need for a settlement. Specific points figured in the talks between Barnala and Balwant Singh and the members of the Cabinet committee. On most of the issues, formulations were prepared on the basis of the talks Arjun Singh had been having with Akali leaders since April. But three issues defied agreement till late in the evening on July 23. They concerned the army deserters and the territorial and river waters disputes.

Akali Dal leaders wanted a general amnesty for all deserters. While on Chandigarh there was no difference of opinion, in the case of Fazilka and Abohar the Akali leaders felt that the two areas cannot go to Haryana without a corridor drawn through Punjab, for which they were not prepared. On the river waters issue, the Akalis were insisting on referring the matter to a Supreme Court judge. The Cabinet Committee desagreed on all three issues.

As negotiations were going on, Arjun Singh had a six-hour-long session with Mr. Bhajan Lal, Haryana Chief Minister, who had landed in Delhi with a high-level official team. The Rajasthan Chief Minister was contacted by P. Shiv Shankar to get his views on the sharing of the river waters.

Shiv Shankar produced a draft agreement the next morning. Akali leaders refused to accept the formulations on the army deserters, territorial and river waters. Another round of talks then took place between members of the Cabinet committee and Longowal's lieutenants. The agreement remained elusive.

Rajiv then called in his Cabinet colleagues. They were firm that on the three issues no concession should be given. But Rajiv Gandhi knew that, if Longowal returned empty-handed, the Punjab problem would take a turn for the worse. And that would have meant the end of moderate leadership in Punjab, giving the hardliners an upper hand in the State politics.

A new formulation was quickly worked out. Deserters were divided into two categories, those who simply deserted and those who took part in the mutiny, the phraseology for the latter category being those who waged war against the State. A commission to look into the territorial claims of Haryana and Punjab was the next proposal. Similarly in the case of the river waters the Akalis' demand that a Supreme Court judge should go into the whole question was accepted.

On July 24 afternoon, Longowal and Rajiv Gandhi met again for two hours and agreed on all the formulations. At 5.45 p.m. they met for the third time accompanied by their aides and signed the 11-point Memorandum of Settlement, which marked the beginning of a new era in Punjab.

Once the agreement was signed, Rajiv invited Opposition leaders to convey the news. Rajiv had been in constant touch with the Opposition leaders on the Punjab problem. He wanted to meet them before signing the document, but last-minute hurdles and the meeting with Longowal made him postpone the meeting which was earlier scheduled for 3 p.m. on July 24. In Parliament when Rajiv announced the accord, Opposition leaders welcomed it by and large. Criticism of the agreement came from Devi Lal, former Haryana Chief Minister, who said injustice had been done to his State.

But the main interest was on the reaction of the Haryana and Rajasthan Chief Minister and the various Akali leaders. Bhajan Lal had been brought around. He thanked the Prime Minister "for fully protecting the interests of Haryana and prescribing a time limit for the implementation of the award, as is evident from the fact that the Ravi-Beas waters will 'start flowing into the Sutlej-Jamuna link canal by August 15, 1986, and the simultanesus transfer of Chandigarh to Punjab and Hindi-speaking areas of Punjab to Haryana." The Rajasthan Chief Minister too praised the accord.

The accord was widely acclaimed by the Press and the public alike. The Herald Review gives two cheers for the statesmanship of Rajiv Gandhi and writes:

"It could not have been more dramatic. The last-minute announcement of a meeting between the Prime Minister and Akali leader Sant Longowal. Two brief meetings over two days to discuss a problem that has dogged the nation for five years. And the announcement of an agreement that, besides appearing just and fair to a nation desperately waiting for the day when it could have a sigh of relief, left all wondering why it had not emerged before.

"Rajiv Gandhi cannot be faulted for the years of waiting. The opportunity to strike an agreement came his way only recently, and he could not have been given less time to arrive at one. The long history of political manoeuvre and administrative default that led up to the burgeoning of terrorist activity in Punjab, the army's storming of the Golden Temple, the tragic assassination of Indira Gandhi and the subsequent riots that led to speculation about an unbridgeable Hindu-Sikh divide all had rendered his task more difficult than that which faced his mother. That he has come out above board, displaying a different style and a willingness to go more than half the way, is an indication of statesmanship that cannot but speak well of the new Prime Minister and his advisers.

"The agreement itself is as crisp and to the point as it is fair. On the one hand, it meets half way the politico-economic demands of the State of Punjab as a whole, paving the way, hopefully, for a more democratic approach to the question of Centre-State and inter-State relations. Chandigarh has been handed over to Punjab, as was promised long ago, with no *ad hoc quid pro quo* to Haryana. Two commissions will be constituted to go into the questions of the areas to be handed over to Haryana in lieu of Chandigarh as well as settle border disputes on the principle of continuity and linguistic affinity, with the village as the unit of delineation of the area concerned. The dispute over the sharing of the waters of the Ravi and the Beas is to be referred to a tribunal to be headed by a Supreme Court judge. And the Anandpur Sahib resolution, in sofar as it deals with Centre-State relations, is to be referred to the Sarkaria Commission. All these are democratic alternatives to the solution of problems that are inevitable in a quasi-federal polity. But they have been resorted to after providing all possible concessions to the Akalis and the State of Punjab, viz, the transfer of the capital project area of Chandigarh, acceptance of the existing quantum of water being used by the State from the Ravi-Beas basin as the minimum beyond which the question of sharing of waters would be raised, and the recognition of the Anandpur Sahib resolution as a position paper on Centre-State relations.

"Finally, gestures aimed at assuaging wounded Sikh sentiment. The agreement accepts within the limits set by national security needs—the need to "rehabilitate" those discharged from the army for mutinying after Operation Bluestar; the need to extend the inquiry into the November riots in Delhi to cover Kanpur and Bokaro as well; the need to compensate the next-of-kin of those killed in the course of the agitation as well as those who suffered damage to their property; and, the need to promote the Punjabi language.

"But that is not all. In what now appear to have been preparatory moves to the settlement, the Prime Minister has in recent times been wooing different segments of the affected population of Punjab in what were no doubt well-planned moves in the wake of Arjun Singh's appearance on the scene. Akali leaders were released, the ban on the AISSF lifted, concessions offered to the peasantry, an inquiry ordered into the Delhi riots and the willingness to negotiate made obvious. This package approach has had one political fallout that is crucial to the solution of the Punjab problem. It has helped Sant Longowal carry the Akali mainstream with him. In the meeting of the party after the agreement was signed he received near-unanimous approval and isolated dissidents like Tohra and Badal. And pre-empting Longowal's isolation from the mainstream can only help isolate the extremists who have yet to respond to what has obviously proved to them also a dramatic development."

Anilkendra Nath, correspondent of the Herald Review, recounts reactions of some prominent personalities on this accord. Inder Kumar Gujral, former Indian Ambassador to the USSR and convener of the Punjabi Group, said: "I welcome the accord because it fortunately shows us the end of the tunnel. I wish to express my deep appreciation of the quality of leadership shown by Sant Harchand Singh Longowal. During the last few months, particularly after his release from detention, he has been following a wise course which has helped clear the mist which surrounded the entire political environment a great deal.

"At the same time I wish to express my deep appreciation of the sagacity and statesmanship shown by the Prime Minister. He has shown a great deal of courage. I would like to repeat an old dictum of Gandhiji: in things like this, there is never a winner or a loser. Ultimately it is the nation and country that has won, and that includes everyone.

"By and large the accord will be acceptable to the people in Punjab. Whatever reports we have been getting in the last few days speak of relief and jubilation in Punjab. You must keep in mind that for the last three to four years Hindus and Sikhs living in Punjab have been under terrific pressure. This (accord) had suddenly offered them relief. The Sikhs by and large have reacted favourably because if at all there was to be a healing touch in totality the accord applies it. The Hindus in Punjab also feel relieved because they have been living under circumstances of intense insecurity.

"The Akali Dal will, by and large, carry the Sikh population with them. Punjabis generally and Sikhs specifically are very productive people. The entire economy of Punjab has been going through terrific strain. People now want to go back to their vocations. Fringe problems are there in every situation but the accord has given to Punjab both a feeling of success and relief.

"Yes, I am aware of the protest made by some Opposition leaders in Haryana. But the very fact that Haryana and Rajasthan have protested will make the task of the Akalis much easier. The reaction in Punjab will be 'if others protest then we must have won.' This will also raise Rajiv Gandhi's image among the Sikhs. With regard to river waters, I feel, we have gone wrong on a national plane in treating resources like water and energy as assets rather than resources. Once you treat such things as property then conflicts arise. I hope the tribunal will look into the river water demands not according to claims but according to needs.

"The main point about the deserters we have to keep in mind is why Indian democracy has survived unlike in the rest of the Third World. This is because we have preserved the apolitical character of our army. Democracy can only survive if the army is insulated from all intra- and inter-party considerations. This does not mean that we want out army to be anything less than compassionate and human. Without our saying so and without a big media campaign the leaders of the army have realised the national temper and are dealing with the situation with compassion. All the tribunals are presided over by Sikhs. Till now all the published punishments suggest that they (the army top brass) have kept the circumstances in mind and shown a great deal of compassion. As a votary of democracy I would rather leave unto the army what is its area."

Khushwant Singh, noted columnist and author, was all praise for Rajiv Gandhi and extremely optimistic about the outcome of the Rajiv-Longowal accord. While conceding the difficulties ahead.

Khushwant was sure that enough goodwill existed on both sides to ensure that the accord worked. The Week met him for his views on the morning of July 26 before the Akali Dal unanimously ratified the accord.

Q: What is your reaction to the accord reached between the Prime Minister and Sant Longowal?

A: "I am very happy and I told the Prime Minister personally in Parliament that he deserves a Bharat Ratna. I think altogether it has been a very happy conclusion to three years of unrest, bloodshed and violence.

"It is not of Rajiv Gandhi's making. It is the legacy he inherited from his mother. But he handled the situation with extreme skill and goodwill. He was assured of his majority in Parliament and so did not have to resort to tactics which his mother did. Having got his electoral victory, he took steps immediately—releasing the Akalis, removing the ban on the Sikh students federation, abolishing special courts. He created a very congenial atmosphere, and let the Akalis blow off steam. And he took the Opposition into confidence.

"Long before the final settlement Rajiv consulted leaders of all Opposition parties and sounded them out about what he was going to do. Fortunately he also included me in these negotiations and so I knew at first hand how they were going. I think this is something people have not realised.

"But the significant point is that all these things were done with good timing. When Rajiv sent for Longowal he readily agreed to every new demand that Longowal made. He considered and conceded on the spot. As a result the entire agreement has been extremely well received."

Rajiv Gandhi has not only made his mark on the domestic front but has left an imprint of his greatness while handling international situations.

He has played a major role in the international arena and has been a catalyst in the non-aligned movement. The three-day extraordinary Ministerial meeting of the Non-Aligned Coordinating Bureau on Namibia was held in New Delhi from April 19 to 21. The unanimous declaration of support to the people on Namibia in their fight against the illegal occupation of their country by the minority racist regime of South Africa was welcomed by one and all. The grant of full diplomatic status to SWAPO by India will no doubt give a psychological boost to the heroic freedom-fighters of Namibia. Mr. Gandhi, who inaugurated the conference in his dual capacity as the Prime Minister of the host country and the Chairman of the Non-Aligned Movement, demanded an early meeting of the Security Council to consider this serious 'challenge to the very authority and credibility of the Council'.

The Prime Minister's assertion of Namibia's inalienable right for freedom and the determination of the non-aligned community to stand by the brave people of their country at any cost has set the right tone for the deliberations.

India's decision to accord full diplomatic status to the South-West Africa People's Organisation's (SWAPO) representative in New Delhi emphasises the country's earnestness in bringing an end to colonialism in the world. This action, announced by Prime Minister Rajiv Gandhi at the inaugural session of the extraordinary Ministerial Meeting of the Co-ordinating Bureau of Non-Aligned Countries on Namibia, is in direct line with the policy that Jawaharlal Nehru had initiated—for helping the then many countries still under colonial rule to achieve freedom. In 1985 this aim has been largely achieved but Namibia is still there to haunt the world's conscience. What makes Namibia's case still worse is that the colonial power, South Africa, is also envorcing the abhorrent apartheid policy there.

Reproduced below is the text of the speech of the Prime Minister, Mr. Rajiv Gandhi, made while inaugurating the Extraordinary Ministerial Meeting of Coordinating Bureau of Non-Aligned Countries on Namibia, in New Delhi, on April 19, 1985:

"More than a hundred nations are represented here today with one purpose—to express solidarity with Namibia, that brave nation yearning for freedom. It is a great cause that brings us together, for the call of freedom is ever exciting and ennobling. The people of India are proud to play host to this meeting. On behalf of them all, I offer you a warm welcome. We specially value the presence in our midst of Mr. Sam Nujoma, President of the South-West Africa People's Organisation and the true voice of Namibia. We greet him warmly.

"India, may I say, has always felt close to Africa. For centuries ships plied between our coasts and built up links of commerce and culture. Colonialism, which was a curse on both of us, tied our political fates closer together. Mahatma Gandhi symbolised this connection. It was in the laboratory of South Africa that he forged that priceless political weapon, non-violent mass action, with which he later won freedom for India.

"A few days from now, in Bandung, a meeting is being held to mark the 30th anniversary of the Afro-Asian Conference of 1955. What Jawaharlal Nehru had said at Bandung three decades ago rings in my ears today: 'There will be no yes-men any longer in Asia and Africa'. About Africa he had siad: 'There is nothing more terrible than the infinite tragedy of Africa in the past few hundred years.'

"This tragedy continues. Even though country after country has won political freedom in Africa since Bandung, the consequences of the brutal economic exploitation and the long suppression of the human spirit persist. The drought and famine, the suffering and death that afflict large parts of Africa today are not the result of the unkindness of weather alone or the incapacity of Governments, but the continuing consequences of the structural imbalances imposed by colonialism. They have been aggravated by the policies adopted by the powerful to prevent many newly free countries from becoming economically viable. The colonialist attitude of plunder has not disappeared. If anything, there is new emphasis on grabbing strategic materials. Besides, in Namibia as well as in South Africa, there is the direct affront of racism. For all of us of the Non-Aligned Movement, the historic battle against colonialism continues. Two years ago, in this very hall, in the Seventh Non-Aligned Summit we declared its support for the Namibian people. We solemnly reaffirm it today.

"It is now more than 100 years since imperialism first cast its covetous eyes on Namibia from across Luderitz Bay. Since the end of the First World War, South Africa has tried directly or indirectly to annex South West Africa and make it its fifth province. The ravages of 'settler-colonialism' imposed by South Africa in the lands under its military occupation are there for all to see. For close to 70 years since its seizure of Namibia, South Africa has practised unabashed deception and illegality. These moves were exposed and castigated, first in the League of Nations, then at the United Nations, yet in clear violation of the mandate of the world community, the South African regime has fortified and militarised the territory.

Today, the regime's military build-up in Namibia has reached a new peak where there is one soldier for every 12 Namibians, perhaps a record in the history of colonialism. This military might is aimed at terrorising the Namibians into withdrawing their support to SWAPO and for aggressive strikes against neighbouring States. How has minority regime defied the world community for so long and with such impunity? Because of open and hidden abetment from others.

"Some countries have sworn by racial equality with their left hand, but with their right hand supported the Pretoria regime. It is their continuing collaboration in the political, economic, military and nuclear fields, that has reinforced South African belligerence. The world organisation has repeatedly asked for a boycott of the minority regime, but its wish has been repeatedly frustrated. We are advised to be realistic and constructive—good sentiments applied to an undeserving purpose. The involvement of important transitional corporations in the economy of racist South Africa and in Namibia is sought to be justified on grounds of benefits that accrue to the black populations there. In reality, the Africans are getting batons and bullets. The recent killings of innocent civilians in Uitenhage is another reminder that the racist rampage continues. Just a few years ago Namibia's progress towards independence appeared so sure. Today it has become a casualty to power politics and multinationals' profit. In the process, the very credibility of the institution that had guaranteed this independence, the U.N. Security Council, has come under question. The issue now is whether a wronged and dispossessed people will be supported or deserted by the world body. It is thus a challenge to the United Nations. Will the U.N., now in its 40th year, fulfil its moral and political obligations or will military and economic might prevail over right?

"The responsibility of the United Nations for the independence of Namibia must once agian be strongly affirmed. Proposals by South Africa to push the role of the United Nations to the background must be resisted. The gathering of the Non-Aligned Movement proclaims that Namibian independence is the direct obligation of the United Nations. The Security Council must seek new ways to enforce Resolution 435 (1978). That Resolution remains the only acceptable basis for a peaceful settlement of the question of Namibia. We oppose any effort to bypass the U.N. and promote spurious schemes of internal settlement.

"The announcement of an interim government in Namibia represents a brazen affront to the Namibian people to SWAPO, indeed, to the entire international community. Is it mere coincidence that the South African authorities have been driven to take a step on the eve of the 25th anniversary of SWAPO? The world can ill afford to sit by the latest actions of the South African regime. History has proved time and again the futility of such efforts to defy the will of the people. I suggest that this meeting should send an urgent telegram to the President of the Security Council registering its strong condemnation of the illegal act of the minority Pretoria regime and calling upon the Council to meet urgently to reaffirm its commitment to an unqualified implementation of Resolution 435 of 1978. This is not a matter merely to be deplored by a question of the Council having to counter a challenge to its authority and credibility.

"Through twenty-five years of travail and tribulation SWAPO has spearheaded the struggle of the Namibian people. We salute SWAPO for the courage and single-mindedness of its brave warriors. Under Mr. Nujoma's inspiring leadership SWAPO has shown farsightedness, determination and resilience in its political and diplomatic responses. It has striven to promote a negotiated settlement of the Namibian question. This attitude has been in contrast to the duplicity and intrigue of the minority regime in South Africa. The latest turn in Pretoria's game is the attempt to set up a "transitional government", with a so-called 'Multi Party Conference' indeed to fabricate possibilities of unilateral declaration of independence on the part of this puppet body. We must not let this pass.

"SWAPO is the sole, authentic representative of the Namibian people. It must receive greater political support as well as more tangible material assistance in pursuing its struggle. Today we observe the 25th anniversary of the establishment of SWAPO. All of us must demonstrate our solidarity with SWAPO through concrete pledges of assistance to the Non-Aligned Solidarity Fund for the liberation of Namibia. India on its part will make a further contribution to the Fund. I am also glad to announce that the Government of India has decided to accord full diplomatic status to the SWAPO representative in New Delhi.

"Our meeting takes place at a time of great international

anxieties. Of late, there have been some encouraging statements on the part of the major military powers seeking negotiations on the arms race. We welcome these moves. But we hope that it will not be a case of 'one step forward, two steps backward'. For we find that each word of peace is accompanied by two of menace. Meanwhile research on new weapons systems continues relentlessly. Death is pursued in the name of life. The happiness, in fact the very existence, of humanity is entrapped in the nose-cones of the frightful paraphernalia of destruction. This is what makes disarmament the great imperative of our day. That is why the Non-Aligned Movement lends its full backing to any initiative that promotes disarmament.

"While the world as a whole has to be made safe for life, each region cries for peace and dignity. No meeting of non-aligned nations can remain silent to the sufferings of the Palestinian people and their righteous struggle for regaining their homeland. We declare anew our support for the PLO. There are tensions and conflicts in South-West Asia and independence of people in Central America continues to be imperilled. We reiterate our support to the endeavours of the Central American countries to pursue their social, economic and political progress without interference and intervention. Another area of the world where the security environment has steadily deteriorated is the Indian Ocean region, where military build-up is being pushed ahead at a feverish pace. The Indian Ocean must be a zone of peace.

"Everything that affects peace, everything that abridges the freedom of nations, everything that aggravates international economic disparities is of concern to the Non-Aligned Movement. But the focus of today's meeting is on Namibia. Its freedom must be expedited. Years ago, at Lusaka, at the only Non-Aligned summit to be held South of the Equator, Indira Gandhi had said that she could hear the heartbeats of Africa. The beats of freedom's drum in Namibia and South Africa reach us here in New Delhi and reverberate all over the world. We must at this meeting draw up a programme of action which will show the brave fighters of Namibia that the Non-Aligned Movement means business. I am sure you will want me to send back this message to our brothers and sisters of Namibia and South Africa: 'You are one of us. We are with you—today and always.' "

Polish Premier Gen. Woijiech Jaruzelski arrived in New Delhi on a five-day official visit and held talks with Mr. Rajiv Gandhi. General Jaruzelski and Prime Minister Rajiv Gandhi voiced the concern of the people of both countries and urged the nuclear weapon powers to pull back from the brink. Speaking at the banquet hosted by Mr. Gandhi, Gen. Jaruzelski observed that militarisation of outer space, in a way, boils down to one power intending to usurp for itself the ownership of outer space. Just like in the past when imperialists used to usurp the ownership of entire countries and continents.

Mr. Gandhi said: "India and Poland have built up a relationship of mutually beneficial co-operation. We have taken advantage of your know-how in mining and metallurgy and in various other areas of economic development. We have endeavoured to increase our trade. There is considerable interest in each other's art, music and literature. This co-operation has grown steadily in the last twenty years owing to the interest taken by the leaders of Poland and Shrimati Indira Gandhi.

"The Poland-India Joint Commission for Economic, Scientific and Technical Co-operation which met recently in Warsaw, drew up a positive balance sheet of the progress made and also indicated the lines of future development. Our own discussions today showed the vast potential there is for further expanding our trade and economic exchanges. We have both agreed that we should move forward to realise the potential.

"Another cause which unites our two nations is our dedication to peace. Poland has suffered in war as few nations have. There are countless families in your country who have personal memories of the agony. India was the victim of another kind of war—colonialism, which too took a heavy toll of human life and pushed us back in the economic race. Today we are running to catch up with history and to shake off the consequences of subjection. Development can take place only if there is peace. We seek peace not only with our neighbours but in every part of the globe.

"The technology of modern warfare has underlined the indivisibility of peace. If there is a nuclear war, it will wipe out the distinction between participant and non-participant. Indeed it will wipe out the whole human race, possibly life itself. Hence the need for a world-wide movement for disarmament. There must be an immediate halt to the production and deployment of nuclear weaponry leading eventually to complete disarmament, applying to both nuclear and conventional weapons. As long as the Bomb exists, humankind lives on parole.

"It is this profound anxiety and the desire to protect man's right to life which promoted the deliberations of the Seventh Summit of Non-Aligned Nations held in New Delhi under Shrimati Indira Gandhi's chairmanship to ask the nuclear weapon powers to pull back from the brink. It was the same concern that underlay the appeal made last May by leaders of Argentina, Greece, Mexico, Sweden, Tanzania and India, to the powerful to undertake earnest efforts towards disarmament. We six met last month in Delhi. Welcoming the decision of the great powers to resume negotiations, we put forth two further steps as being of urgency—the prevention of an arms race in outer space and the conclusion of a comprehensive test ban treaty banning underground nuclear weapons tests. Our call has evoked a positive resonance from many parts of the world. We are glad that the Polish People's Republic and other socialist countries have welcomed it.

"All of us are worried at the continuance of old conflicts and the emergence of new crises in different parts of the world. We must continue the efforts to bring the tragic conflict between Iran and Iraq to an end, to provide justice and dignity for the people of Palestine, as well as to eradicate racial discrimination and oppression in South Africa. The famine that stalks many countries in Africa calls for prompt action by the world community.

"In the region around India, tensions have increased because of the induction of sophisticated armament and the building of bases. This militarisation will be a setback to development, which is the foremost need of our peoples. We should all work for the day when swords are beaten into ploughshares and the vast sums now going into the industries of destruction can be diverted into the redeeming arts of human development.

"Poland and India have worked side by side to reduce international economic disparities. The participation of the President of Poland in the meeting of world leaders in New York in September 1983 contributed to the efforts to bring the developed and developing countries. We appreciated Poland's efforts to promote cooperation between East and West. I am sure our two countries will never be found wanting in any call made on behalf of international harmony."

On April 2, 1985, the Prime Minister, Mr. Rajiv Gandhi, welcomed the Prime Minister of Mauritius and recalled that "Mauritius and India are linked by ties of history and culture. The same ideals inspire us. The same ocean washed your coast and ours. In recent times, after the achievement of independence by both our countries, we have drawn even closer. In size we differ greatly but our problem and concern are similar. Both our countries are multi-religious and multi-lingual. We are building modern societies based on equality and justice. We are dynamic democracies. We are engaged in shaking off economic backwardness and absorbing modern science and technology. Jawaharlal Nehru described the building up of a new India as a mighty adventure. We are glad to have shared our development experience with other countries and to have co-operated with you in your development."

Mr. Gandhi observed that Shrimati Indira Gandhi had special affection for Mauritius, which she lovingly described as a "great little country".

Due to the tactful handling of the situation by Mr. Rajiv Gandhi the tension between India and Sri Lanka has also greatly lessened. Due to an ethnic crisis in Sri Lanka the Tamil refugees were crossing the border and coming to India in large numbers. It became a problem for the State of Tamil Nadu. Hence an all-party delegation from Tamil Nadu led by the Chief Minister, Mr. M.G. Ramachandran, met Mr. Rajiv Gandhi on April 23, 1985, and submitted a memorandum regarding the latest developments in Sri Lanka. It was pointed out that the influx of refugees is continuing. Traditional activities of Indian fishermen in the Palk Straits had been affected. The situation was critical. The delegation requested the Government of India to take up the matter with the Sri Lankan Government for restoration of peace and normality so that the refugees in Tamil Nadu can return home and traditional economic activities resumed on both sides.

Mr. Rajiv Gandhi assured the delegation that the Government of India was following the developments in Sri Lanka and their repercussions on India with concern. They have been in continuous touch with the Sri Lankan Government, both through the normal channels and through special visits. In view of the prevailing situation Mr. Rajiv Gandhi agreed to convey to President Jayewardene India's distress and anxiety and the need to arrive at a speedy and viable solution of the problem on a political basis acceptable to all parties concerned. In view of the gravity of the situation, Mr. Gandhi set up a Special Advisory Group to continue efforts for resolving the problem.

Thanks to the efforts of Mr. Gandhi, Mr. Jayewardene arrived in New Delhi for talks on June 1, 1985. On June 2, Mr. Jayewardene had talks in cordial atmosphere with Mr. Gandhi.

The frank and cordial talks between the two leaders seem to have helped them to appreciate each other's stand on the ethnic crisis. India is in no way interested in weakening Sri Lanka's territorial integrity. It has at no stage supported the demand for Eelam. But India is very much concerned about a political settlement of the ethnic crisis because the Tamil refugees are becoming an increasing burden for it.

Thanks to the efforts of Mr. Rajiv Gandhi, Mr. Jayewardene's Government has realised that there cannot be a military solution to this problem and he has felt the imperative need of a political solution to the ethnic crisis. He was convinced of this after his talks in New Delhi. India under Mr. Rajiv Gandhi can certainly play a major role in evolving such a solution and would play such role in the near future.

In the field of national economy Mr. Rajiv Gandhi has blazed a new trail with his first budget which is a historic event in the political economy of post-Independence India. It marks a major discontinuity or "change" in regard to both rhetoric and action.

Obviously the 1985 budget is a curtain raiser towards the new political economy under Mr. Gandhi. The next few months will perhaps make the strategic details more explicit. The 1985 budget is certain to invigorate the economy as never before. In fact, it was truly an extraordinary budget which gladdened the heart of almost everyone while displeasing and practical budgetary exercise has been undertaken exemplifying how a budget can favourably influence the course of the national economy. The sole intention is to stimulate growth, improve efficiency and provide relief where needed.

For tribal folk in Madhya Pradesh, Mr. Gandhi's four-day visit to their areas must truly have been the best thing that ever happened. The visit afforded him with an opportunity to know tribal problems at first hand. Wading through mud and slush, talking directly to the people to find out their grievances and by providing quick relief, the

Prime Minister has endeared himself to the tribals.

Mr. Gandhi, who was on the first leg of a four-day tour of tribal areas of Madhya Pradesh, did not make any speeches but preferred to talk directly to the tribals.

Reaching Devigarh village in Thandla block by helicopter Mr. Gandhi visited the Panchayat Bhavan and held discussions with members of the Panchayat. He also visited two schools and enquired from the students what they read and how many miles they have to walk to reach school. He evinced keen interest in what the villagers told him about the functioning of the Government's various welfare programmes and the actual benefits derived from them by the villagers.

The villagers told Mr. Gandhi about the acute shortage of fodder due to drought and the difficulties they were facing in procuring loans under the Integrated Rural Development Programme (IRDP).

They said nearly 800 buffaloes had been given to tribals in the Meghnagar development block under IRDP, but due to marketing difficulties, they were not getting remunerative prices for their milk.

Prime Minister Rajiv Gandhi's tour of tribal areas in Madhya Pradesh represented a welcome departure from the usual routine of VIP visits. The normal media hoopla and a surfeit of speechifying were hearteningly absent. It was clear that this was no high profile publicity event; the Prime Minister obviously desired to be personally aquainted with the various problems facing the tribals.

Mr. Gandhi preferred to mingle with the tribal people and talk directly to them about the difficulties afflicting them and there is no dearth of problems. Often the schools are few and far between and the children have to traverse long distances to get to them. The government has a number of welfare programmes, but it is moot point how much of the benefits accrue to those for whom they are intended. There are loan facilities under the Integrated Rural Development Programme, but far too often the road between the application and the actual acquisition of loan funds is strewn with difficulties created by unimaginative bureaucratic procedures and rapacious middlemen.

The welfare programmes are sometimes half-backed. In the Meghnagar development block of Jhabua district in Madhya Pradesh, for instance, the tribal villagers complained to the Prime Minister that although 800 buffaloes were given to them under IRDP, they were unable to get remunerative prices for milk due to lack of marketing facilities. There seems to be a marked need for co-ordination in these programmes among the various sectors that encompass them.

Tribal problems are not confined to Madhya Pradesh alone although the State is probably more representative of them. Bastar is the biggest district in the country, larger in area them the State of Kerala.

Mr. Gandhi visited villages of other States including Orissa and Rajasthan.

In Orissa Mr. Rajiv Gandhi met, during his visit to backward and drought-hit areas of the State, a shepherd woman and a poor tribal woman. They were Panasi Punji, a 35 years old shepherd woman in Amrapali village in Kalahandi, and Saboti Pradhan, a tribal woman of Phulbani. Saboti was a beneficiary of anti-poverty programmes and her plight convinced Mr. Gandhi that the programmes were not necessarily effective.

Panasi's grit and determination surprised all those who met her. Undaunted by the pressure from officials and politicians who reportedly coached her with cooked-up stories she admitted to the Prime Minister tht she had indeed sold her sister-in-law for Rs. 40 to feed her three starving children.

Her statement put to naught the massive cover-up operation launched by the State administration to hid the real condition of drought-hit people in Kalahandi. Mr. Gandhi was very much moved by hearing this pathetic tale.

Mr. Gandhi also visited the tribal areas of Rajasthan. A number of poor and unemployed Adivasis narrated their plight to the Prime Minister in Raja village in Kherwada district. Groups of Adivasis waiting on the hillocks moved down as soon as Mr. Gandhi arrived in the village. Most of the semi-clad Adivasis complained in unison to the Prime Minister about the neglect of their area which did not have any basic amenities. Several were heard pleading with Mr. Gandhi to give them employment and establish some industries as they had been without any means of livelihood for ages. Some complained that influential people in the area were taking away their land. One Adivasi told Mr. Gandhi that although he had won a court case relating to land, he not been able to till his land which was still in the custody of a landlord. Even the police has not been of any help, he said.

The Prime Minister assured the Adivasi that his land would be restored to him and asked Chief Minister Harideo Joshi, who was standing near by, to take strong action.

When the Prime Minister asked about the land, all the Adivasis said there was no water and during drought they had to migrate to the neighbouring districts of Gujarat for food and work. They also complained that no irrigation schemes were being implemented in their villages.

Many said that even for medical treatment they had to travel long distances to Udaipur, Dungarpur and sometimes even to Gujarat. The few dispensaries in the area did not have any medicines and facilities for treatment of any ailment.

Aoma, another Adivasi, told Mr. Gandhi that 16 years ago his land, along with that of 13 other families, was submerged in the Godavari waters. More than 100 people had died but till date no compensation or alternate land had been provided. Mr. Gandhi asked the Chief Minister to look into the matter.

The Prime Minister was received at Dabok airport by Rajasthan Governor O.P. Mehra, Chief Minister Harideo Joshi, his Cabinet colleagues and senior administrative and police officials.

Mr. Rajiv Gandhi suggested that to make the programme for alleviating poverty effective, preference should be given to the poorest while choosing beneficiaries.

He said that in the first instance families with the lowest range of income should be picked up so that help was given to those who had been reduced to absolute levels of destitution. Participation by locally elected representatives in the selection would help to obviate the aberration noticed in the identification of beneficiaries.

Mr. Gandhi said the task of reducing poverty to at least 10 per cent by 1994-95 was a national goal and had to be achieved. He sought the co-operation of all party leaders in this national endeavour.

"My government is the one that works faster", quipped the Prime Minister when asked by a correspondent how he compared his government with that of his mother which had been described by her as "the government that works".

At the 75-minute Press conference at Vigyan Bhawan, New Delhi, on July 7, 1985, the Prime Minister handled a wide range of questions crisply and confidently with occasional quips and pieces of advice to the journalists present.

Mr. Gandhi made his opening statement in Hindi and answered questions in the same language they put in.

After his Press adviser had called for the "last question", Mr. Rajiv Gandhi on his own picked out another questioner. This questioner wanted to know if the twin responsibilities of heading his government and the Congress were not a bit too much for him to shoulder. "Are you comfortable?"

"Yes, I am quite comfortable," Mr. Gandhi quipped amid laughter and thus ended his first Press conference at home on a lighter note. He went on to explain that it was the party which had put him in this position and it was up to it to decide.

Favouring consensus on all domestic and international problems, the Prime Minister, rated the chances of normalcy returning to Punjab and finding a solution within the framework of the Constitution as "high" though President's rule in the State might have to be extended if holding of elections before October 6 was not feasible. He also hoped to begin talks soon with the leaders of the Opposition parties both on the Punjab and reservation issues.

Answering a wide range of questions on both international and domestic issues at his formal Press conference on Indian soil since he took over as the Prime Minister, Mr. Rajiv Gandhi said that though there were differences between India and the USA, particularly on the latter's regional policy, the discussions he had with President Reagan would pave the way for closer co-operation between the two countries. India was also in favour of closer relations with Pakistan as with all the neighbours. However, on the nuclear issue India would have to "react" if Pakistan acquired a nuclear weapon, the Prime Minister stated.

While answering a question on the possibility of holding elections in Punjab, the Prime Minister described the situation in the State as "very fluid and sensitive". He said that the Government would very much like to hold the elections in Punjab before October 6, but it might be difficult to do so. He further said that if necessary President's rule in the State would be extended. He was happy that not only the Akalis but the entire nation was against terrorism and violence.

On the foreign policy also, the Prime Minister seemed to be satisfied with the results achieved except in the case of relations with Pakistan. He said that progress had been made at the recent meeting of the Indo-Pakistan Joint Commission with regard to trade. He was hopeful of improvement in ties in the course of future talks. He said that it was for Pakistan to respond to several positive proposals that had been made by India.

He told a Pakistani correspondent that India was not in favour of the no-war pact that had been proposed by Pakistan and would prefer a more comprehensive treaty of peace and friendship. He would also not agree to a joint inspection of nuclear installations as India feared that Pakistan would not be able to give adequate guarantee and might use it for "clandestine" production of nuclear weapons. He said that Pakistan was "fairly close" to manufacturing a nuclear weapon. He said India felt that if Pakistan produced a nuclear weapon it would change the entire situation in the region and "we will have to react to this development in some way."

Replying to a question on disarmament, the Prime Minister stated that the non-aligned countries were working for complete disarmament. Answering another question, he criticised the United States' Star War programme as hindrance in containing nuclear arms race. He expressed the hope that the close and age-old relations with the Soviet Union would further improve with Mr. Gromyko becoming the Soviet President. Referring to the Soviet proposal for convening an international conference on making Indian Ocean a zone of peace, Mr. Gandhi said that India supported any initiative taken in that regard.

The overall impression in the various replies given was that the Prime Minister was in favour of working for peace and consensus on both domestic and international issues while at the same time dealing firmly with terrorist and violent activities.

Addressing the national Press, Mr. Gandhi however categorically declared that there was no question of changing or altering the reservation available to Scheduled Castes and Scheduled Tribes.

Replying to a question on the anti-reservation agitation in Gujarat, Mr. Gandhi said he had no plans to convene a meeting of

Chief Ministers to evolve a consensus on reservations. He would meet Opposition leaders and explore the possibility of bringing about a consensus. He added that the agitation in Gujarat was a political agitation in which many Opposition parties were involved. These parties must not exploit narrow parochial feelings and must rise above them in national interest, he added. About the prevailing situation in Gujarat, he said the new Chief Minister would tackle it.

A correspondent sought to know if action would be taken against the former Chief Minister, Mr. Madhavsinh Solanki, who has been accused by even Congress (I) men of fanning communalism.

Mr. Gandhi said many charges had been made in the Press but nothing has been substantiated. "It is easy to level charges. There is need to evolve a system where a person who levels such allegations is held responsible if the charges are not substantiated," the Prime Minister said.

Mr. Rajiv Gandhi said that the Government would proceed against the Haryana Chief Minister, Mr. Bhajan Lal, if the corruption charges levelled against him by Opposition leaders were substantiated.

In reply to another question, Mr. Gandhi said the Government would try to evolve an effective system to look into charges against the Prime Minister and other Ministers. The Lok Ayukt and Lok Pal were working in several States with varying degrees of success.

A correspondent referred to Mr. Gandhi's promise to cleanse political life and wondered how partymen who were denied tickets in the Assembly elections were now being made Chief Ministers and Ministers. Mr. Gandhi said corruption and bad image were not the only reasons for denying tickets. In some cases tickets were denied to those in whose Assembly segments the party had not done well in the Lok Sabha elections. He added tht the party had not rehabilitated anyone against whom there were serious corruption charges.

Another correspondent asked why the Government had decided not to take any follow-up action on the report of the Vaidyalingam Commission, which inquired into charges against two former Prime Ministers. If this was the fate of reports of inquiry commissions, what sanctity would such commissions have?

Mr. Gandhi said the commission did find prima facie cases in respect of three charges, but the Government felt it was not necessary to go into the matter any further because the people had given their verdict on these issues in the 1980 parliamentary elections.

The Prime Minister, Mr. Rajiv Gandhi, refused to be drawn into a discussion on whether the economic policy pursued by his Government was "left, centre, or right". Asked by a correspondent to define his Government's policy within these parameters, Mr. Gandhi said the main question was what was good for the country. The economic policies followed by Jawaharlal Nehru and Indira Gandhi have to be modified taking into account the present conditions on the ground. "We have to produce a package which does not deviate from the basic Congress ideology," he remarked. The Government's priorities had already been spelt out and its biggest task was in the field of agriculture. At the same time, it would strive for better capacity utilisation in industry and improving the performance of public sector undertakings.

Mr. Gandhi pointed out that the inflation rate in the past three months was only 3.1 per cent which was the lowest in recent years. But there was at the same time a need to keep a watch over the price situation.

The draft of a new education policy was expected to be ready within the next two months, he told a correspondent. The new policy should be such that in 15 years people were made aware of new technologies that would be developed.

The Government, on its part, had chalked out certain policies which would enable Indian scientists and technologists abroad to return to their motherland and work here, he said, adding that some people had already returned to the country to work.

A correspondent wanted to know how the country could be said to be moving towards self-reliance when it was importing goods like sugar and coins. "Self-reliance does not mean that you do not import anything," replied the Prime Minister pointing out that even developed countries like Japan could not go without imports. Some items needed to be imported to meet the country's immediate needs and yet others to enable the country to produce more.

Asked about the recent recommendation of the Information Ministers on the need for a code of conduct for the Press, Mr.

Gandhi said the Government was against imposing any kind of code. The Press should evolve one on its own. He made it clear that the Government would not like to take the responsibility for implementation of such a code.

As regards AIR and Doordarshan, Mr. Gandhi once again ruled out total autonomy. "We are not ready for total autonomy for radio and television. We are not giving it at the moment," he said.

On the occasion of 38th anniversary of India's Independence on August 15, 1985, Mr. Rajiv Gandhi unfurled the national flag at Delhi's historic Red Fort. In his address to the Nation he observed:

"Thirty-eight years ago, Pandit Jawaharlal Nehru for the first time unfurled the tricolour at this very Red Fort. Indiraji should have been here today but she has been snatched away from us. The task has fallen on me. I did not see the struggle for independence. When the tricolour was unfurled here for the first time, I was only three years old. Today, two-thirds of the people of India are like me, who have not participated in the country's struggle for independence. A new generation has come to the fore. The struggle for independence is as much our inheritance as the Himalayas, the Ganges, the Plateau of Deccan, Ajanta, Taj Mahal and Mahabalipuram, the arts, philosophy and science of India. The independence struggle, along with all these, is part of India's heritage.

"Who is not filled with pride when thinking of the Buddha, Kabir, Nanak and Gandhiji? We are filled with pride when we think of the sacrifices by our freedom fighters who trailed a new path of truth and non-violence during our freedom struggle".

Talking about the economic development Mr. Gandhi observed:

"In the last 38 years we have been able to lift nearly 63 per cent of our population above the poverty line. A new middle class has emerged. We have become self-sufficient in foodgrains. The entire world wonders at the way we have been able to mould and advance our science and technology, our independent foreign policy, our democracy, liberty and secularism. The journey, however, is still very long and difficult. We have to battle with poverty and eradicate it altogether. This is the only path for us to follow and we have to eliminate poverty with all the strength at our command."

Mr. Gandhi told the countrymen that regional imbalances in

the growth of various parts of the country would be removed. He said: "We shall ensure that all citizens of the country—Harijans, tribals, the youth and the minorities—get full opportunity to contribute their mite towards India's progress. It is towards this end that we have formulated the Seventh Plan which aims not only at economic development but the total advancement and strengthening of the Indian polity. The framework of this Plan will be shortly before you. It is our hope that the country will progress substantially under the Plan and that in the course of these five years we shall advance more than what we have been able to during all these years."

Cautioning the people about the internal dissensions based on religion, caste, language or region, Mr. Gandhi said: "We must make sure that these dissensions do not acquire extremist dimensions. We have also to ensure that such disputes do not weaken the foundations of our democracy. They weaken the country and act as a drag on its progress. Many people have fallen victim to extremism. Thirty eight years ago Gandhiji and only ten months before Indiraji fell victim to it. Communal conflicts have done immense harm to the country and we have to root out communalism from the midst of us all...Today the country has to make a pledge to end communal differences and raise its voice against terrorism. We have to make sure that we use our energies for creating an atmosphere in which we can live like brothers."

Summing up the achievements of his Government during the last 41 weeks Mr. Gandhi said: "In these 41 weeks, we have done many things to redeem our pledges. The biggest challenge confronting us was to maintain the unity and integrity of India. Ten months ago, the world was watching whether India will disintegrate into pieces. Today, that question just does not arise. The world now finds a strong India. We had the problem of terrorism in Punjab. We took steps and, a few weeks back, an agreement was signed. We hope that complete peace will be restored in Punjab and the State will make rapid progress on the road to development. The tension that existed has eased and the country can now move rapidly ahead."

Mr. Gandhi was very happy to announce that the Assam problem had been resolved. He said: "The other problem was of Assam. It had been there for many years and a solution had eluded us. I am happy to tell you that an agreement was signed between the Assam students and the Government of India. We hope that with the signing of this agreement, another element of tension will be removed and the country will be able to devote its attention to development. During the elections, we had promised that we would wage a battle against corruption. We have taken a couple of steps and we are in the process of taking a third one in this direction. First of all, we brought the anti-defection Bill at the first opportunity, get it passed and implemented it, removing thereby a great infirmity from our politics. Secondly, we allowed political parties to accept donations. This will minimise corruption. We are now ready to take the third step and introduce the Lokpal Bill. We hope his Bill will be presented soon and a major cause of complaint will be removed."

Mr. Gandhi said that efforts were on to improve relations with all neighbouring countries including Sri Lanka, China and Nepal. He said: "We had also pledged to strive for peace in our neighbourhood. We initiated talks with Sri Lanka and these talks are being continued today in Bhutan. We hope that just as we have been able to resolve the problems in Punjab and Assam, we will also be able to bring about peace in Sri Lanka. This will lead to an easing of tension in the South and our people will be less worried. We are trying to improve our friendly relations with Bhutan, Nepal and China. We are also talking to Pakistan and have made some progress. However, there is one thing which is coming in the way. Their Atomic Energy programme makes us feel that Pakistan is moving towards developing an atomic bomb. If there is to be complete friendship and confidence between two countries, Pakistan should reconsider this programme."

Before ending his speech Mr. Gandhi asked the people to rededicate themselves to the cause of the unity of the country and help it move faster towards its cherished goal of uplifting the poor and downtrodden.

The agreement on Assam issue is another feather in the cap of the young Prime Minister. Coming soon after the Punjab accord it marks the fulfilment of the promises Mr. Gandhi had made earlier. The Assam accord was signed at 2.45 A.M. on August 15, 1985, bringing to an end another long and tragic chapter of discord. Mr. Gandhi has once more shown the will to resolve issues without standing on mere formalities and keeping in mind a larger perspective. Accoridng to the accord, January 1, 1966, has been accepted as the "cut off" date. Illegal migrants found to have entered the State between that date and March 1971 will be struck off the rolls and disenfranchised for a period of ten years. All foreigners who have infiltrated into the country after 1971 would be detected and all possible legal steps taken to send them back to their country.

Ten months after becoming the Prime Minister Rajiv Gandhi remains a popular, largely non-controversial figure. The press likes him, magazines queue up to do sycophantic interviews, and the foreign media act as though he is the last hope for India. Political observers, too, are generous with their praise.

P. Chidambaram, a member of the Congress (I) Parliamentary Party, says: "In months only Rajiv Gandhi has got a primary position on the world scene. Our friendship with the USSR has never been more wooed by the USA. He has been accepted on the international scene as an authentic interpreter of non-alignment. His role in the peace movement will grow and India will become an important factor on the world scene.

"Rajiv's principal achievement has been that he has reassured the people that their hope and vision of India will not disintegrate. We underestimate the importance of this. Moreover, he has impressed upon every government organisation that they will be held accountable. The government had gone down in people's esteem because people thought that it was not accountable to them. Rajiv Gandhi has changed that."

Mr. Rajiv Gandhi wants actions and results. According to Arif Mohammed Khan efficiency in government offices has increased. "The Prime Minister has succeeded in removing red tapism and simplifying procedures. In my Ministry, people have never before been able to get their projects cleared in 90 days. The emphasis now is on delivery—on showing results."

Vishvjit Singh, a Congress (I) member of the Rajya Sabha, feels that Mr. Gandhi is responsible for the rebirth of democracy within the party. He says: "When the anti-defection Bill was being discussed at a party meeting, true to form, nobody wanted to get up and criticise even those provisions which would obviously lead to authoritarianism. But Rajiv exhorted them to speak up without fear or favour. When some members got up and started criticising certain clauses, he didn't stop them—he asked for more criticism and a show of hands. Nobody has ever done this before. As the majority didn't want those clauses, they were discarded. That, according to me, was the rebirth of democracy within the party."

What attracted Sonia to Rajiv during their Cambridge days? According to her it was not the handsome looks or the high family connections that attracted her to Mr. Rajiv Gandhi during their Cambridge days.

"I could find an inner beauty in him. He was somewhat different from others, deeper and wiser than his outward looks", says Sonia Gandhi in her first ever interview granted to any publication.

Recounting their student days in Cambridge, she tells Mrs. Pushpa Bharati who interviewed her for the Hindi weekly, Dharmayug, that Rajiv's distinguished family background and his position in society and the politics of the country never made him arrogant or conscious of his status. He was honest and soft.

Emphasising that their love was deep and sincere, Sonia Gandhi said when she came to India first before her marriage, she did not have any fears whatsoever. "When one is in love, that love gives the person an extraordinary strength of mind. The strength wards off any fears. The sole aim is to unite with the lover. Once this is accomplished, everything is unimportant. I wanted Rajiv and Rajiv is my greatest security," she said.

The nation, too, wanted Rajiv in their hour of crisis and Rajiv is their best security.

You name a great man and I will place a woman behind him, is an old adage. Two women have influenced the life of Rajiv Gandhi. One was Indira Gandhi and the other is his wife Sonia Gandhi.

What kind of person is the PM's Italian-born wife? Madhu Jain, a noted journalist, has answered this question in The Sunday of February 10-16, 1985. According to her Sonia Gandhi is a very private person, her whole world centres on her husband and their two children, Priyanka and Rahul. Says a friend: "She loves her family and her husband in her life. You should see that when one of them walks into a room, the way the face of the other lights up..." The house is the centre of the universe and the kitchen a very important part of this universe. Sonia Gandhi loves to cook. She has mastered the art of Kashmiri cuisine. Good bread is one of the weaknesses of the Gandhi household. In more carefree times, when their circle of friends was larger and not under the supervision of the security-men, she would often make special dishes and take them to friends' houses for dinner.

Sonia Gandhi has another duty now. With Indira Gandhi no longer there, she is the one to be concerned with the larger Nehru family. When, recently, the Jawaharlal Nehru award for International Understanding had to be given, it was Sonia Gandhi who made frantic phone calls to trace the various members of the Nehru family and invite them for the function. She shares with her mother-in-law an eye for detail and the ability to remember the smallest of facts. Says another friend: "She is so considerate. She will remember to send a particular kind of *heeing* (a kind of spice) to a Kashmiri relative, or what there was for dinner when so and so came years ago."

Languages interest Sonia Gandhi. She speaks Russian, French, Portuguese, Spanish, English, Hindi and, of course, her mother tongue, Italian. In fact, it was while learning English at the School of Languages in Cambridge that she met Rajiv Gandhi. Art is another love. She learned restoration of paintings at the National Gallery of Modern Art. Music, especially opera, interests her a great deal, adds Madhu Jain. Sonia Gandhi's shyness notwithstanding, she has played an important role behind the scenes in her husband's political life, though by and large over the telephone. She may, as her friends say, have been reluctant to let her husband enter politics, but once he decided, she played the ideal supportive role. For two years, up to the elections she went to Amethi for three days every month to visit the villages and distribute medicine. Her Italian-oriented Hindi went down well with the villagers. "Bahu rani, do not come here, we will vote for you anyway," they told her. And, they did.

Sonia Gandhi provides a happy home. This helps Rajiv give out his best for the nation, confident that every action of his has a firm supporter at home and a vast populace all around the nation.

This book covers about 300 days of the Prime Minister of India, Mr. Rajiv Gandhi. This is too short a time in a nation's life. Yet, it is enough to reveal the qualities of a leader of a nation, to assess his abilities to lead his people, to maintain order and system, to initiate action to advance economic growth and political stability, to build bridges of understanding with other nations, to effectively concretise the concept of universal brotherhood.

In response to a question from a correspondent Mr. Rajiv Gandhi noted that his Government would work faster. He has already proved that his government can move really fast by sorting out the Punjab tangle and the Assam problem which had been hanging uncertainly refusing to be diffused even with the best of efforts for the last few years

The resolve to tackle the continued problem of poverty of the masses has been clearly indicated by the new directions he gave to Indian economy while presenting the first budget of his government. Since then Rajiv has been moving around, visiting pockets of poverty in Madhya Pradesh, Orissa, Andhra Pradesh and other States, gauging the extent of poverty so that the strategy for the fight against poverty could be evolved. Ultimately Rajiv's place in the history will be decided by how he wiped out poverty and provided the minimum need of the populace. This is the golden test. Given time and public co-operation there is no doubt that Rajiv will succeed in this endeavour. Rajiv is India's best bet and he is gearing the country for meeting the challenges and opportunities of the 21st century. We do hope that he would be around captaining the ship of the State at the dawn of the 21st century.